POWER
PERFORMANCE

POWER
PERFORMANCE

Multimedia Storytelling for
Journalism and Public Relations

Tony Silvia and Terry Anzur

WILEY-BLACKWELL

A John Wiley & Sons, Ltd., Publication

Blackwell Publishing was acquired by John Wiley & Sons in February 2007. Blackwell's publishing program has been merged with Wiley's global Scientific, Technical, and Medical business to form Wiley-Blackwell.

Registered Office
John Wiley & Sons Ltd, The Atrium, Southern Gate, Chichester, West Sussex, PO19 8SQ, United Kingdom

Editorial Offices
350 Main Street, Malden, MA 02148-5020, USA
9600 Garsington Road, Oxford, OX4 2DQ, UK
The Atrium, Southern Gate, Chichester, West Sussex, PO19 8SQ, UK

For details of our global editorial offices, for customer services, and for information about how to apply for permission to reuse the copyright material in this book please see our website at www.wiley.com/wiley-blackwell.

Library of Congress Cataloging-in-Publication Data
Silvia, Tony.
    Power performance : multimedia storytelling for journalism and public
relations / Tony Silvia and Terry Anzur.
        p. cm.
    Includes bibliographical references and index.
    ISBN 978-1-4051-9868-4 (hardback) – ISBN 978-1-4051-9869-1 (paperback)
    1. Mass media–Authorship.   2. Broadcast journalism.   3. Reporters and reporting.
4. Public relations–Authorship.   I. Anzur, Terry. II. Title.
    P96.A86S55 2011
    070.4'3–dc22

                                                            2011001827

A catalogue record for this book is available from the British Library.

This book is published in the following electronic formats: ePDFs (97814443406170); Wiley Online Library (9781444342192); ePub (9781444340624)

Set in 10.5/13 pt Minion by Toppan Best-set Premedia Limited
Printed and bound in Malaysia by Vivar Printing Sdn Bhd

1   2011

Contents

About the Authors

COURTESY MELANIE MARQUEZ

TONY SILVIA

Tony Silvia is Professor of Journalism and Media Studies at the University of South Florida St. Petersburg, and the author of four other books, two of those titles, *Student Television in America* and *Global News: Perspectives on the Information Age*, published by Blackwell. He is a regular presenter at national conferences, consults with newsrooms, corporations, and non-profits, and is a frequent contributor to seminars at the Poynter Institute. His career in television news spans more than two decades, as a general assignment, political, consumer reporter as well as anchor at local stations. In addition, he regularly consults with newsrooms and non-profit organizations on issues like effective storytelling, media ethics, and diversity. His work has appeared on CNN, where he served as a features correspondent in the network's science-technology unit. He holds both a master's and doctoral degree from the University of Birmingham, England.

COURTESY BOB LASKY

TERRY ANZUR

International journalism educator Terry Anzur consults broadcast and online video outlets on talent development and is a news anchor at KFI-AM in Los Angeles. She developed her coaching techniques while on the faculty of the Annenberg School for Communication and Journalism at the University of Southern California. She holds an AB in Communication from Stanford University and was a Benton Fellow at the University of Chicago. Her on-air experience includes a national talk show on the network that became MSNBC, as well as anchoring and reporting for KTLA-TV in Los Angeles and CBS stations in Los Angeles, Chicago, New York and West Palm Beach. She has reported from Washington for the NBC-owned stations and has anchored at local TV stations in Houston, Miami, Atlanta, Providence and Charleston, WV. She began her career in print journalism at the *Trenton Times* newspaper, United Press International and the Associated Press. She is a Fulbright senior specialist and was the lead consultant on the Maldives Media Training Project. For more information, visit: http://www.terryanzur.com/.

Foreword

COURTESY NBC

LESTER HOLT

NBC News/MSNBC

Job: Co-anchor, Weekend *Today*
Anchor, *NBC Nightly News*, Weekend Edition
Market: National, based in New York City
Hometown: Sacramento, CA
Education: Attended California State University, Sacramento
Career Path:
  Internships: KCRA TV and local radio, Sacramento, CA
  Radio reporter and weekend anchor, KCBS-AM San Francisco, CA
  Reporter, WCBS-TV, New York
  Weekend anchor and reporter, KCBS-TV, Los Angeles
  Weekend anchor and reporter, WCBS-TV
  Anchor and reporter, WBBM-TV, Chicago

Reporter, CBS News magazine, *48 Hours*
Anchor, MSNBC, Fort Lee, NJ
Anchor, NBC, New York

I started working in the news business while I was still in high school. I worked at a radio station in Sacramento and I was interning at a TV station. In 1979, when I was just starting my junior year of college, I left school to take a job at KCBS-AM news radio in San Francisco. It was one of the first broadcast stations to have a computerized newsroom. I was a morning drive reporter and I anchored on the weekends. They had a little promo for me. It said, "Breaking news with Lester Holt, the fastest mike in the West." I loved breaking news; I was always the guy with the scanner in the car, chasing police cars and fire trucks. Later, when I moved to New York, that experience translated into being very comfortable on TV in front of a live camera and at the anchor desk. You become more conversational because you are telling people a story as opposed to just reading it.

How I deliver the news as a network anchor came from years of doing live coverage on a pay phone or a two-way radio. On the *Today* show, I spend most of my time preparing for interviews, doing my homework. There's a lot of adlibbing because that's the nature of the show. For *Nightly News*, I write quite a bit in the first block of the show. I go through every piece of copy. My days as an anchor on cable at MSNBC taught me to read up on stories and be ready for anything. Suddenly a story breaks and you have to be an instant expert. My preparation is to be aware of the stories we are doing but also scan the wires, read the papers. Be aware that a story that has been bubbling on the back burner of the stove could suddenly flare up. I am constantly making sure that I understand the stories and their bigger meaning. I tell students that one of the most important things we do is give perspective and more information. It's not just the words, but your tone and what you choose to emphasize.

One thing I've always missed about radio was the immediacy. I could push a button on my walkie-talkie and be live. I could drop a dime at a pay phone and be on the air. For much of my career, television has been very cumbersome. Your report depended on whether there was a live truck or a satellite truck available. With multimedia tools, the world has shrunk considerably. I was in Haiti not long ago, making the drive from the Dominican Republic to cover the earthquake. I took my BlackBerry and pointed it toward myself, shot video and began to give narration as we were driving through the country. I emailed it and I was on the *Today* show a few minutes later. I didn't need a crew, I didn't need a producer. I didn't need anybody. Blogging and tweeting add another dimension. It's another way to add perspective. Sometimes you can't fit everything into a 90-second *Nightly News* spot. But you can offer more texture, or still photos, in a blog or a tweet. People know we're out there and it's added value. I'm a big proponent of the multimedia revolution because it allows us to do our job better and more efficiently.

Technology enhances storytelling. With tweeting and blogging we can be a bit more informal. There's something about the TV camera that implies more formality. We choose our words more carefully because it's a big stage. But then we get on our BlackBerries or iPhones and start tweeting and it becomes a more personal reflection on the story, what it smells like, what it feels like. It can give people the background and the texture for the entire story. Shrinking resources are the new model. We see people having to do more than they used to, because there are fewer people in the newsroom. I really love what I do. I love telling stories. The thrill has never worn off for me. I work with a small group of tight-knit people. As we draw down in terms of resources we become more focused and rise to the challenge of getting the broadcast on the air. In a war zone or a disaster zone like Haiti, you have to become creative. I've used Twitter, cell phone video and Skype. I probably wouldn't think of those things when doing a story in Manhattan. But when you're in a difficult place, you start thinking out of the box and realizing you have a lot of tools in the box. You eventually find the right digital outlet. We have a lot more ways to get the story out, even if it's just a tweet.

I always tell people that if you want to be an anchor, you have to love reporting. You have to enjoy that moment of being the first to tell somebody something.

My son is anchoring weekend mornings on a station in Florida and he sent me a photograph from the control room, with him in one monitor and me in the other, competing with each other. I talked to Stefan a lot before he got his first job. I tell all journalism students that they are learning the actual tools of the trade. You no longer go to college and they teach you stuff, and then start a job and find out that none of it applies. If you are shooting on DV and editing on Avid or another computer program, you are doing what the professionals do. I told Stefan that it's hugely important to be coming out of school with all of the tools. All you are lacking is the experience. When Stefan was looking for a job, I told him that you want to end up in a market where there is room to grow and where there are people with experience to be your mentors. You want to be a small enough fish in a big pond where there are people to look up to.

I also feel strongly about respecting the people we cover. If I ask you to do an interview, I owe you respect. It doesn't mean I will avoid the hard questions, but I don't believe in badgering people or looking down on them. At one point, Stefan thought he might be going to Haiti. He asked me for some advice. I told him to remember that you are not better than the people you cover, simply because of a cultural or socio-economic difference. Just because we're the media doesn't make us special. It's crucial to respect the people that we cover and talk to them as equals.

The book you hold in your hands is a fine step in the direction of making the news business better. The authors, both highly respected for their work in the industry and as journalism educators, help provide a strong foundation for the next generation of storytellers. The ability to adapt as new technologies develop, to use what we now call multimedia skills to tell better stories across more media, is at the heart of *Power Performance*. Both those now in the classroom and others already in the newsroom can benefit from the advice given and the skills taught in the pages ahead. As it takes me back to my own beginnings in radio, I'm reminded that we all have to get our start somewhere. This book is a great place to begin.

Everyone says the news business is in trouble. It's not. We just have to learn to adapt. I believe there will always be a need for people who can put words and information with pictures. Whether people will still be watching it on television 15 years from now, I can't say. The screen could be on a refrigerator or a mobile phone. But the need for video/audio content won't go away. We need good people and good storytellers. If you are coming out of college now, all you have known is shooting and reporting your own stories, but it's not so different from back in the days when I was a beat reporter on the radio in San Francisco with a tape recorder playing audio through the telephone. At the end of the day, it's basic, raw reporting. It means asking the tough question. Technology allows you to go more places and be better. Don't get discouraged. You'll figure it out.

Introduction

The constantly changing universe of multimedia is the focus of much study and endless debate. This book is about what does *not* change: the basic human need for a good story. As a storyteller in the present day, your tools may be a camera, a microphone, and a computer. But you are carrying on a tradition that dates back to the first person who used the wall of a cave and piece of charcoal to draw pictures that might point the way to a successful hunt, or the first sculptor using stone as a tablet to record the outcome of an epic battle. From the beginning of human history, we have depended on storytellers to pass on our legends to the next generation, to share practical information needed for survival, to encourage our sense of community and to inspire our faith in something greater than ourselves. And, yes, we also want to be entertained while we are being informed.

Effective storytelling has long been a blend of words, sounds and pictures. In the days when most people could not read, religious stories often came to life through images and music in a house of worship. Wandering minstrels spread the news of the day while performing their songs. Playwrights and actors gave us insight into the human condition by portraying archetypal characters and dramatic situations on a stage. The printing press made it possible for storytellers to reach a wider and more educated public, leading to the development of worldwide mass media in the present day. What all effective storytellers throughout history have in common is the ability to engage the audience, not merely capturing attention, but challenging the users, viewers, listeners or readers to process information and apply it to their own lives.

We recognized the need for this book because of the way in which multimedia has broadened our own experience in the newsroom and the classroom. There are many textbooks that address the fine points of writing and reporting for the page or for the airwaves, but they are often limited to "how to write the news in English for an American audience." Today's multimedia storytellers must think globally while they are reporting locally. A local story on a community web site can be downloaded by someone halfway around the world.

Even in many countries where the official media is government-controlled, student journalists can view global media online and via satellite. They not only watch CNN, they can also upload their own reports. We hope that this book will give all students – and especially those in emerging democracies – the tools they need to tell their unique stories to the world. We also hope to remind those in a free society not to take for granted their right and responsibility to tell the truth. In a worldwide marketplace of information, where all journalists face the challenge of developing a business model that will support their passion for reporting the truth, storytelling skills are vital.

While traditional journalism texts often downplay or ignore public relations (PR), this book presents PR as the other side of the multimedia coin. The best public relations practitioners think like journalists when pitching stories or crafting a client's image and journalists must acquire the public relations skills needed to manage their own brands. All must be accomplished storytellers across multiple platforms, including social networks. Future careers in multimedia communication will likely incorporate elements of both journalism and strategic public relations.

In writing this book, we are trying to pass along the best traditions of print and broadcast journalism to a new generation of multimedia storytellers. Each chapter contains at least one example of what we call a "Power Profile." These profiles are structured in the form of a social networking page, with some basic information, followed by questions and answers. We'd like to think they simulate the experience of having each of these outstanding professionals appear as a guest speaker in your classroom. Because we are still in the transformative stage of multimedia, writing a book about a moving target was no easy task. Illuminating the conversation about change with those who are in the middle of it every day is, we believe, a good starting point.

We sincerely thank those professional journalists and public relations practitioners who shared their insights. Their work exemplifies the ways in which leading storytellers have adapted to new technologies and multimedia platforms. NBC and CNN were especially generous in allowing their journalists to participate, while ABC, CBS and Fox News declined. Along the way we discovered numerous local TV journalists and web casters, print and radio reporters, and public relations practitioners who are developing their own brands, whether they are freelancing or working as staff members of a major media organization. They stand as excellent role models for future journalists who are still finding their voices.

You may be reading this book for a journalism course, or you may be a citizen journalist learning the basics of the craft on your own, or a professional multimedia storyteller who is ready to take your journalism and power performance to the next level. Our goal is to give you the skills and insights needed to identify, gather and present compelling stories, whether your audience is one person or the entire multimedia universe. As the great broadcast journalist Edward R. Murrow once said, "Just because your voice reaches halfway around the world doesn't mean you are wiser than when it reached only to the end of the bar."

1

The Role of the Storyteller

It's one day after the death of Michael Jackson, June 25th, 2009. All across the country, newsrooms have expended the level of resources once reserved for covering political conventions, presidential elections, and the passing of heads of state. In our burgeoning celebrity-first culture, that part is not surprising. What is remarkable is the path the story takes, not through any one news medium, but across many: newspapers, radio, television, the Internet, and social media.

The first contact with the story of Michael Jackson's death was, for many, through social media followed by the web, then radio and television, and, finally, newspapers – and by extension, other print media, such as magazines. Within an hour of the pop icon's death, the message was being received and relayed by people with cell phones, Facebook or MySpace pages, and Twitter accounts. For the current generation, there will always be the memory of where they were when they got the news that Jackson had died; in many ways, it is similar to those of another generation who will never forget the details surrounding how they learned of the death of President John F. Kennedy over four decades earlier.

For the news media, the difference was palatable. It wasn't so long ago that when a major news story broke, the path to an audience was first and foremost through a traditional medium: print, radio, or television; then and only then would thought be given to posting it for the web, and social media weren't even on the horizon. Now it's web first. Just ask Mark Douglas of Tampa's WFLA-TV. Douglas, a 30-year veteran of television news, would think television first. Not any more. "I sometimes joke that I'm a web reporter who every once in a while does television," he says. In fact, a 2010 story Douglas wrote about a regional coyote infestation "broke" first on the station's web site and didn't end up on its TV newscast in a different form until weeks later.

His parent company, Media General Corporation, also owns the *Tampa Tribune*, WFLA radio, and the news web site tbo.com. Their "converged newsroom" concept dates back to the 1990s when theirs was one of the first newsrooms in the country to adopt a multiplatform approach to newsgathering and storytelling. It is illustrative of the very different

Power Performance: Multimedia Storytelling for Journalism and Public Relations, First Edition. Tony Silvia and Terry Anzur.
© 2011 Tony Silvia and Terry Anzur. Published 2011 by Blackwell Publishing Ltd.

demands placed upon journalists today. In a word, these demands can be summed up as "multimedia."

What is Multimedia?

First and foremost, it's an approach to storytelling that bestows new power, both on the storyteller and the audience. Control over the elements of a big story is no longer the exclusive domain of the print reporter, the broadcaster, or even the web journalist. It's the domain of the storyteller, the person whose skills and judgment contribute to a story that has maximum impact both for and with the audience. We call that level of storytelling *Power Performance*, because it harnesses the power of today's multimedia to tell the story in a more compelling way. It involves every aspect of the storytelling process, from print to broadcast to web. It invites the audience to be part of the process by including them through all forms of social media. There is much misunderstanding about the role of multimedia. Is it just applying new technology to old skills? Or is it an entirely new form of storytelling that requires a whole new set of skills? In many ways, that discussion is framed by the rapid development of online media compared to the adoption rate of traditional media. The Internet is unique for its exponential growth over an incredibly fast period of time.

Johannes Gutenberg invented the printing press in the mid-1400s, but cost and distribution meant it was hundreds of years before books were adopted by a significant segment of the world's population. Compare that to the growth of television, which we think of as having always been part of our media experience. It took over three decades to reach just half of the American public. By contrast, it took the Internet ten years to reach the same audience level. As for social media, five years after its inception in 2003, Facebook alone had reached 350 million people. In 2011, that figure rose to half a billion. As author and media watcher Ken Auletta puts it, "That's extraordinary."

With the tools available to us, it's useful to distinguish what is expected of us as storytellers in today's multimedia environment. In doing so, let's summarize what separates best practices in multimedia storytelling – *Power Performance* – from those approaches that neither advance the story nor the storyteller.

POWER PERFORMANCE IN MULTIMEDIA IS:

- Recognizing the major elements of any story, regardless of media platform.
- Approaching storytelling across every media platform available (print, audio, video, web).
- Learning from the best practices in each medium by taking advantage of the unique elements of each.
- Becoming proficient with the tools of each medium.
- Thinking visually about each element of the story, including your own place in it.
- Using all means available to interact with and engage the audience in the process of storytelling.

POWER PERFORMANCE IN MULTIMEDIA IS NOT:

- Creating a story simply to accommodate the technology available.
- Cutting and pasting a story from another medium onto the web.
- Creating stories quickly and without much forethought.
- Having only a rudimentary knowledge of each medium's strengths.
- Ignoring opportunities for interaction with the audience, who often possess defining elements of the story.

Keep these points in mind as you begin to consider why it is important to become proficient in the performance elements of multimedia; some might say it's as important as being well versed in the nuts and bolts of basic journalism. Both have elements in common: solid writing, good storytelling, and credible research. Multimedia is, in many ways, a combination of the *enduring values* of good journalism and the modern visual tools available to deliver a more compelling story.

The oldest form of news writing has always been traditional print or newspaper reporting. While the influence of newspapers on other forms of media has been greatly diminished, early broadcast journalists took their lead from the local newspaper. Why? Not only because it was easy to do, but also because newspaper reporters generally spent time researching a story before writing it. Your venture into writing for other media in today's newsrooms should, similarly, take time. As a general precept, keep in mind this paraphrase from a popular wine commercial of the past, "No story should be written before its time."

In fact, for generations of journalists, the distinction between time spent on a story and the depth achieved in that story defined the qualitative difference between print and broadcast reporters. Newspapers were often defined by their appeal to the cerebral side of human beings and broadcast (TV especially) to the visceral side of our nature. What, then, of the Internet? Does it engage both our brains (cerebral) and our emotions (visceral)?

The web, with its multimedia potential, is the biggest change in the way people read and absorb information since Gutenberg invented the printing press. It is, as Eastman and Ferguson write, the primary example of "discontinuous change," meaning it is unlike any change in media that predates it. While it's "like" a newspaper, radio, and television, it's none of the above, nor is it a simple combination of all of the above. It is an entirely new medium that exists, but doesn't eclipse those media that came before it. In the best sense, it is the repository medium for most of what we think of as multimedia. As such, it has defined and redefined many of the traditional roles we think of in journalism, all of which, thus far, have been derived from what we often describe as "old" media.

Newspapers and Broadcast News

There are both similarities and differences between today's so-called "converged" newsrooms, driven as they are by multimedia demands on reporters, and the manner in which the relationship between newspapers, radio and television developed in and around each other. To start with, those who owned newspapers found radio stations to be both competitors and allies. Fearing competition, newspaper owners intimidated the Associated Press into embargoing its news to radio stations until after 9 a.m. (when presumably everyone had already read the morning paper) and 9 p.m. (when they had already read the afternoon paper). This led radio stations to hire and develop their own news staffs, ultimately benefiting the station and the public.

Over time, newspaper owners came to see the promotional value of owning radio stations. Radio was a great way to give listeners some of the story and refer them to the parent company's newspaper for the rest. Does this sound familiar? Today, newspapers use television to drive readers to their print product, while both use the web to entice the online audience. However, the staff for each medium – print and broadcast – were once separate and reporters had specific, defined duties related to the medium in which they worked. And, while they shared the same parent company, equality did not exist. The newspaper was primary; radio (and later television) was there to serve the paper's best interests – and profits.

Of course, all of this began to change once radio started to garner the lion's share of the company's profits; it certainly changed once television became its profit center. Still, a "wall" of sorts existed between the print side of the news operation and its broadcast "second cousin." Big stories were routinely withheld from the nightly newscast until after they first reached readers the following morning. Until the 1980s, broadcast news operations were often seen by a newspaper's executives as a necessary evil – albeit a profitable one – but certainly media that should be avoided by the newspaper's "real" journalists, lest they be tainted by broadcasting's supposed superficiality and personalities.

Similarly, established radio newsmen shunned television in its early days; those who emerged as TV news stars were those willing to give the new medium a try. More recently, some television news managers have held back exclusive stories for the next scheduled newscast instead of allowing themselves to be "scooped" by their own web sites. Each established medium was reluctant to accept the presence of a new technology.

One example is WEAN, in the 1980s, an all-news radio station in Providence, RI, then owned by the *Providence Journal-Bulletin* corporation. Each afternoon a printed copy of the top stories to run in the following morning's *Journal* would be delivered to the radio newsroom, which existed in rented space several streets away from the spacious newspaper facilities to prevent cross-contamination. Today, that information in, say the *Tampa Tribune*'s newsroom, would be used to coordinate multimedia coverage across all the company's platforms. In 1985, it was for informational purposes only. The radio news staff was forbidden to develop or air any of the stories the newspaper staff was developing until the following day, well after they had been published and read by the paper's audience. It's difficult to absorb in today's multimedia-rich environment, but print reporters had their place and so did broadcast reporters, but they were in two different – and disconnected – worlds, sharing only the name of the corporation that owned them. How times have changed!

Today's print reporter

Those who have spent most of their lives in a print newsroom are often nostalgic about the days of "ink-stained fingers," synonymous with a time when newspapers were the premier medium and led the way for other news media to follow. It seems a better time, when everyone knew the tools associated with their job and security came from honing the use of those tools into a sharply defined set of skills. Jenny Cromie spent six years as a reporter at the *Anniston Star* and writes about the often difficult transition from print reporting to multimedia journalism:

> It was a time when most people still took the Sunday paper. Computer-assisted reporting was just coming into vogue. And long, in-depth story features still had not met the short attention spans of online readers. Good old-fashioned print journalism still prevailed. And if you had a big story package in the Sunday paper, you could stay late in the newsroom, listen to the kerthunk, kerthunk, kerthunk of the press running in the background, and grab the first few copies of your above-the-fold story – barely dry ink and all. It was a great time to be a reporter.

Her reminiscences bring with them this reality check: the timeframe in which she worked as a print journalist wasn't the 1940s, 1950s, or even the 1960s or 1970s. It was in the mid to late 1990s. It's a strong reminder of how quickly the job of traditional print reporter has changed – and how those occupying what were once essentially newspaper jobs have had to change and, more importantly, *adapt*. In order to be successful, today's print reporter must be not only a wordsmith, but a visual thinker across all media. He or she must become proficient with a digital still photo camera and small hand-held video camera, as well as develop an understanding of graphics, slideshows, streaming audio and video: the major elements of reporting for the web.

A typical day for today's print reporter might look something like this timeline. The assignment: cover a breaking news story centered on a chemical plant explosion just outside the downtown of a major metropolitan area.

6:40 a.m.   Arrive on scene. Take several quick "snaps" with your digital camera. Interface camera with laptop or cell phone to send photos back to the newsroom for posting on the web.

7:00 a.m.   Interview fire chief and eyewitnesses using digital audio recorder or small video cam, preferably the latter, since it captures both image and sound – the sound can later be extracted for radio and the web; the video for the web and television.

7:10 a.m.   Using basic facts gleaned from the interviews, file a quick story for the web. Continue to gather facts and interviews.

7:45 a.m.   File second story, with updated information, maybe a few new photos, audio or video. Think about elements for TV story. If the only reporter from that news organization, he/she may do a "live shot" for the co-owned or partner television or cable outlet.

8:20 a.m.   Collaborate from the field with web editor to determine best way to present larger-scale package on the story, using not only the elements gathered in the field, but graphics, slideshows, history of the plant, identify former workers to provide perspective, either through profiles/sidebars or for audio interviews and/or podcasts.

9:15 a.m.   Begin to think about the broader, detailed story for the next edition of the newspaper.

Notice that it is over an hour and a half before the "print" reporter begins to think at all about her/his newspaper story. During that time, he/she is doing jobs formerly reserved for colleagues in radio and television news. And we haven't even begun to include the additional possibilities, such as shooting, producing and presenting a video story for the next morning's television newscast. It might include narration and a "standup," in which the storyteller appears on camera. There is increasing pressure to put the finished package into a form that will be posted on someone's mobile phone or other device. And when all that's done, the reporter must be sure the story goes out to the newspaper's followers on social media, and find time to post her/his thoughts and observations on covering the story via the news organization's web site or on a reporter's blog.

Under these circumstances, is it accurate or fair to describe what you've just read as the domain of the "newspaper" reporter? Probably not. Multimedia storyteller is a better term for the actual work being done. This is not to suggest that in every instance the newspaper reporter is always on her or his own to cover a story across all media, only that the probability exists, together with the need to be ready if called upon to do so.

Print reporters who once dismissed broadcast media as "superficial" now must embrace the same skills used by TV journalists in order to be successful. That requires a major shift in approach, a new level of skills, and a very different mindset. But, as with most things, history reveals that what appears to be new really has its roots in some incremental changes made in the way news organizations operate and, more importantly, *collaborate* – both within and outside corporate boundaries.

Storytelling collaborations

One early example of a newspaper staff collaborating with a television news staff came in 1994, when Philadelphia's WPHL-TV launched an innovative newscast together with the then Knight-Ridder-owned *Philadelphia Inquirer* newspaper. Titled *Inquirer News Tonight*, what was then referred to as a "hybrid" newscast (today's equivalent of "converged"), it incorporated *Inquirer* staffers – print reporters – contributing the stories they were doing for next day's newspaper. Considered an "experiment," one that raised tension levels in both newsrooms, it survived only two years. Its legacy, however, was to pioneer the television skills newspaper reporters would need in the future, once newspapers and television stations were not cooperative, but co-owned.

Suddenly, the previously anonymous writers from the newspaper side of journalism had to learn what their counterparts knew intuitively: not only how to write a story in fewer words, but how to present that story using the visual skills of the television journalist. First, there were the on-camera skills, both verbal and non-verbal. Where and how to look into the camera when addressing the viewer was a challenge for the print reporters, as was body positioning, gestures, makeup, hair, clothing, and accessories. Suddenly, people who thought of themselves as writers were forced into recognizing a new dimension to their storytelling for a very different audience. And because it was television, not the printed page, visuals were important. In many ways, albeit on a very limited basis, those *Inquirer* reporters were indulging in multimedia reporting.

Other news operations were watching, including the *Providence Journal-Bulletin*, which owned both newspapers and television stations and, up until 1987, had owned WPHL. The idea of sharing resources and combining staffs was appealing, if not primarily from a journalistic standpoint, then from an economic one. In 1995, a reporter named Jim Hummel was in his thirteenth year on the print side of journalism. He pitched an idea to his then-bosses at the *Journal* for a story on trading places with a broadcast reporter. The broadcast reporter would learn the skills needed in a print newsroom and vice versa. Admittedly, the idea was a gimmick, seized upon by the management of television station WLNE to create curiosity and boost viewership during a ratings period. The unpredictable happened, however. Hummel, once he learned the ropes of television news, found he preferred the visual medium and remained at the television station.

More recently, in St. Louis, former newspaper reporters have nicely meshed into news operations at public TV station KETC. Part of the motivation in St. Louis is simple survival. That city's *Post-Dispatch* downsized its reporting staff, resulting in 14 reporters looking for work. They found it, not in another newspaper city room, but in a corner of the TV newsroom at KETC, where they publish their own newspaper as the *St. Louis Beacon* online (www.stlbeacon.org).

Similarly in 2009, KCTS-TV in Seattle brought on board 20 journalists laid off from the *Post-Intelligencer*, absorbing them into its web operation. KCTS president Moss Bresnahan said there were strengths the print reporters brought to his news operation. "We were doing some strategic planning at the station, looking at what public media will become, and that coincided with the closing of the paper," Bresnahan said. "We called some of our contacts at the *P-I* and started actively exploring how to find a viable business model to support an in-depth, integrated multimedia site."

Part of that business model, as we shall see, comes from the integration of print journalism with television and the web. For today's print reporter, that means learning the visual skills long associated with TV news and now a major element of web news. It also means becoming proficient at many of the same skills that today's TV journalist needs to learn, especially those that involve doing more with less, creating opportunities to become valuable players on the landscape of multimedia. It's still journalism, but it's less about medium than message, a form of storytelling that stresses interactivity over authority. And it shares control over the story with the reader, viewer, and user. While embracing the enduring values of journalism – accuracy, objectivity, fairness, and balance – today's print reporter has had to add another dimension to her/his work: *versatility.*

Today's television reporter

Television has traditionally been divided into small, medium, and large markets, as defined by a locale's population size and demographics and as established by Nielsen Media Research of Oldsmar, Florida. The designation has, in many ways, dictated the resources allocated for broadcast news according to market size. In large television markets, reporters do just that: report. They cover their stories, doing interviews, stand-ups, record the narration and sometimes introduce their stories as part of what has become known in TV news as a "live shot" or "set piece," where the reporter is on the news set with the anchor for purposes of interaction through a question and answer exchange.

Traditionally, in large markets (sometimes referred to as "major" markets), reporters had a "crew" which included a videographer (updated since the days when film was used for TV news and the term was photographer) who shot the visuals for the story, a field producer, who helped decide the locations to shoot and the subjects to interview, as well as consulting on the story's writing, and an editor, who put the whole prerecorded "package" together, wedding video to narration and sound bites. The reporter might suggest or look in on these processes, but mainly concentrated on his/her role in presenting the story.

In medium-sized markets, reporters might be expected to take on some of the tasks of others on the news team, possibly editing the final piece for airing, but would still be assigned a videographer to shoot the story's visuals, including the standup. Some reporters might know how to shoot and edit video, but it was usually neither expected nor encouraged. Similar to a major market, others did the visual work; as a reporter, you concentrated on the words, keeping the story short, sharp and accurate. Visual skills helped, but they weren't expected.

In small markets, the term television *reporter* was really a misnomer. In these markets, due to economic pressures and fewer resources, the reporter was expected to do it all. That meant setting up the story, deciding who to interview, doing the interviews, shooting the interviews, shooting your own standup, writing the script, recording the narration, picking the video, editing the video, doing the live shot or set piece or, possibly, even anchoring the whole newscast of which the story is a part. This arrangement came to have a term of its own. It was called being a "one-man band" and one of the incentives for moving up in market size was the opportunity to cease doing every job and just concentrate on reporting. Again, how times have changed!

Fast forward to the year 2010. In one of our Power Profiles, you'll meet Joe Little. He is the contemporary version of the "one-man band," but with a difference. A reporter at San Diego's KGTV, Little thinks of himself (and his employers label him) as a "digital correspondent." Still, like the "one-man bands" of TV's yesteryears, he writes and reports his stories, shoots all the video that goes into them, including standups, and edits the final product on his laptop's hard drive.

For today's *digital correspondent*, accumulating the visual skills needed to tell the story across platforms is not an option, it's a necessity. Whether the medium is print or TV makes little difference. For this generation of storytellers, carrying a hand-held camera for taking still photos or video, a digital audio recorder, and a laptop seems as natural as carrying a spiral-bound notebook was to reporters of previous generations. If you are a student or a working professional, success ultimately depends upon recognizing that you can no longer think of yourself as a reporter *or* a photographer *or* an editor. You will be expected to have all three skills and perform each at least competently, if not exceptionally.

Multimedia performance skills are not limited to local television stations, nor are they limited to local stories. As early as 2003, what were then termed "a new breed of multimedia television reporters came to global attention" on the battlefields in Iraq. The term then was "sojos," for "solo journalists." A news article written at the time described them this way:

> Whether they operate independently or with the support of a news organization, the gear package – all originally developed for consumer use – is similar: a DV camcorder, a laptop computer (usually an Apple Macintosh Powerbook G4), video editing software such as Apple's Final Cut or Avid's DV Express, compression software to squeeze the images, and a laptop-sized satellite telephone to transfer the pictures and sound back home.

A skilled multimedia journalist, equally adept at writing/reporting, audio and video recording and editing, with on-camera skills and enough proficiency to operate a small satellite telephone, can tell a story from anywhere in the world. As it was described back in 2003 and as it has been refined since, the multimedia reporter – having mastered several traditional trades – first prepares the story, writes the copy, and shoots still and/or moving images, including his own "standup" in front of the camera. Then, the reporter creates a voice narration, edits the images and completes an edited video news report on the laptop. Finally, the report is "compressed" and sent as a video data file back home through the satellite telephone.

Preston Mendenhall is an NBC news veteran with a TV news background. He describes himself as a "one-man band" and is a prime example of someone who has mastered the skills of multimedia reporting. In his backpack is about $15,000 worth of video equipment that he uses to snap photographs and shoot video in war zones around the globe as an international editor for MSNBC.com. "You get a connection, set up the camera, point it at yourself and just do it – you're live," Mendenhall said.

Some question the wisdom of having one person do the job of many – reporter, editor, camera and sound operator. On the other hand, no one disputes that for today's journalism students and those currently working in the field, it is a reality. And it can be a benefit to those who do it well, giving them ultimate control – one might say *power* – over their stories and their own performance. Whether you have a predisposition toward or talent for print or television journalism, begin thinking of yourself now as a multimedia storyteller. You'll see that term (along with similar ones like "digital correspondent") used in job postings for most major news organizations. It represents more than a change in titles or position descriptions.

Chances are good that even if you begin your career as a newspaper reporter, you will eventually do television reporting, especially if the paper for which you work is part of a larger media corporation that owns television stations, if not radio outlets as well. Knowing how to present your story in these media is essential. And every newspaper and television station, regardless of its overall ownership profile, has a web site. There you will be required to think "web first."

For television reporters, it is inevitable that you will be asked to contribute to the parent company's print product, either through text or photographs, not to mention the web site. If you go into TV reporting or already work in it, you can expect that you will do more than simply report. And you won't just have competition from print reporters, many of whom now must be adept at the presentation skills necessary for performance on TV or the web; there is a whole new movement toward multimedia performance in the field of public relations – one that can put effective PR storytellers front and center.

Public Relations Professionals

There is often a misconception that public relations practitioners are not reporters, at least not in the same sense as journalists. The reality is that, while news reporters and PR professionals have very different goals, they share the same sets of skills. The common denominator: effective storytelling. Everything we've said so far regarding the need for print and television reporters to adapt their skills for multimedia storytelling is true of PR professionals. Why? For one, the field of PR is increasingly a world driven by capitalizing on opportunities to speak directly to the audience, unfiltered and bypassing what was traditionally the "middle" man – the reporter, print or broadcast. To a certain extent technology has made this possible. To a large extent, social media have made it compelling.

If you work or aspire to work in public relations, you should plan to think as much about telling your own stories to a targeted audience as persuading print or broadcasters reporters that they should give you coverage. The "old" days of writing a news release about a client's issue, product, or cause are fast fading. No longer is the PR person's principal job to mail or fax the release, follow up with a phone call, and maybe even drop by the desk of a reporter for additional persuasion. Today's public relations professionals are more reporters than "flaks," a somewhat derisory term employed back when the principal job of the PR person was to deflect bad publicity about her or his client. Today, it's preferable to convey direct, unfiltered good news about that client.

A decade or two ago, a PR person might hope to "lure" print and broadcast reporters to an event staged on behalf of his or her client's rollout of a new product line by writing a traditional news release, containing basic facts and providing some background information. The goal was to spark interest among the print and TV reporters, the conduit to the audience you wanted to reach. Journalists might tell your story to their audience, but only if it first interested them. So, a news release might be drafted that would look like the one below:

Anzur and Silvia Associates
For release: August 4, 1992
Contact: Terry Anzur, 640-5555; Tony Silvia, 640-5514
LOCAL FIRM DEVELOPS FIRE ANT CURE

The end to annoying fire ants is now at hand, thanks to a revolutionary new product developed by scientists at Pest Free America, a Los Angeles firm. On August 21, firm officials and those who developed the ANT EATER will demonstrate its effectiveness at company headquarters on Hollywood Blvd. The ANT EATER uses scalding hot water, injected several feet down into the soil beneath it, through a series of hoses hooked to one master pump. It's portable, safe, and uses old-fashioned "boiling" to rid yards and gardens of red ants, also known as "fire ants." The pest populates mostly southern and western portions of the US and is especially troublesome to those who work outside or do landscaping. While some people are allergic to the ant's bite, for others, it can be fatal. This is the first affordable home application for what promises to be a hit with consumers and a relief for farmers.

Then there would be a list of people from the company who would be available for interviews on-site the day of the news conference. A so-called "press kit" (since renamed a media kit) would most likely accompany the release, containing still photos of the invention, testimonials from test groups if not actual customers, perhaps a schematic explaining the operation of the ANT EATER, etc. The PR person's job would be to get the print and television reporters to the news conference site by engaging their sense of what a "good" story was for their particular audiences. Certain "beat" reporters – those who cover specific kinds of news as opposed to general assignment reporters, who cover anything and everything on a given day – might be targeted. In this instance, it might be those who write about science, the environment, or technology.

Keep in mind that the entire goal was to convince others to provide you, the PR person, with news coverage for your client's product. Toward that end, yesterday's public relations person simply "baited" the coverage, but had no control over whether it actually reached the proper audience for the product. In other words, PR people, while possessing similar writing and researching skills to their journalist counterparts, were completely at the mercy of print and broadcast reporters to spread their message – or not. Their only tools from the 1920s until the 1970s consisted of the typed news release, the telephone, and, later, the fax machine. Beginning in the 1980s, public relations practitioners enlisted a new resource called the Video News Release (abbreviated as VNR).

The VNR was intended to look just like a finished television news story. It contained interviews with all those associated with the story and was narrated by a person who sounded and looked very much like an actual television news reporter or anchor. Often there was a reason for this similarity: the person in the VNR sometimes was actually a former TV reporter or anchor who switched jobs from journalism to PR – not an uncommon career path, as you'll see in Ann Kellan's profile in Chapter 6. The hope was that a well-produced VNR, fitting within the TV news time frame of less than two minutes, would run in its entirety on a local newscast. That might actually happen in smaller television markets. In larger ones, portions of the VNR might be edited into a story done by the local TV reporter or anchor. Either way, the PR practitioner – still very much at the mercy of the reporter – considered it a "win" for her/his client. And, as a bonus, sometimes the visuals and overall storytelling might capture the attention and support of a newspaper reporter as well.

As exposure on television became more important, the VNR became more slickly produced. Company interviewees became more polished in their presentation skills, usually as a result of coaching by the PR practitioner. With more sophisticated visual elements, the overall "look" of a VNR became vastly more appealing than a flat typed news release, no matter how well it was written. PR people, whether trained journalistically or not, began to take on more of the storytelling role of the print or broadcast journalist – no longer simply "pitching" the story for coverage, but orchestrating that coverage themselves. Multimedia has accelerated this trend, making a strong case for PR practitioners to have the writing, producing, and performance skills that once were the sole domain of their print and broadcast colleagues.

The effective public relations professional today is no longer in the background of news coverage. Managing a client's image now includes everything from designing multimedia-rich news releases – replete with opportunities for audience interaction – to appearing on-camera, either on traditional television or via the web, possibly even on a cellular phone screen. Increasingly, PR people reach out not only to journalists, but directly to consumers, encouraging them to drive the story through social networking media, according to James Lee, president of the California-based Lee Strategy Group (see his Power Profile in Chapter 6).

Today's Citizen Journalist

Of course, today anyone with a laptop and Internet access can produce and distribute informational content that once was the domain of the print/broadcast journalist or the public relations professional. The term "citizen journalist" has come to represent a person who uses all the tools of the multimedia journalist – text, audio, video, graphics – to tell a story that might otherwise not receive coverage in traditional or mainstream media. His or her motivation may stem from an interest in a certain subject or loyalty to a specific cause or community. The main difference is that, while newspaper and broadcast reporters as well as PR practitioners are professionals, paid to do their jobs, civic journalists sense a need in their community and fill it – usually without pay and sometimes with a small audience base.

Often the forum is a blog (the term that arose from the combination of "web" and "log") on the Internet and some civic journalists even develop a relatively large following. One upside to citizen journalism is its strong roots in the democratic tradition of connecting with a community, using readers, viewers, and users as a resource for what is sometimes seen as a "conversation" between those with a stake in the outcome of an election, a zoning board decision, a tax increase, or construction project. The downside to citizen journalism is that it can look amateurish in terms of its overall look and production values. Citizen journalists often have little formal training in journalism or media and many see their work both as a balance to corporate-owned news media and as an important contribution to public dialogue.

Citizen journalists face the same performance challenges as professional journalists and public relations practitioners. They need the skills associated with producing "value-added" content, rich with video, audio, graphics, and interactivity. They must also develop presentation skills, whether for a community cable television show, a web site, or a social media outlet like Facebook or Twitter. After all, whether you seek to be a print or television reporter, a PR professional, or a citizen journalist, your goal is the same: reach an audience in the best way possible.

An Inventory of Needed Skills

So, if you're a print reporter or studying to become one, what skills must you develop in order to be competitive in today's media job market? What if you're a television reporter or in college learning to become one? How about a public relations professional or student? And what skills do community journalists need? A list of skills for each is given below; a fuller exploration of each is contained within the chapters related to that specific media job. As you might expect, this inventory contains much overlap, but the intent is to suggest what skills in general each traditional job holder or seeker currently has and which skills he/she needs to develop or refine.

Which skills do you have and which do you need to be an effective storyteller in the multimedia environment? It is a question often asked by students and professionals alike. Our inventory is a good place to begin assessing your *power performance* skills. Choose from the check-list below the traditional media career path that best describes where you are or where you want to be.

General skills check-list

Job description: Newspaper reporter

- Traditional skills possessed: writing for print, editing for print, some web writing/editing skills.
- New skills needed: still photography, photo taking, video shooting, presentation skills (on-camera and voice), video editing (putting finished story together on laptop), graphics design, podcasting, refined web writing skills, social media skills.

Job description: Television reporter

- Traditional skills possessed: writing for broadcast, editing for broadcast, video editing, presentation skills (on-camera and voice), and some web writing skills.
- New skills needed: writing for print, editing for print, still photography, video shooting skills, refined web writing/editing skills, graphics design, refined web writing skills, social media skills.

Job description: Public relations practitioner

- Traditional skills possessed: writing news releases for print and TV, producing video news releases, planning news conferences, arranging interviews for media, serving as spokesperson for client.
- New skills needed: creating multimedia packages for print and TV, performance skills (on-camera and voice), coaching skills for clients to appear on web, TV, or social media.

The check-list above is not intended to be exhaustive, since there are no doubt individuals in each traditional job category who already possess to some degree the skills from other media that are suggested as "new skills." But many do not and, further, do not know where to begin.

Self-Inventory: The Right Stuff

The qualities of a successful multimedia journalist

Now it's time to determine specifically where *you* fit as a storyteller in today's multimedia environment. Take a few moments to assess your strengths and needs in each of four key areas: personal qualities, reporting and writing, presentation skills, and technical know-how.

Evaluate yourself in each of the categories listed below. Identify:

- skills you have not yet developed
- your areas of strength
- skills you already have begun to develop that are targets for improvement.

Review your list with someone who knows you well enough to be honest. Does that person agree with your self-assessment? Why or why not?

Personal qualities

Table 1.1   Personal qualities

	Must learn	*Strength*	*Needs improvement*
Curiosity			
Persistence			
Energy, enthusiasm			
Strong work ethic			
Honesty			
Self-confidence			
Takes initiative			
Open to new ideas			
Open to viewpoints I disagree with			
Good listener			
Sensitive to feelings of others			
Responds well to criticism			
Works well under pressure			
Team player			
Well organized			
Meets deadlines			

Reporting and writing

Table 1.2 Reporting and writing skills

	Must learn	Strength	Needs improvement
Can get information			
Can verify facts			
Attention to details			
Asks good questions			
Can get people to talk			
Solid news judgment			
Can write for broadcast			
Can write for print			
Uses correct grammar			
Uses correct spelling, punctuation			
Can identify more than one side of a story			
Learns quickly			
Writes clearly			
Can simplify complicated information			
Draws on education/life experience			
Can see the "big picture"			
Knows the audience			

Presentation skills

Table 1.3 Presentation skills

	Must learn	Strength	Needs improvement
Has a pleasant voice			
Good posture			
Correct breathing			
Uses variations in speed and pitch			
Avoids filler words like "um"			
Proper pronunciation			
Speaks clearly and distinctly			
Emphasizes what is important			
Can improvise or "ad lib"			
Makes an emotional connection to the story			
Listens and reacts appropriately			
Uses meaningful gestures			
Non-distracting hairstyle			
Appropriate use of makeup			
Wardrobe is suitable for situation			
Encourages a positive response from the audience			

Technical know-how

Table 1.4   Technical know-how

	Must learn	Strengths	Needs improvement
Word processing			
Internet search			
Operate digital camera (photos)			
Operate video camera			
Record audio			
Use lighting as needed			
Edit audio and video			
Post text, photos, and video to the web			
Knowledge of web design, HTML, Flash, etc.			
Social networking			
Embraces new technology			

Adapting to New Media

Obviously, you will need to learn additional skills and adapt to new job descriptions as multimedia continues to evolve. Today's journalists perform many more tasks than their predecessors of previous generations. It is, however, worth noting that some of the earliest of those we now revere as the pioneers of broadcast journalism worked in what we might call an early incarnation of multimedia. Edward R. Murrow, often termed the "father of broadcast journalism," worked in print journalism, for a news wire service, radio, and television. He even worked for the US Information Agency, in what might today be described as a public relations job, following his departure from CBS. One can only imagine that if the Internet had existed in the 1950s, Murrow would have readily embraced it as yet another medium to disseminate his reporting. His seminal documentary program, *See It Now* would have been not only broadcast, but streamed on the web. It would be available as a podcast or a download to mobile devices.

To suggest an example, Murrow's politically charged program on Senator Joseph McCarthy would be adapted to the web in an interactive manner. Viewers would be able to delve further into the life of this enigmatic man to decide for themselves if his mission to rid the US of communist infiltration during the 1950s was patriotic or frightening. There would be a Facebook page where fans of the show and of Murrow himself could "friend" the broadcast icon, exchanging updates and messages. Other social media would allow Murrow to keep his audience aware of reaction from politicians, sponsors, and other viewers. He could promote upcoming shows, not only *See It Now*, but *CBS Reports* and *Person to Person*, the celebrity interview program for which Murrow was also famous.

No one, of course, can say with certainty what Edward R. Murrow or others of his generation would have thought of the Internet and social media. Based upon his stated belief to an assembly of radio and television news directors in 1952 that the medium of television was nothing more than "a box of wires" if it failed to educate the viewing public, one might surmise that Murrow would have been excited by the web's expanded opportunities for illumination of difficult issues. On the other hand, he might have also bemoaned it as one more distraction from what he saw as the serious business of news. This doesn't detract from the primary point: Murrow, like others of his generation, moved fluidly and flexibly from one medium to another. Half a century before the term "multimedia" was invented, Murrow and his colleagues thought nothing of writing a story for a newspaper, doing another version for one of the wire services – Associated Press or United Press International – anchoring a radio newscast, and going down the hall at CBS to read the news on-camera for its television network. Job titles come and go, but *power performance* of storytelling skills is a constant – no matter what the job is called.

Whatever the specific media platform on which you work, your personal *brand* as a storyteller is a combination of the skills you have, the integrity you reflect, and the value you bring to an audience. Keep in mind that, as a storyteller in today's world, you are, indeed, a brand. That brand is reflected not only in your newspaper by-line, but through your television persona and your online presence, every time you post, blog, tweet or interact on Facebook. Maintaining your place as a multimedia brand means knowing what others around you are doing – and what you need to do just to keep up.

News anchor or digital host?

Legendary newsman Walter Cronkite was a print journalist before he assumed the role of anchor of the *CBS Evening News* and became what many polls called him: "the most trusted man in America." When Cronkite died in July, 2009, among the many tributes paid him was one by NBC's Brian Williams who referred to him as "America's anchorman." Cronkite began his professional career as a wire service reporter, having first worked at his college radio station. Before transitioning to TV, he anchored news on the CBS radio network. Upon his death, one story mentioned the vast number of reporter's notebooks he had saved over the years, each filled with fine details of stories covered, each a resource for writing longer versions of those he found especially compelling. Cronkite's legacy in many ways was this ability (similar to Murrow's) to move fluidly and flawlessly between media platforms – print, radio, and TV – without missing a beat.

When President John F. Kennedy was assassinated in November, 1963, Cronkite first delivered the fateful news to a nation on television over a slide announcing a "CBS News Bulletin." He did not appear on camera until later that hour. History tells us that the television crew was on its lunch break and there was no one to turn on or operate the cameras. Cronkite fell back on his radio skills, doing the best he could with voice only. He also wrote his own copy, not just on that day, but on most days for most broadcasts.

Cronkite, like ABC's Peter Jennings, kept a manual typewriter near the anchor desk and was known to write or change copy during commercial breaks. He was a writer and an editor; he used his voice and his visual presence, knew when to rely on film to tell a story best and when it was sometimes better to reassure a nation using the warmth and confidence radiated by his own image on-camera. He could do it all. Sound familiar? Again, it is in many ways the same expectation employers have of today's journalists.

Broadcast historians note that Cronkite was responsible for the coining of the term "anchor" following his reporting from the Democratic National Convention in 1952. The term was meant to describe someone who was at the center of the storytelling, the person who "held it all together." Cronkite personified this new job description at a time when TV news was just coming into its own, expanding from a nightly 15-minute news "round-up" to a full half-hour broadcast. TV was hiring those with strong writing and editing skills honed in other media, principally newspapers, wire services, and radio, as well as the ability to adapt to a changing media landscape. In many ways, it was a time similar to our own. Multimedia is creating new job descriptions, such as "digital host."

The term was first seen on the job listing site of the Poynter Institute for Media Studies in 2009 (poynter.org), amid other ads looking for applicants with web design, online writing, digital editing, and multimedia skills. The qualifications stressed all of the above. Formerly, the collective skills sought in three or four individuals, the job title itself implies someone who can do it all and, like the anchor of a previous generation, "hold it all together." The media platform listed was online, appearing on-camera to provide a thread between audio and video clips, slideshows, and graphics. Without over-generalizing from a single job listing, it is just one example of a new description for an evolving job across media platforms: the person who can guide an audience through a myriad number of stories by using her/his skills to create and present content in a credible manner. If the audience for Walter Cronkite misses his calm reassurance and credibility on television, the online audience is still waiting for his counterpart on their computer screens.

Cross-Platform Influences

To return to where this chapter began, let's think again about how the world of media – and with it the role of the storyteller – has changed between November 22, 1963, the date of the JFK assassination and June 29, 2009, the day of Michael Jackson's death. If you've ever watched the television coverage of the former, you can't help but recall the stark black and white images of the networks' news anchors – principally Cronkite on CBS and Frank McGee, later joined by Chet Huntley and David Brinkley, on NBC. These two networks dominated the coverage, with ABC, a fledgling news operation, barely in its infancy. Video (it was actually film in those days) was virtually non-existent. The processing time plus the distance from Dallas made it impractical for purposes of "breaking news" on television. The only extant film clip of the actual moment the bullet struck the president was captured by a home movie camera; it was operated by Abraham Zapruder, a bystander to the event.

Two things are remarkable from viewing television's coverage of this major event in American history. First, nearly all the TV coverage depended on reports not only from the networks' own correspondents in the field, but also from wire service reports (Cronkite got his first confirmation from one) as well as newspaper and radio reporters on scene. It was, in that sense, a sharing of resources across several media platforms, not unlike the cross-platform journalism of today. A primitive telephone hookup served as the live link for questions and answers from the anchors to the reporters. They used the phone, the only tool they had, to weave the story together from many sources and correspondents working in many different media. One might say they were *resourceful*. Or you could use the term *multimedia*.

Second, platform aside, what is most remarkable and enduring is the *storytelling*. Over four decades ago, as the nation mourned, without knowing they were doing so, the journalists of another generation used what they had at hand to tell the story that an anxious nation awaited. They were *innovative*. As the great jazz musician and band leader Count Basie once told *Downbeat* magazine in 1975: "I don't find innovation very interesting as such. The real innovators do their innovating by being themselves." The rules hadn't been invented for how to cover a story of this dimension or where the media boundaries were drawn. So, they crossed all the boundaries. In that sense, it could be argued they were practicing a form of multimedia storytelling even back then, complete with a citizen journalism component (the Zapruder film).

The TV networks got their information on the Kennedy assassination from other journalists within the established media corps: print, radio, or wire service reporters. From the first report of Kennedy's shooting to the final pronouncement of his death in a Dallas hospital, broadcasters relied on other reporters for the story they disseminated. They did not rely on the audience (with the admittedly major exception of Zapruder's film) for details or insight into the assassination or its aftermath. Most of the news came from officials, both in Dallas and Washington, and was relayed through reporters from various media at or near the scene. The audience for the story was passive, not active, and certainly not interactive. If anyone from the general public knew more than the officials, experts or journalists who dominated the coverage, they had no way to contribute.

Today, it would be difficult to imagine news coverage of any major event without the Internet and its social networking sites. When the government of Iran expelled all foreign media from the country in 2009, news coverage of improprieties within that country's elections didn't end; it shifted instead to Twitter, as ordinary citizens were motivated to spread the story beyond their sealed borders. In fact, when Twitter followed a planned shutdown for upgrading on the day of national elections in Iran, it sparked such a protest in the US and elsewhere around the globe, that the upgrade was delayed so the election story could continue. With today's cell phones, digital cameras, wireless Internet access and other communication alternatives like Skype, as well as Twitter and Facebook, interactivity to and from the audience becomes a vital part of every journalist's repertoire.

An unprecedented collaboration between CNN and Facebook during the 2008 US presidential election resulted in an audience on the social media site that far exceeded that of the network's television viewing audience. It is not hard to discern why the partnership was successful. Given that it has become commonplace for politicians to communicate with their supporters through social media (Barack Obama being, if not the first, certainly the most visible and effective candidate to do so), the news audience is already conditioned to receive information through this medium. Using it as one more tool can make today's multimedia journalist both *resourceful* and *innovative* – the same qualities that made those journalists covering JFK's assassination successful.

The opposite of those qualities involves what sometimes appears to be desperation or resignation by traditional news media in their approach to covering a major story. If the JFK assassination coverage in 1963 was among journalists' finest moments, it shared little in common with the coverage of Michael Jackson's death in 2009. Because so many in the audience already knew about Jackson's death not from radio, TV, or newspapers, reporters struggled to come up with new angles. That struggle led to the Internet, the place where celebrity news (in fact, increasingly, most news) often "breaks" first. The sight of an *NBC News* correspondent structuring his television story around the "exclusive" web cast of the 911 call that followed Jackson's death is telling on a number of levels. The correspondent waited during his live shot for the tmz.com audio clip off the Internet to load, and then simply amplified it for the TV audience to hear.

This scenario should provoke some questions for you to consider. Discuss the following, either in class or among your friends:

- What makes this a story, if you believe it is?
- What did the reporter in this situation provide his audience beyond what they could easily get for themselves by going directly to the web?
- What does this say about how the media landscape has changed?

We ask these questions for a very important reason. Beyond the specific tools used by today's journalists, consideration must be given to the process of storytelling itself – what it is and how it has changed. If multimedia adds anything to storytelling, it should bring added value to that process – audio, video, graphics, slideshows, an illustrative standup, anything that makes the story clearer, more understandable, and more interactive. In Chapter 2, you will learn how to tell compelling stories that begin with solid writing, strong research, and a keen sense of audience. Then, we will show you how the thoughtful inclusion of multimedia can make a good story even better!

A Multimedia Exercise

In this chapter, reference was made to news media coverage of President John F. Kennedy's assassination in 1963. The only existing film that day derived from a home movie camera. If a sitting American president were assassinated today, how would the story be covered across media platforms? Imagine that you are in charge of coverage for a newsroom where you have the obligation to cover that story for your parent company's newspaper, radio station, television station, and web site. What elements would you assign to each medium and how would they differ across platforms? What role would social media play in covering the story? Finally, how would multimedia be used to the greatest possible advantage?

Works Cited and Further Reading

Auletta, Ken. "Nonstop news," *The New Yorker*, January 25, 2010.

Cromie, Jenny. "Ink stained memories, multimedia futures," January 28, 2009. Retrieved from: http://www.everyjoe.com/articles/ink-stained-memories-multimedia-futures-15/.

Eastman, Susan and Ferguson, Douglas. *Media Programming: Strategies and Practices*, 8th edition. Boston, MA: Wadsworth Books, 2006.

Glor, Jeff. "How e-books are changing the printed word," *CBS Sunday Morning*, January 10, 2010. Retrieved from: http://www.cbsnews.com/stories/2010/01/10/sunday/main6079170.shtml.

Konrad, Rachel. "Technology enables backpack journalists," *Editor and Publisher*, March 25, 2003. Retrieved from: http://www.editorandpublisher.com/eandp/news/article_display.jsp?vnu_content_id=1848424.

Mendenhall, Preston. "Multimedia reporters debut on the battlefield," *Broadcast Engineering*, March 31, 2003. Retrieved from: http://broadcastengineering.com/news/broadcasting_multimedia_reporters_debut/.

Sefton, Dru. "Not too strange new bedfellows: print refugees," *Current*, March 30, 2009. Retrieved from: http://www.current.org/news/news0906printrefugees.shtml.

Tompkins, Al. "How one-man-band journalist handles multiple roles reporting, shooting, editing video," Poynter Institute for Media Studies, February 3, 2009. Retrieved from: http://www.poynter.org/column.asp?id=2&aid=157859.

COURTESY NBC

BRIAN WILLIAMS

NBC News

Job: Anchor and Managing Editor, *NBC Nightly News*
Market: National, based in New York
Hometown: Elmira, NY, and Middletown, NJ
Education: Attended George Washington University and Catholic University of America, Washington, DC. Left college for White House internship.
Career Path:
    Assistant administrator, National Association of Broadcasters political action committee, Washington, DC
    Reporter, KOAM-TV, Pittsburgh, KS
    Chyron* operator, reporter, WTTG-TV, Washington, DC
    Reporter, WCAU-TV, Philadelphia
    Anchor-reporter, WCBS-TV, New York
    Correspondent, *NBC News*, New York
    White House correspondent, NBC, Washington, DC
    Anchor, managing editor, MSNBC, New York

What life experiences prepared you to become a journalist?
I never had a dime for college. I've worked since the day I turned 14 and qualified for working papers in the state of New Jersey. Because of the lack of money I had to start out at a community college after high school and I was working two jobs, and fighting fires as a volunteer. I transferred to two different four-year schools, but eventually had to drop out. I've regretted that decision, but it wasn't a credential that has stood in my way in a business where, if you can write and report, that's all the bosses are interested in.

Note: *A chyron operator is a technical support person who types the on-screen titles that will be superimposed over video during the live newscast.

If you didn't learn it in college, how did you learn to report and write?

Role models are really crucial. The anniversary of Apollo 11 (the first landing on the moon) had me thinking back to watching Walter Cronkite every night as a kid. You couldn't eat dinner until the *CBS Evening News* was over. It was kind of like having a master class in broadcast journalism every night on a black and white television in our living room. It's that simple. I had the very best role model. Decide whose work you like and make the decision for sound reasons, not cosmetics, but on the quality of the work. Does it look like they wrote it? I can usually tell when I fly into a city and watch the local 11 p.m. news I can tell you who went out to dinner between the 6 and 11 and who stayed in the newsroom, got takeout and wrote the copy. Selecting as a role model a professional that you admire in terms of work ethic, work quality, and presentation is part of it because it's a visual medium.

How did you land your first job in broadcasting?

I got work by answering a classified ad in the *Washington Post* for a typist. The job happened to be at the National Association of Broadcasters, the lobbying arm of the industry. After working there for a long time I confided in my boss that my real goal was in television news. A station in Pittsburgh Kansas was willing to take me on as a rookie. I ended up moving out there, to the Midwest, starting a new career for $168 a week in 1981.

Was it worth it?

After 13 months in Kansas, I wasn't even at the poverty level in this country. I assumed it was a failed experiment. I couldn't get hired anywhere: Springfield, Missouri, Jefferson City, Tulsa, Wichita and Topeka were too big for me. I took all my accrued time off and got in my car with a bunch of tapes, trying to get the attention of news directors. Nobody would hire me. I ended up moving back to Washington where I knew I could find something.

So why didn't you give up?

I've always said that the term "hustler" isn't a pejorative. I hire hustlers, I'm attracted to them. A hustler is someone who knows how to make a living, survive and make their own luck. I knew I could hustle a job or two and put food on the table. So I went back to DC and got a job from another classified ad doing weekend chyron* at the independent 10 o'clock news station, WTTG. That was the break. I had a news director just take a liking to me. She took a leap of faith and put me on the air. Then someone at CBS saw my tape and they put me into their Philadelphia (station), WCAU.

I was able to work my way up to New York. But that was by hustling as well. I called the (WCBS) assignment desk and said, "Can you send me a (microphone) flag?" Atlantic City was just opening. Casino gambling had gone through and (Donald) Trump was flying in and all these other companies were building casinos. I was doing lots of pieces (for the Philadelphia station) that were of interest to New York. So I would take off the Channel 10 mic flag and talk the crew into shooting a new standup close for Channel 2. I would (send) tapes up to New York and they started airing my stuff. My motivation was simple: #1 market, both parents were still alive and I figured if I could come home they would be able to see me on TV and know that their boy had become something.

Do you write your own copy for *Nightly News*?

I am still forced to write my copy because I can't read anything cold. I have almost a kind of dyslexia when it comes to reading someone else's writing. It's not that mine is better, but how could they know what I was going to say? How could they possibly know how I was going to tell this story? I'm compelled to write and put everything in the broadcast in my own words. Some days I wish I was one of those who could look in the prompter and just go, but I've never been able to do it.

What's your thought process when you tell a story?

It really helps to know your audience. During my time at CBS, (a researcher) came and told us that everyone in our audience has a Sears credit card, what used to be known as America's largest retailer. Having grown up in a

Sears credit card household, that told me everything I need to know. I have a mental picture of John and Mary Viewer, including an average age, military experience or not, in some cases a room full of people of various ages, races, ethnicities. That's what I'm thinking about when I sit down to do the writing. Nothing matters but how the viewer is going to perceive it.

I always say the camera is like an MRI; it goes right through to your soul. People who watch our broadcast regularly have a pretty good idea who I am and I can tell they are trying to confirm that when I encounter them at airports and stores and restaurants. They start to know your sensibilities, the kinds of stories I like to tell. On the stories where you can show a little opinion and attitude, they know I'm kind of a libertarian and that I'm a friend of the military and they know I was a fireman. You'd be surprised how much they can know about you.

Is it more of a two-way conversation with the audience now because of multimedia technology?

Every day I have a blog due in the afternoon. It's a whole new deadline. It's not like I was sitting around with free time that I hadn't allocated. We post a lot of the behind-the-scenes stuff, the background from interviews. Or I'll use the blog to say, "You know what? We screwed up last night. We got something wrong, we omitted this or that, it wasn't our best effort." It's a nice reporter's notebook outlet for me. If Cronkite had written one of these things as a kind of viewers' guide to the broadcast, I would have loved it.

The *New York Times* has called your coverage of Hurricane Katrina "a defining moment." Was it your most memorable story?

Katrina was one where we were there before the first responders. We were there before the storm, in the Superdome, and we just watched it unfold. I've never truly witnessed a story unfold like that. These were Americans floating past me face down, the victims of a terrible, embarrassing, botched federal response. These were people no different from me, and their government just didn't seem to care that much about them or their plight. When you see dead citizens on the streets of a major US city, it was an outrage and a lot of us said so. I could not believe what was happening to my fellow citizens there. I get it that the storm was nobody's fault, but, boy, those first hours and days afterwards sure were.

What's your advice to multimedia journalists?

Talk to people the way you talk to the people you love. You wouldn't patronize them or announce something to them. You wouldn't use a different voice or a big persona. Envision your audience and just talk to people.

**Image of the Journalist
in Popular Culture**

RESOURCE

THE IMAGE OF THE JOURNALIST
IN POPULAR CULTURE

Web site: http://www.ijpc.org/

What: The IJPC Database is available to anyone and includes more than 75,500 entries on the image of the journalist in popular culture.

When: Founded in 2000 and used daily by scholars and researchers worldwide.

Where: A project of the Norman Lear Center and the Annenberg School for Communication and Journalism at the University of Southern California in Los Angeles, CA.

Why: To investigate and analyze – through research and publication – the conflicting images of journalists in film, television, radio, fiction, commercials, cartoons, comic books, music, art, video games – demonstrating their impact on the public's perception of news gatherers.

Who: Joe Saltzman, a professor of journalism at the USC Annenberg School for Communication and Journalism, is director of The IJPC.

How has the image of the journalist changed over time?

Ancient journalists offered news of the day from the beginning of recorded history to the fall of Rome. In ancient Greece, news gathering was an oral tradition, with so-called historians, who were more like journalists, "broadcasting" to the town square or discussing current events and history with their students. The epigrammatists of Rome were doing exactly what gossip columnists do today, writing about the bad or funny things people do.

The image of the journalist hasn't changed much in more than 2000 years. It's a continuing dichotomy. The reporter or editor could get away with anything as long as the end result was *in the public interest*. The journalist could lie, cheat, distort, bribe, betray, or violate any ethical code as long as the journalist exposed corruption, solved a murder, caught a thief, or saved an innocent. Most films about journalism end with the reporter or editor winning the battle, if not the war. At the same time, the most indelible image may be that of the journalist as scoundrel, as evil, as the worst of villains because they use the precious commodity of public confidence in the press for their own selfish ends. If the journalist uses the power of the media for his or her own personal, political, or financial gain, if the end result is *not in the public interest*, then no matter what the journalist does, no matter how much he or she struggles with his or her conscience or tries to do the right thing, evil has won out.

It's a fallacy that the image of the journalist today is not as good as it used to be. The news balladeers of ancient times would go to see a hanging and write a poem or a ballad that they would sell to the crowds leaving the event. In 1625, Ben Johnson wrote "The Staple of News" launching a vicious attack on newsmongers because they were making money from information. In the eighteenth and nineteenth centuries a host of novelists wrote parodies of the well-known editors of the day. Popular novelist James Fenimore Cooper, for example, wrote two novels about Steadfast Dodge, an editor who was as corrupt as a journalist can be. Many films have been based on novels about journalists. *Five Star Final*, released in 1931, is one of the most vicious attacks on journalism you'll ever see. The last shot is a picture of a newspaper in the gutter with mud being swept on it. The editor washes his hands throughout the movie as if there is something dirty on them. Boris Karloff, who made his fame playing Dr. Frankenstein's monster, is one of the sleaziest reporters in the history of the movies, masquerading as a minister to get the story. He plays a despicable character who looks as creepy as his ethics. The film was based on a Broadway play written by a newspaperman who worked on the tabloids. Everybody talks about *The Front Page* as one of the great movies about journalists in film history. But the reporters in *The Front Page* behave unethically by today's standards. Journalists in films of the 1930s and 1940s did terrible things, but they were played by the most popular actors of the day, so people transferred their love of the actor to the character and forgave them almost anything.

Is there a difference between a journalist and a storyteller?

A storyteller can make up a fictional story. By the 1950s, journalists established an ethical framework within which to tell the story. The journalist has to be a storyteller within the confines of accuracy and fairness, or he's a bad journalist. If the journalist is good, he or she will tell compelling stories with interesting characters. But a lot of journalism is simply transmitting information efficiently. There isn't a journalist, real or fictional, who doesn't feel that working for a newspaper or a TV station or a web site is beneath their skills. In the old days they wanted to be novelists or playwrights. In the present day, they want to write movie scripts and TV pilots. They want to get respect and most journalists believe that journalism is a stepping stone to something better.

Journalists can also be commentators, columnists, critics, cartoonists, and editorial writers. These people write from very specific points of view. They may be lying or you may just disagree with them. But it's not just news gatherers and reporters. The word *journalist* came from the act of writing in a journal, which was usually stating an opinion. Most of the journalists in history had a point of view. The whole notion of not having a point of view, of being "objective," is a fairly new term from the mid-twentieth century. It became the code of the journalist to be fair. Now everybody fears that we are losing it again and going back to the way it was. During the Civil War, for example, you couldn't find a paper in the South or North that was going to write a fair account of a battle.

How are journalists viewed in a multimedia world where anybody with a computer can be a journalist?

I believe the Internet is what democracy was supposed to be. Many Americans in the eighteenth and nineteenth centuries envisioned that freedom of the press in America meant that everybody would have a press and write a newsletter, that everybody would have the opportunity to speak, and out of this chaos would come truth. That belief proved to be a fantasy. There was a whole history of itinerant printers who would go from town to town creating newspapers for a livelihood. But along the way it became expensive. Only people with money could afford a press. Nowadays we all have our own press. Anyone can write a blog and each reader will evaluate what it means to him or her. You are seeing more bloggers in fiction. There's a TV show called *Ghost Whisperer* in which a blogger played a key role, revealing information and causing problems. In the movie *State of Play* a young, inexperienced Internet journalist is paired with a seasoned (print) reporter and they work together to expose corruption.

What can multimedia journalists and researchers learn from this database?

This database includes entries on film, television, fiction (novels, short stories, plays, poems), radio, commercials, cartoons, comic books, video games, the Internet and all aspects of popular culture. The database is a comprehensive roadmap, a starting place. But the actual research, scholarship and writing are up to the individual. You have to actually watch the films and read the novels. For example, it is fascinating to trace the mythology of Superman and Clark Kent from 1939 to today. Whether it's a comic book or a radio show or a film or a TV program, the mythology never changes. It's one of the great stories of the image of the journalist in popular culture because young people who are discovering the TV series *Smallville* may not realize that these are the same images established in comic books more than seven decades ago. Lois Lane is still a feisty female reporter, Clark Kent is still the loyal, hardworking journalist trying to be fair and accurate. Perry White is still the crusty editor, yelling at the reporters all the time. The comic books have taken Clark Kent into television, and recently some of the *Daily Planet* staff were fired due to cutbacks.

How does the image of the journalist appear in diverse cultures?

In the 1940s, there were black editors and reporters in "race movies" made for the African-American audience, but there weren't many black reporters portrayed in the mainstream media until Sidney Poitier played a photo-journalist in *The Bedford Incident* in 1965. Some 30 years later, Denzel Washington played an investigative journalist in 1993's *The Pelican Brief*. From the 1980s on, many African Americans were featured portraying weather or sports reporters, and they can be seen in anonymous groups of reporters, but there are few Asian or Hispanic reporters visible until the late twentieth century and most of them can only be seen in groups of reporters trying to get a story at a press conference or a courtroom.

Numerous regions and countries are represented in the IJPC database: Australia, Canada, China, Great Britain, France, Germany, Italy, Mexico, Poland, Russia, Spain, and especially India. Nearly every Bollywood film has a reporter running around. The database can be indexed by country.

What lessons from the database will be useful for the multimedia journalists of the future?

By studying the image of the journalist, young journalists can see in bold letters that it's an important profession. What a journalist does matters. Whatever you write or say, people are reading or listening. And it makes a difference. Without journalists, no democracy can survive. It is crystal clear, when you see a dramatization of the journalist on the big or small screen, that it's important to do the job of a journalist well. If you do not serve the public interest, you are in for a bad time.

2

Reporting Stories across Media

In Chapter 1, we made the case that all storytellers, regardless of their specific job title (print, broadcast, or PR) should have an understanding of what multimedia skills are and when it is best to use them for maximum impact on the audience. The ability to do so is what we call *power performance*. The first step in that process is *getting the story*. There are scores of books that focus on how to generate story ideas, pitch them to your editor or news director, then generate the research, do the interviews, and report the final story, creating an easy-to-follow narrative that includes a clear beginning, middle and end. That is the *linear* process of news reporting and writing; it has served traditional print and broadcast journalists well for hundreds of years. What we will do in this chapter and those that follow is focus more upon how multimedia reporting adds additional elements to that process, creating a *non-linear* approach to storytelling that enriches the experience for your audience.

Before returning to a consideration of what effective multimedia storytelling is and isn't, it may be useful to explore the advantages of each media platform: print, television, and web.

Platform Advantages

- Broadcast news offers:
  - immediacy
  - impact (sound, visuals and emotions)
- Print news offers:
  - depth
  - detail
  - permanence

Power Performance: Multimedia Storytelling for Journalism and Public Relations, First Edition. Tony Silvia and Terry Anzur.
© 2011 Tony Silvia and Terry Anzur. Published 2011 by Blackwell Publishing Ltd.

- Web journalism is:
  - on demand
  - interactive
  - innovative

Television news offers immediacy, the sense that what we are seeing is happening right now; as we are watching, it unfolds before our eyes. On September 11, 2001, when terrorists attacked New York's Twin Towers, TV news was the first place most Americans turned and for a reason. In the aftermath of the attack, cell phone and Internet access were either erratic or non-existent in parts of Manhattan. Another reason is simply habit – the fact that whole generations of Americans had turned to TV (and before its advent, radio) for breaking news.

Television also has impact, largely related to the visual effect it has on the viewer. Television is a visceral medium; because viewers process information differently from readers, the entire experience is tied less to the cognitive side of our brains and more to those areas chiefly responsible for emotion. It is why a strong visual in a story, say, the close-up of a person in tears over losing a loved one, provokes a visceral reaction in the viewer that is far more powerful than words on a page. Where words engage the brain, images capture the heart. The latter is when TV news, most practitioners agree, is at its best.

On the other hand, TV news has never been especially good at conveying stories that require specialized knowledge in such fields as politics, economics or science. The advantage for in-depth coverage has traditionally gone to newspapers and magazines. One reason is that there is more room for detail in print media, which also has traditionally enjoyed the advantage of permanence. During most of its history, the *New York Times* has been referred to as the nation's newspaper of record, in part because of the quality of its coverage, but also because newspapers in general were traditionally considered less ethereal than television news, where the story is aired once and then is gone forever. Newspapers were archived and, therefore, retrievable for research and historical purposes.

Of course, the permanence aspect, along with most other traditional assumptions surrounding news media, has changed considerably since the advent of the web. Television news has an infinite shelf-life today on the Internet, as does every other form of media. However, web journalism brings an entirely new component to storytelling. Unlike newspapers, it is not time-locked, meaning online readers can read and retrieve any content they want any time they want. One of web journalism's greatest advantages is the fact that all information is available on-demand.

In addition, web journalism, unlike print and television, is interactive. Users not only respond to the content they read, but contribute to it, either by posting comments, expressing opinions, asking questions, requesting more information, or sending e-mails to the story's reporter: possibly even providing details not included in the original story or suggesting new angles to the story. For that reason – and many others – for those who want to report compelling stories, web journalism is *the* platform. It is a nexus for the kind of innovation that leads to power performance in multimedia.

Finding the Story

It may seem counter-intuitive, but often the biggest challenge for a storyteller is finding a story to tell. Sometimes, if you're lucky, the story finds you! Usually, that's called *breaking news* – the story that's right in front of you is a "can't miss" proposition. Most stories, however, regardless of their eventual platform, must be conceived (the idea), developed (the research), expanded (the interviews), and constructed (the writing and editing). Before you can report any story, you must gather its essential elements. That process begins with knowing what makes a good story and then deciding which is the best medium through which to tell that story – print, audio, video, or the combination of all three, with graphics, slideshows, and additional story links. That combination we call multimedia.

What makes a good story? There are as many answers to that question as there are storytellers. One answer is that it begins with knowing your audience. To be a good storyteller in any medium, it could be argued that you need to be a good observer of human behavior. Below are things to keep in mind when measuring the interest a story idea might engender in the audience:

- Know your audience: *Who* are you trying to reach? This means understanding what are called the demographics of the audience: their age, gender, etc. It also means understanding the audience's psychographics, often known as "lifestyle" data: their hobbies, buying habits, education, even religion.
- Know what your audience knows: *What* information does your audience already have about the story that will help you in telling it? This means reviewing recent news coverage of similar stories.
- Know what your audience doesn't know: *Where* in your story is there information that your audience is likely not to know? This means recognizing those aspects of the story that require knowledge of a specialized nature in order to understand it fully.
- Know what your audience needs to know: *When* is the timing of a story important? This means assessing the optimum time when the audience is more likely to need the information in your story. At different times of the year, for instance, some stories may generate higher interest than others.
- Know what your audience wants to know: *Why* would anyone want to read, view, or listen to your story? What is the potential benefit they will gain from it? This means evaluating what your audience cares about, thereby increasing the probability they will care about the story you're telling.
- Know your audience's value system: *How* will your story fit in with what the audience already believes to be true? This means knowing what your audience values. What do they already like? What do they dislike? What do they fear? What are their hopes and dreams? Obviously, it's difficult to make assumptions about every member of your audience, but people who live in a certain city, town or region generally share some common values. To the extent you can create a "fit" with those values, your job as a storyteller is much easier.

Note, each of the key words in italics above is the same as journalism's check-list of journalism's essential storytelling elements: the five Ws and one H:

- *What* happened?
- *Who* is involved?
- *When* did it happen?
- *Where* did it happen?
- *Why* did it happen?
- *How* did it happen?

Evaluating a story's potential is the same as evaluating its meaning for your audience, not your competitor's audience, but *your* audience. When doing so, it is wise to keep in mind the words of Kenn Venit, a veteran television news consultant: "Don't overestimate the audience's knowledge; don't underestimate its intelligence."

Journalism's Enduring Values

Now that you have defined your story, you are ready to gather and verify all the facts you need for power performance storytelling. In gathering the five Ws and one H, there are several prime considerations:

Accuracy

If you don't get the facts right, why bother? Verify every fact in your story, including the ages of your subjects and the proper spelling of names. Just because you read it online or believe it to be "something everyone knows" doesn't make it true. Observe the old newsroom adage, "If your mother says she loves you, check it out." If you are not sure of something, don't report it as a fact. If an unconfirmed fact is important to the story, you might say that you are still working to verify the information. Otherwise, when in doubt, leave it out.

Attribution

Your audience deserves to know where you got the information. Journalists call this "attribution." It is especially important in situations where the facts are in dispute, or could be in dispute. For example, in a crime story you would use attribution this way: "*Police say* John Doe shot and killed the shopkeeper during a robbery; *Doe says* he wasn't even in the neighborhood when the shots were fired." Not every fact requires attribution, but most do. You can probably say that it's a hot summer day without attributing your personal observation, but if you are reporting that it's the hottest July temperature ever recorded, you had better name a source like the National Weather Service. Put most simply: If the fact you have just reported causes the audience to say, "Oh, really? Says who?," you need attribution.

Fairness

Even if every fact in your story is verified and attributed, it is possible to be totally accurate – and completely unfair at the same time. News stories must have conflict, which implies that there is more than one side to the story. You may have to make an extra effort to get all the relevant viewpoints. For example, you are reporting the grievances of striking workers on a picket line. You need to make a phone call or check the company's web site to get the employer's side of the story. If one side is unavailable or won't talk, disclose to the audience that you made the effort to be fair. You may run across someone who hopes to stop your story by refusing to talk. In that case, you should let the audience know that the person was given an opportunity to comment and declined. Yes, there are some stories that are overwhelmingly dominated by one viewpoint. But never hit the "send" button until you are sure you have considered the possibility of alternative views.

These standards for power performance storytelling apply to all platforms. In the chapters ahead we will address the presentation of your story and how to adapt to the unique requirements of television, radio, print and the web.

Human Elements of Storytelling

No matter what the subject of a story, to be compelling, it should include a human element. Compelling news stories are, after all, *stories* and good stories are about people. That's what makes them intrinsically interesting and what separates a story from other forms of writing. As Don Hewitt, the architect behind one of television's longest-running news programs, *60 Minutes*, puts it: "No child has ever said to his parents, 'Daddy, mommy, please tell me an article.' Every kid says, 'Mommy, daddy, please tell me a story.'" It's also useful to remember that stories don't happen. Events happen. Stories are *built*. And they are successful to the extent that they build a vital connection between you and your audience.

Keep in mind that stories are written for people, not for other reporters. Given that, there are some aspects of human nature that are useful to know when planning the approach to your story. The major points below will help you find the human element in every story.

• People want to *connect*.

Humans have a basic human need to connect with one another. That need fuels the drive toward sharing common experiences, whether a sporting event, a concert, or a religious service, among the many other communal activities we undertake in society. One might even deduce that the explosion of social media like Facebook and Twitter is an extension of that need for people to connect with each other from across the office, down the street, or around the globe. Stories that remind us of our common humanity reflect this need to connect.

- People want to *care*.

In times of tragedy or devastation, the outpouring of emotion and support for those suffering, by neighbors or even total strangers, is remarkable. The sharp increase in financial donations to charitable organizations that help victims of tragedy is just one indication of the human capacity to care about others in their time of need. Stories that include a strong emotional element reflect this human capacity for caring.

- People want to *commit*.

The human need to connect with others, coupled with the inclination to care about others, together lead to a desire to do something, what those who work in the philanthropic field refer to as a "call to action." No one wants to feel powerless to change a bad situation. Most are looking for a way to help. Stories that provide the audience with a solution to a dilemma, their own or someone else's, reflect this human need for commitment.

- Give them a *reason*.

It's not as hard as it might sound. Human beings listen and watch selectively, screening out information that they don't find relevant to them. They also key in on those elements of a story that give them a reason to do all of the above: connect, care, and commit. Stories that embed universal truths, strong emotion, and solve a problem answer the question every audience has about any story: "Why should I invest my time and energy in what you're telling me?"

Building a Story

Once you've established a connection for your story, the building begins. We said it above, but it bears repeating: events happen; stories are *built*. For instance, the fire down the street is an event, what we often refer to as "breaking news." The event "tells" itself: the flames, smoke, sirens, engine companies on scene, etc. are all self-evident. But the story that results from that fire is what we, as storytellers, "build": the predicament faced by the fire's victims, the firefighter who loses his life saving a child inside the burning building. News stories are built around a number of principles that help create interest and ensure success:

- *Impact*: What's the effect and on how many? The principle of the greatest good for the largest number of people. This comes from the English philosopher John Stuart Mill and is one of the foundations of American journalism.
- *Interest*: What are people talking about on the subway? In barber shops? At the local grocery store? Generally, stories have interest to the extent that people are already talking about them where they work, live, or shop. The news consulting group called Broadcast Image put it this way: News is what people are talking about or *should* be talking about.

- *Immediacy*: Proceeding from interest, there are things we are more interested in now rather than later or later rather than now. Ask yourself: what does the audience want to know NOW, not tomorrow or next week?
- *Currency*: How does it fit in with other stories that are "top of mind" in the news cycle? What are the other stories that day competing for the audience's attention?
- *Proximity*: We're generally more interested in things that happen near where we live or work. The closer a story's setting is to our neighborhood, block, or section of a town/ city, the greater the interest. There is also another kind of proximity, what we might call psychological proximity. Not everyone lived in New York City on 9/11, but all Americans felt "close" to those in Manhattan, regardless of where they lived across the rest of the country.
- *Characters*: Successful news stories share something in common with a good short story, play, or novel. They have people in them who, like those in literary works, are strong, appealing characters. Ask yourself: are the people interviewed for your story likable, sympathetic, and, therefore, compelling? For instance, producers for NBC's *Dateline* talk about "casting" their stories.

To the extent that they are any or all of the above, your story will probably be memorable to the audience. To paraphrase former CBS News president Van Gordon Sauter, to be successful, every story has to have a moment that is magical, one that the audience will carry with them, that moment they will remember long after the story is over.

Stories as Conversations

Think for a moment about the most memorable verbal interactions you've had with other people throughout your life. Were they lectures? How about monologues? Most likely, the answer is neither. It's more likely they involved talking *with* another person, not being talked to *by* that person. There's an old adage in the news business: write as if you are telling your story to one person, not to a massive audience. Doing so means writing the story as if it were a conversation, not a lecture or a monologue. So, as you write – in fact, even before you write – keep the following guidelines in mind:

- The best stories are conversations with the audience and result in "reverb" coverage.

If a story hits a chord with an audience, it often finds its way into other media, in one form or another. For example, a story that begins in the *Wall Street Journal*, if it is compelling, is replicated on the *Today Show*, local news outlets, and web sites. Lawrence Grossman, the former president of NBC News, once called this the "reverb effect," meaning that good stories begin as conversations and the conversation spreads beyond the original sources. In today's storytelling environments, that conversation often spreads through various social media. If people are talking about it to their friends on Facebook or tweeting about it via Twitter, there's reason to believe it's not just a good story, but a big story – one that *connects* with a broad audience.

- Simplify, simplify, simplify.

Think about the way people speak. Have you ever heard a person say in any conversation "I was in an unfortunate mishap when another motorist's automobile collided with my own vehicle"? Of course not. This is not the language of conversation. "Real" people use informal language when they speak. You probably have heard something like "I was in a bad crash when another driver hit my car."

- Minimize ambiguity and reduce complexity.

Stories should be written in a manner that helps your audience understand, not in a manner to create misunderstanding. Most of us feel uncomfortable with ambiguity – the sense that there is no possible answer to what's being discussed. The answer could be this; on the other hand, it could be that. News stories, because they give both sides of an issue (as they should), can create confusion for the audience if each side is not presented clearly.

Similarly, complexity works against clear understanding of the story being told. Don't go into every minute step or detail in a complex process like how an innovative new gadget works. The audience doesn't care. When friends talk about that story, the emphasis will be on the fact that the gadget exists, that it does work, and where it can be bought – not the fine points of what makes it functional.

- Use familiar words.

Going back to the adage "simplify," try to avoid specialized jargon used only by experts in a given field. Those experts will understand what you're talking about, but no one else will. How many times have you felt left out of a conversation because those around you are using language that is a total mystery to you? Think about that before using terms like "environmental dimensions of a communication-based scenario assist in maximizing sound potential" instead of a familiar interpretation like "room size affects how well people hear."

- Focus on people before property – the best stories are about people, not material things.

Picture this scenario: a tornado has destroyed 75 percent of a small Texas town. In the midst of the devastation is a young 8-year-old girl clinging to her cherished stuffed animal. Behind her is her demolished home. Do you care more about the girl or the house? Certainly, it's sad that she lost what may be the only home she has ever known. But she's alive. A house can be replaced; a life cannot be restored.

The fact that the little girl survived is the story most people will talk about, not one about yet another house (as important as that house may be to the girl and her family) in a long path of destruction. The one piece of property that might be part of the conversation and, therefore, should be in the story is that stuffed animal. They both survived the storm and that constitutes a poignant image few in the audience will ever forget.

- Look for "People like us" – create a parasocial relationship.

Generally, people have conversations with those who they feel share certain things in common with them. Those things might be where they went to school, where they work, where they vacation, what movies they see, what foods they eat, what cars they drive, etc. It's a long list of what we might call affinity factors: those things that determine whether we feel others are more like or unlike us. To the extent we sense an affinity – that someone reminds us of us or our own situation – we are more or less likely to pay attention to the story we're being told.

For example, if a story is about people who work hard, are paying higher taxes all the time, and still facing foreclosure on their home, we may have more interest in that story if we are in the same situation – or fear we may be soon. That person becomes more "like us" than not. We begin to identify with his/her plight and there the conversation begins. If you are really successful, the audience may even develop what's sometimes termed a "para-social (one-way) relationship" with the subject of your story. At that point, the audience feels like they know the person so well that they begin to think "Wow, this is someone I would have a cup of coffee with to talk over what we're both facing."

- Look for "microcosm-macrocosm" – specific to the general.

Notice that, in the examples above, the emphasis has been on individuals as subjects for your story, not groups of people. This is based on research suggesting that successful stories personalize or "put a face" on a broad subject or issue. It's hard for people to grasp the plight of "the seven out of every ten women who contract breast cancer." It's a great deal easier to sympathize with the plight of one woman whose challenges are representative of the larger group. By focusing on the specific person affected, your story has a better chance of interesting the audience in the general topic.

- The best stories utilize the environment: observe what's physically around you.

Television reporters are always looking around them while covering a story, in search of the best background against which to do their standup (the portion of the video story in which they appear on-camera). The choice should be a spot that's integral to the story, giving the reporter the opportunity for movement, gestures, etc., if not certain "props" that help illustrate a major point (see Chapter 3).

This helps with creating both a sense of conversation with the audience and the para-social relationship between reporter and viewer. However, when reporting a story, all journalists should train themselves to observe the small details of what surrounds them. The small detail could lead to a story's "hook" – the single most important element for peaking audience interest.

Chip Scanlon, a former newspaper reporter, now on the faculty at Columbia University, relates how he once went to the home of a woman whose son had died because of a drunk driver a year before. He was to interview her on the anniversary of her son's death and the work she did on behalf of MADD (Mothers Against Drunk Drivers). As he entered the front door, he noticed the porch light was lit. It was mid-morning.

Scanlon wrote on his pad "porch light," as a reminder to ask the mother if it was significant. It could easily have been that she forgot to turn it off the night before. When he asked, she replied that it had never been turned off since the night her son left home and never returned; it was left on as a sign of hope that he might one day walk back through the front door. That small detail, based upon an observation many reporters would have completely overlooked, became the driving element behind the eventual story.

Storytelling Formulas

Once overhead in a television newsroom: "There are six basic formulas to every story; all we do is vary them." There is some truth to this statement, however simplified it may seem. Certainly, however, there are more than six variations on the theme of storytelling. Each of the "formulas" below are timeless ways of structuring a story, most dating back centuries to the classical age of Greek tragedy and the works of Homer, Aristophanes, and Sophocles, among others. Shakespeare, though obviously not a journalist, was a storyteller. He used these same tested formulas for writing his greatest plays. They have survived for a reason: they work.

- Hero against the odds.

Stories that focus on someone who accomplished a deed or has overcome a disadvantage to succeed are compelling because, in our own lives, we all like to think it's possible to beat the odds and win big – whether that means getting the top job, marrying the best-looking spouse, or capturing the biggest lottery win.

In terms of more substantial achievements, stories about the "unlikely" hero – for instance, the frail old woman who refused to be robbed in her own home, instead putting up a fight and driving the thieves out of her house. That's an actual story that garnered great interest, even prompting a segment on the *Today* show in 2009.

- Self-sacrifice for family.

Stories that focus on a family member who gives up something of value for the sake of others in his or her family or, alternately, someone else's family are compelling because they demonstrate the kind of selfless behavior we want to believe is possible. A parent who foregoes a lucrative job or a prestigious honor in order to care for a physically challenged child would be one example.

For example, there is the actual story of two girls involved in a car crash. One survived, the other died. Due to the extent of the injuries suffered by the surviving girl, identification was difficult. As it turned out, the identities of the two girls were reversed; the girl thought to have died was alive, and vice versa. The family of deceased girl, rather than being bitter once the truth was discovered, instead befriended the family of the girl whose life had been spared. In doing so, they put their own grief aside and embraced the happiness of the other family at having their daughter alive. This form of sacrifice, in this case for a family other than one's own, creates an extraordinary storyline.

• Self-sacrifice for friends.

Stories that utilize this approach are compelling because they reinforce the belief that friendship is an inviolable bond between us and those to whom we are closest outside our immediate families. Most people have many acquaintances; many of us, if we are fortunate, have a few people we classify as "friends." When we sacrifice for one of them or they do so for us, that's a great storyline.

For example, the person who volunteers her/his kidney for a lifelong friend who will die without an organ transplant creates a story in which many in the audience can see themselves – either as the recipient or the donor. We can empathize with the plight of both parties and, therefore, are intrinsically drawn to such a story. We marvel at the level of strength it takes for one friend to give and for the other to receive.

• Self-sacrifice for strangers.

Even more compelling are stories in which an individual risks life or limb to prevent harm to someone who is a total stranger. Stories about this form of self-sacrifice reinforce in the audience a core belief in the essential goodness of humanity.

For example, during the war in Iraq there have been many stories of heroism by service-men and women who throw themselves in harm's way to protect the life of a fellow service-man or woman who they don't even know. Closer to home are those instances of people who run into burning buildings to save a total stranger from death, sometimes at the cost of their own lives.

• Man's conflict against nature.

Conflict in general is a good formula for storytelling. However, anyone who has ever had to battle against a natural disaster, be it a hurricane, flood, tornado, or typhoon, knows first-hand the severity of the conflict people face in these situations. Fighting the elements, win or lose, creates a compelling storyline with which people in most parts of the country can, at one time or another, identify.

During Hurricane Katrina, the outpouring of support for survivors from all corners of the US was a direct result of the universal awareness that nature is capricious; any of us can find ourselves in conflict with its fury. Despite hardships and relief efforts that were slow in coming, New Orleans residents persevered. Stories about the bravery and resiliency of others in this situation can be inspiring.

• Man's struggle against bureaucracy.

People struggling against big corporations or social institutions – especially those that are perceived to be inefficient or unfair – creates a situation in which the audience cheers for the average guy in his fight against city hall. At some point, everyone feels as if the "system" has mistreated them, whether it is an undeserved traffic ticket or an unfairly high tax bill.

The General Motors dealer in New Jersey who went on CNN in 2009 to announce he wouldn't stand still for being one of those closed down by the big corporation is a great example. The dealer brought his plight to the television cameras, vowing that no matter how long it took or how much it cost, he would not go down without a fight. Stories of this kind interest us precisely because that dealer is fighting back, something we would like to do, but often don't. We live vicariously through his actions.

- Man's battle against self.

How many stories do we read and watch every day that deal with others battling against a myriad of personal problems from drug and alcohol addiction to failed relationships and shattered careers? It's the stuff of celebrity news, but this formula has found its way into all forms of storytelling.

In 2008, one of the biggest stories in sports was Josh Hamilton of the Texas Rangers baseball team. The year before, Hamilton had been released by the Tampa Bay Rays after numerous, very public efforts to kick drug and alcohol habits were unsuccessful. Two teams later, Hamilton was the poster child for what can happen when one faces his own inner demons – and wins. Stories of this kind suggest that it's possible to overcome one's baser instincts while celebrating the personal redemption we like to believe is possible for all of us.

Crisis, Conflict, Resolution (CCR)

Each of the above story formulas involves conflict. Think back to the stories you enjoyed as a child. Fairy tales often begin with "once upon a time," then "something happened" and "they all lived happily ever after." The story is satisfying because it has a beginning, middle and end. Screenwriters and playwrights speak of dividing their stories into three acts, or thirds. Romance writers rarely stray from the basic formula of "boy meets girl, boy loses girl, boy gets girl back." In multimedia storytelling, the standard three-part story structure is crisis, conflict, resolution, which we will abbreviate as CCR (Table 2.1).

The "crisis" element is easy to identify when it is literally a crisis: someone is murdered and police are hunting for the killer, or a family loses everything when their home burns

Table 2.1 Crisis, conflict, resolution

Beginning	Once upon a time …	Act I	Boy meets girl	The starting point	Crisis
Middle	… something happened …	Act II	Boy loses girl	The central question	Conflict
End	… happily ever after	Act III	Boy gets girl back	The ending point	Resolution

to the ground. Other times it is more like a problem to be solved: an angry consumer who wants a refund, or a parent trying to figure out how to help her kids do better in school. The term "crisis" can refer simply to the catalyst or starting point of a story: a new product on the market, or a change in a government program.

Of the three elements, the most essential ingredient is conflict. Stories without conflict are boring. The "conflict" can usually be summed up as a central question with competing answers. By identifying the conflict and presenting more than one side, the journalist determines the focus and direction of the story. Perhaps the purest example of CCR comes from the world of sports: Two teams meet on the field to decide the championship, they have a conflict on the field, and the game is resolved with a final score.

The skill of the storyteller comes in defining the conflict between the two teams, in terms of the athletes, the coaches, the fans, the key plays or other factors. In sports, there is usually a resolution: one team wins, the other loses. It is also possible that the resolution may be less about the final score and more about what a particular team or individual has achieved in the process. The term "resolution" refers only to the ending point of your story, which may be a decisive ending or some version of "tune in tomorrow for the next installment."

You may be questioning the CCR rule, especially when it comes to a "good news" feature. Consider the example of a student who is volunteering in a soup kitchen for the homeless. Reporting that Susie Student is a good person only scratches the surface, and is probably only interesting to Susie, her friends and family. To tell a compelling story you must take a closer look and identify the CCR:

- *The crisis (or problem to be solved)*: Susie wants find a way to help the hungry and homeless people in her community.
- *The conflict*: In this case, there are several possible angles:
  - Can the efforts of one student really make a difference? We would talk with Susie, some of the people she is trying to help, and a program organizer or an expert on local homeless issues.
  - Are soup kitchen volunteers helping the homeless or making the problem worse? This question might focus on the conflict between volunteers like Susie and angry neighbors who want the soup kitchen to close.
  - What personal conflict will Susie experience? Perhaps she was once homeless herself, or comes from a comfortable background and is deeply moved by what she learns from volunteering.
- *The resolution*: Susie won't resolve all the problems of the homeless or calm down the angry neighbors, but may achieve her own resolution by planning to return next week to do what she can, or winning an award for her work, or deciding to quit.

There is usually more than one way to approach a story. In this case, we could have focused on the crisis experienced by neighbors when the soup kitchen opened, their conflict with the homeless people and the volunteers, and the resolution that neighbors plan to protest at the city council meeting next week. Or we could have focused on the CCR from the viewpoint of a homeless person who is caught in the middle of the debate over the soup kitchen. As the storyteller, you must choose the CCR that will be most compelling to your audience.

CCR will help you define a story that can be told with the time, space and reporting resources available to you. Beginning journalists often express interest in a topic, such as "the homeless" or "student volunteers." But no one wants a storyteller to "tell me a topic." You must identify the compelling stories within your chosen subject area, and find a way to tell them within the attention span of your audience. A broad topic, such as health care reform, can be broken down into CCR stories focusing on a patient, a doctor or a Congressman who must vote on the reform bill and must confront other lawmakers or angry constituents.

CCR and public relations

CCR can also help you avoid stories that are predictable and obvious. For example, no one is surprised when a company puts out a news release touting the virtues of a new product. Of course, the company thinks its own product is great. The challenge for the public relations practitioner is to define the CCR:

- *The crisis*: A problem or consumer need that is addressed by this product.
- *The conflict*: How does it compare to competing or previous products? What research breakthroughs or regulatory challenges were involved in bringing it to market?
- *The resolution*: When or how consumers can get the product and what happens next.

What's in it for me? (WIIFM)

The multimedia audience demands that every story "tell me something that I don't know." Your audience also wants a reason to care, what the media consulting firm Broadcast Image has defined as WIIFM or "What's In It For Me?" Your WIIFM may simply be a CCR narrative that surprises, entertains or inspires the audience in some way, or it may be a specific benefit like learning how to save money on your electric bill.

Stories with strong CCR and WIIFM tell themselves. On April 11, 2009, a frumpy woman from a small town in Scotland took the stage for the television talent show *Britain's Got Talent*. The crisis was immediately obvious in the reaction of the audience. Susan Boyle didn't look like the other would-be pop stars competing for the spotlight. She didn't belong there, a classic fish out of water. What would happen when she opened her mouth to sing? Boyle began her rendition of the ballad "I Dreamed a Dream" from *Les Misérables*, and suddenly the audience was plunged into conflict; the woman they had pre-judged as a loser had the voice of an angel. Her performance was followed by a standing ovation and praise from the show's harshest judge. The resolution of the story allowed her to advance in the talent competition. *The Washington Post* reported that the video clip of Boyle's stunning song went on to attract more than 90 million online views within the following week, and comments on the performance set new records on social networking sites. And the WIIFM? Each individual in a worldwide audience was surprised, entertained and educated about the pitfalls of judging someone by their appearance alone.

One last thing about storytelling formulas; there is an exception to the rule that stories must have conflict. Some just deal with subjects that are just plain strange, where others bring us to tears, appeal to our basic love of a good "animal" story, or play off the parental devotion to children.

- The unusual or rare – "Hey, Mabel"

A prevalent school of thought has always been that news is about what's outside the realm of everyday expectations – in a word, what's unusual. If we expected it would happen or if it happened every day, the thinking goes, it wouldn't be news, would it?

A true story about an elephant and a stray dog that became best friends is both unusual and rare. The two became inseparable and their story made the front pages of newspapers around the world. The owners of the elephant sanctuary where the dog took up residence made the rounds of all the network morning and evening news broadcasts. Disney even wanted to make the story into a movie (the sanctuary's owners declined). It's the kind of story that, as newsroom lore would have it, causes a husband to call out loudly to his wife who's in another room: "Hey, Mabel, come here. You've got to see this!" Or, in multimedia terms, it might go viral as users are compelled to share it.

And that brings us to our final storytelling formula, which is really three formulas in one.

- Tears, terriers, and tots!

Classic movie comedian W.C. Fields once famously advised "never work with kids or animals." The belief was that either would upstage your performance. In the movies, that might be true. In news writing, along with emotion (tears), animals (terriers), and kids (tots) are among the best vehicles you have for telling a compelling story.

During a massive manufacturing mill fire in Lowell, Massachusetts, in the 1990s, news stories focused on those who were killed or injured, and property that was destroyed. Donations to the American Red Cross poured in for victims and their families. On the day after the fire, rescue crews found a dog that had survived the blaze, but was badly burned. The story about this lucky canine made local and national headlines, complete with photos and a text that read donations were needed to help with the dog's veterinary care. Within hours, money poured in, outpacing what had been donated for the fire's human victims. Never doubt how much people love their pets.

And there is the story of Jessica McClure, a little girl who fell down a well in a small Texas town some twenty years ago. Beyond those in her immediate family and the small number of residents of that town, an entire nation was captivated by the little girl's plight. Why? Parents (and, by extension, sisters, brothers, grandparents, aunts and uncles) could put themselves in the place of those parents and imagine that little girl as one of their own children. Never doubt the power of a child in trouble to drive a story forward.

In fact, the first live, unscripted news story to be covered by two competing local TV news stations involved another small girl who fell into an abandoned well casing – in 1949. Even with the primitive technology of the time, the Kathy Fiscus story brought Los Angeles

Table 2.2 Writing styles for each platform

Print	Broadcast	Web
More complex sentences and concepts, rich in detail and depth	Written for the ear, simple sentences, active verbs, present and future tense, video-driven	More like broadcast, short and simple sentences. Rich in graphics to provide details on demand, invites interactivity

to a standstill and captivated the world through newspaper and radio reports. The child did not survive, but the event is credited with transforming the perception of TV sets, from a newfangled gadget to a must-have appliance bringing essential news and entertainment into the home.

Emotion – giving the audience for your story a reason to care – is the driving force common to most compelling stories, whatever their eventual platform. Al Tompkins, broadcast group leader at the Poynter Institute for Media Studies, gives the following advice. When considering how best to tell your story, says Tompkins, "Write for the ear, shoot for the eye, but aim for the heart."

Good Writing as the Foundation

All forms of storytelling begin with good writing. Traditionally, differences between print, broadcast, and web writing have centered on a story's length, the brevity of its sentences, and the extent to which visuals play a role in the language used. Of course, all forms of media writing have begun to look more similar than different over time, beginning with the advent of *USA Today* in 1982, a newspaper written more from a broadcast (specifically television) news perspective than its long-form predecessors. In addition, today's web writing resembles more closely the short, sharp, to-the-point writing style of broadcast writing than it does the newspaper.

Still, there are distinctions in the way you write for each of these media. Telling your story in print is very different from writing it for television; similarly, writing for the web means using language that encourages the user's response to your story. Table 2.2 summarizes the major differences between writing for each individual platform. At this point, it serves only as a brief overview of those writing principles that will be explored for each storytelling platform in subsequent chapters.

How Storytelling for Multimedia is Different

Now that we've discussed those elements that are common to all stories, regardless of the platform on which they're presented, let's revisit those elements that make some stories more adaptable to a multimedia approach than others. Before considering what we suggested multimedia storytelling is and is not in Chapter 1, it's useful to look at the work done in this area by the Knight Digital Media Center. Drawing upon work done by researcher Dr. Paula Messina, in 2007, Jane Stevens of the Knight Center put together a course for journalists from other platforms to follow when adapting their specific skill sets to multimedia. In it, she defined a multimedia story as "some combination of text, still photographs, video clips, audio, graphics and interactivity presented on a web site in a nonlinear format in which the information in each medium is complementary, not redundant." She went on to define the term "nonlinear":

> Nonlinear means that rather than reading a rigidly structured single narrative, the user chooses how to navigate through the elements of a story. Not redundant means that rather than having a text version of a story accompanied by a video clip that essentially tells the same story, different parts of a story are told using different media. The key is using the media form – video, audio, photos, text, animation – that will present a segment of a story in the most compelling and informative way.

Among the elements that a multimedia story could include, according to the Knight Center model, are:

- databases
- timelines
- infoboxes
- lists of related stories
- links to other resources
- online forums

The goal is to create a story that "gives the reader a sense of the context of a story and where it fits in with other stories on the same topic." Doing so, whether you're a print or broadcast reporter in a traditional newsroom or a public relations practitioner, takes advantage of what the Knight Center calls two of the most "important characteristics of storytelling on the Web – context and continuity."

That's a starting point for what multimedia storytelling is, but the Knight Center model goes further, suggesting that while many sites have text, video clips, audio, still photos and interactive graphics, many do not create a distinctive medium that is separate from the component parts borrowed from traditional media. In looking at sites like CNN, *The Washington Post*, NPR and MSNBC, each is, in many ways, simply an extension of traditional media. The Knight Center's survey of these and other sites found that

> The video is usually the same version that appears on television. Rarely are video, text, still photos, audio and graphics integrated into the same story. Usually, they are stand-alone stories, each produced for a different media about the same subject, that are then aggregated into multimedia packages.

Here's the difference: stories that simply transfer the same content from other media onto the web are not true multimedia stories because they do not maximize opportunities for interactivity with the audience. Essentially, they are (like most stories on most news web sites) reporter-, producer- or editor-driven, with all the decisions about what is most important to the user made by those in control of the content. The audience simply consumes the stories in a manner similar to reading a newspaper or magazine or watching a TV newscast. They are still in "linear" mode – one story follows another, the order predetermined by the journalists who prioritize stories and present them in what is far too often a form that is unchanged from its original form in the newspaper or on television. They are, simply put, a collection of stories under a specific banner or brand, not a whole new method of storytelling. That's not true multimedia, not because we say so, but because there is research to support the assertion that audiences don't find this approach fully satisfying.

Research: When is Multimedia Most Effective?

In 2002, a study done by researchers at the University of Minnesota sought to identify some essential "Elements of Digital Storytelling" (www.inms.umn.edu/elements) by looking at a variety of attributes of digital stories. Called the DiSEL study and headed by media design experts Laura Ruel and Nora Paul, the aim was "to compare the impact on user attitude and experience between different approaches to content and user action" on the web.

They used two different approaches to telling the same story: what they termed a "static" approach – what we might term "traditional" newspaper and broadcast style – and a "dynamic" one, related to the web's built-in interactivity. Both conveyed essentially the same content, related to BBC's material on health effects of recreational drugs; one was "the static, encyclopedia-type page display," the other "the dynamic interactive package."

Using graduate students to conduct their study of user satisfaction with each story's approach, Ruel and Paul were able to make some general observations of when a multimedia approach to storytelling is, in their words, "worth it." Among their findings:

- Stories can be designed with either static content (the material just sits there, there is no movement) or dynamic content (the material moves).
- In terms of how the user must engage with the content, stories can be designed to be passive (once the user has clicked to the page, they can sit back, there is no action to be taken) or active (the content is designed so that the user must engage with it in order to fully experience the full set through selection of options or clicking to see the next portion).
- Dynamic/active content is the type that is typically crafted using Flash. There is motion and choice. Static/passive content describes HTML coded, there is no motion and what you see is all you get.

The entire study is quite detailed in terms of an audience's motivation, real or perceived, to acquire information from different story approaches as opposed to simply seeking entertainment. The most important findings are quoted below from the study's web site posted at what's called the *On-Line Journalism Review*, available at: http://www.ojr.org/ojr/stories/070210ruel.

DiSEL Study: Findings

This comparative study showed that for the two sites tested.

Interactive presentations work best when …

- You want users to spend more time with the presentation.
- You want users to describe the experience as "enjoyable."
- You want users to recall more of the information.
- You want users to recall your brand.
- You want users to feel entertained.

Static presentations work best when …

- You want users to "click to" all of the presentation's materials.
- You want users to perceive the site navigation as easy.

Ruel and Paul conclude "that the choices made in presenting information will have significantly different impacts on the audience." They suggest that "No one presentation form is going to be the most effective by all measures that you have in your newsroom for determining successful design."

Here, however, are two important things that the research "does seem to reveal," according to its architects:

1. Highly interactive content results in more time spent online with the material and a greater level of reported "enjoyment."
2. The Flash version of the story seemed to help people recall the information being presented.

Ultimately, Ruel and Paul put it this way: "If your goal in presenting a story – particularly one that has potential for a long 'shelf-life' – is to entertain, inform, and keep people online longer, then investing in a creative, interactive presentation could be well worth the effort."

Other similar research done as part of the Poynter Institute's "Eyetrack III" study (2007) confirms many of Ruel and Paul's major findings. Eyetrack researchers used two different and distinct story designs. Text versions of two news stories from NYTimes.com were compared with multimedia presentations of those same stories. A summary of their findings, quoted from the study, is given in the box.

Eyetrack III: Findings

This study shows that:

Interactive presentations work best when ...

- You want users to recall unfamiliar terms and processes/procedures more effectively.

In one test story an animated graphic showed how cast iron pipes are made – an essential component to understanding the overall story content. Those who received this graphic had better recall of the terms and processes involved than those who received the same information in text form.

Static text works best when ...

- You want users to correctly recall specific factual information, such as information about names and places.

It was found that with both stories, individuals had better recall of the names of people involved and the locations of specific story events if they read the text version.

However, a multimedia approach to storytelling, while desirable and clearly effective for the audience, is also time-consuming and expensive – not to mention that it also often involves learning new skills. How do you decide if a specific story is, to put it as Ruel and Paul did, *worth it*? One major outcome of both the studies outlined above is a story check-list that you might keep consider downloading to your laptop. It suggests a series of seven questions to ask in advance of committing to a multimedia approach to storytelling on an individual basis. As you'll see below, the decision is largely dependent, as we previously suggested, on knowing your audience.

Should we present this story as an interactive?

Before undertaking any large story project, be sure to ask:

√ Who is the target audience for this story?
√ What do we hope to accomplish in telling this story to them?

Then use this check-list decision-tool to see which approach to storytelling is best supported by the research in these studies:

1. Does the story concern elaborate or unfamiliar processes/procedures?
   - Yes – 1 point
   - No – 0 points

2. Is the level of interest in the topic high enough that people would be willing to figure out story navigation?
   - Yes – 1 point
   - No – 0 points
3. Does the story have value beyond the first few weeks? Is it likely to be a topic in the news again?
   - Yes – 1 point
   - No – 0 points
4. Is entertaining the audience more important than simply informing?
   - Yes – 1 point
   - No – 0 points
5. Is it important that the audience be able to recall specific facts from the story?
   - Yes – 0 points
   - No – 1 point
6. If the story is told in separate components, it is essential that all the components be viewed by the audience?
   - Yes – 0 points
   - No – 1 point
7. Do you hope the audience recalls where they saw the information?
   - Yes – 1 point
   - No – 0 points

According to the check-list's authors, "If you get five or more points, then you should strongly consider an interactive story approach."

Of course, if a story fails to score enough points to merit interactive packaging, you might consider that it is still suitable for a static medium, such as print or broadcast, without going to the extra effort of crafting multimedia elements.

Once you decide to use the multimedia approach, you need to know which tools are required to create your interactive story. Whether you are a print or TV journalist or a public relations practitioner, the same multimedia tools apply. They include some acquaintance with what constitutes good design, a basic knowledge of HTML and, increasingly, the program called "Flash" alluded to above. You don't have to be an expert in any of the above, but you at least have to speak the language in order to be proficient when communicating with what are often termed "digital natives" – those of a certain age who have never known a time when there was no web, cell phones, or iPods. If you are already of this generation, you already speak the language. If your background is in traditional media, this is a language you *must* learn.

Using Multimedia Tools

Let's begin with an understanding of basic web story design, not how to build a web page (there are plenty of online tutorials and text books that do this), but what constitutes a good, appealing design that's attractive to visitors. Why do you need to know this as a print or TV reporter or a public relations professional? In today's media world, design is part of the storytelling process. A cluttered, poorly designed web story misses its mark with the audience in much the same way as a visually unappealing story on television or a confusing headline on the front page of a newspaper.

Successful multimedia stories begin with design elements that help the user understand the story and encourage your audience to become part of the storytelling process. These include:

- *Creating a straightforward page that's easy to read.* This is sometimes referred to by design experts as creating a story template that is "clean," meaning there aren't a lot of distracting elements that take away from the story you are trying to tell.
- *Identifying major story elements in places where the eye is drawn.* This means keeping it simple, putting photos, links to audio or video clips, graphics, slideshows, etc. in obvious locations on the page.
- *Using design to complement content, not the other way around.* While it's tempting to use multimedia "bells and whistles" on a story simply because you know how to, the well-worn adage "content is king" is as important in a multimedia story as in any print story.
- *Recognizing how story continuity is different on the web from other media.* Never, repeat NEVER, continue to tell your story below the point on your screen where the reader is forced to scroll down. Research shows that online readers, unlike the newspaper audience, have no inclination to scroll down to retrieve the rest of a story. Print audiences are accustomed to the familiar "jump" carrying them from one page of a story to its continuation on the next; web audiences are not.

After a basic understanding of the foundation that design elements provide for multimedia reporting, it is essential to know the differences between terms like HTML and Flash. The latter is fast becoming the standard for adding multimedia to news stories, but knowing how the two differ is important to knowing which to use when – and why.

First, HTML. The term, simply put, is an abbreviation for Hypertext Markup Language. It's the way web pages are encoded, using language that leads the reader to a site where you want to direct them. How much do you need to know about HTML? At least enough to be conversant with colleagues whose job may be to help you bring your story to the web in its most effective form.

A great resource for jumpstarting your knowledge of HTML comes from the University of Southern California, Annenberg School for Communication. That web site, designed for the school's National Summit on Arts Journalism, gives a simple overview of what to type into a story to convert it into HTML language. At first, it may seem like learning a foreign language. It doesn't have to be. All languages are, after all, divided into conversational and fluent. Your goal as a multimedia storyteller is to become conversational with the language of HTML and Flash. Fluency is up to you. There is no one book that can teach it all to you. Only time spent doing and perfecting the process can make you an expert. There are many resources, however, that can jumpstart that learning process. One is specifically targeted toward learning HTML in its entirety. A tutorial created by the

Knight Center for Digital Media, http://multimedia.journalism.berkeley.edu/tutorials/, is a self-described "crash course in basic HTML – enough to get you up to speed."

In addition to HTML, having basic knowledge of the multimedia storytelling tool called Flash is essential for today's journalist. A brand of the firm Adobe, Flash was once referred to as "Macromedia Flash." Today, it functions as a tool for journalists to create interactive and animated web sites. Simply put, it helps create motion for your photos, graphics, or video online. An online tutorial called w3 schools.com (http://www.w3schools.com/Flash/flash_intro.asp) can give you a clearer idea of what Flash is, what advantages it has, and how it compares to other programs that create the same effects.

As an online storyteller, you must speak the language that is used by the people whose job is to translate your stories using this technology. You *do* have to understand something about the *process*. From there, as you'll read in web editor Owen Michael's profile in Chapter 5, you can usually use a template to post your content.

Revisiting Power Performance: Keeping the Promise

As a storyteller in any medium, you are making a tacit promise to your audience every time you interact with them. That promise involves essentially saying, "If you stick with me, I'll take you here, tell you this, and show you that." Remember that every time you create a story in any medium, you are asking a lot of the reader, listener, or viewer – not the least of which is their time and attention. If you create enough interest, the audience will give you a chance. From there, it's up to you to deliver on the promise.

In Chapter 1, we made a promise that we would revisit the major elements of what we call "Power Performance in Multimedia" and elaborate on each once you had the background necessary to put it all in context. Now is that time.

POWER PERFORMANCE IN MULTIMEDIA IS:

- *Recognizing the major elements of any story, regardless of media platform.* Storytelling is timeless and enduring – a good story is a good story, regardless of the medium used to tell it.
- *Approaching storytelling across every media platform available (print, audio, video, web).* Storytelling is cross-platform – a good story told across media platforms brings added value to the storytelling process.
- *Learning from the best practices in each medium by taking advantage of the unique elements of each.* Storytelling can be learned – there are "best practices," tried and true ways of telling stories from which you can learn and improve.
- *Becoming proficient with the tools of each medium.* Storytelling uses more than words – it uses all the tools that today's technology makes possible.
- *Thinking visually about each element of the story, including your own place in it.* Storytelling helps the audience visualize – it uses photos, video, infographs, databoxes, timelines, slideshows, anything

that assists the audience's comprehension and engagement, including any place in the story where the storyteller appears on camera.

- *Using all means available to interact with and engage the audience in the process of storytelling.* Storytelling should be creative and dynamic, not static. Use all the resources available to you and be creative. Think of the technology you have at your fingertips, on your laptop, as the conduit toward making your audience a partner in the storytelling process.

POWER PERFORMANCE IN MULTIMEDIA IS NOT:

- *Creating a story simply to accommodate the technology available.* We've all seen stories that have what is sometimes called "whizz bang" – visual effects included in a story simply for the sake of showing that the storyteller knows how to use the technology that produced them. Ask yourself: does this specific element, be it an animation sequence using Flash or a fancy graphic, help tell a better story or is it simply a substitute for a weak one?
- *Cutting and pasting a story from another medium onto the web.* Too many online stories are simply taken verbatim from a version in another media – radio, TV, or newspaper – and posted on a web site. There is nothing magical, let alone powerful, about transferring what is essentially a print or broadcast story to the web. As pointed out earlier in this chapter, the online platform is unique because it is interactive. Take advantage of that unique advantage and use it to tell the kinds of stories that thrive on interactivity.
- *Creating stories quickly and without much forethought.* It's tempting to turn out a story quickly, if only because we can do it so easily. Today's technology makes it possible to produce stories in real time at a furious pace, especially compared to the time once needed for printing presses to roll or film to be processed. Even more so in this age of multimedia, take time to reflect on the story you're telling. It will be more powerful in the end if you think about it first.
- *Having only a rudimentary knowledge of each medium's strengths.* You are not going to be an expert in every medium. No one can be. The old adage that "a little knowledge is a dangerous thing" does not apply to multimedia storytelling. Even a little knowledge of each medium and an understanding of its basic strengths are mandatory to be a successful storyteller in today's world. Like most of us, you may always feel more proficient in one medium than another, but you should feel sufficient across all media.
- *Ignoring opportunities for interaction with the audience, who often possess defining elements of the story.* Doing a story about, for instance, a raging wildfire in the hills of southern California and failing to take advantage of the insights and perspectives of those who live there or near there (or those with loved ones in the affected area) constitutes a missed opportunity. As we'll suggest, effective multimedia storytelling often means letting the audience help tell your story by determining the direction it takes and the elements it uses.

Multimedia as a State of Mind

Beyond the specific skills needed to excel as a multimedia storyteller, there is the need, first, to *think* like one. For a traditional print or broadcast journalist, that means adjusting the entire approach to a story from the beginning. Ask yourself the following pivotal questions to guide you through that thought process:

1. *What elements might this story need that are easier to gather now rather than later?* So often we gather facts, quotes, and background information to tell our story, but the elements that would later turn it into a multimedia package are either forgotten or neglected. NPR's Vice-president for Diversity, Keith Woods, the former Dean of the Faculty at the Poynter Institute for Media Studies, says he is always surprised that in today's multimedia storytelling environment, reporters still approach their stories "word first" – that is, doing their interviews, taking notes, etc. Once they have the text of their story, they return to take a few photos, shoot some video, or re-interview a subject on audiotape. Rather than having to re-create the elements of your story after the fact, be proactive.

2. *Think multimedia first and you won't have to rethink your story for multimedia later.* The task is easier if you carry the tools with you, in your backpack, handbag, laptop case, whatever you find easiest. The "must have" devices below should be part of your stock in trade, and updated as improvements are made. Your multimedia tool kit is similar to the medical bag a doctor would carry, filled with first-aid essentials.

A multimedia "must have" list includes:

- *a digital audio recorder, with a USB port.* This device makes it possible not only for you to have your interviews for transcript or quoting purposes, but also to download them into an audio file. From there, they can easily be inserted into a multimedia version of the story.
- *a hand-held flip video recorder.* This may also double for audio. Lightweight and simple to operate, it enables quick, easy download of on-the-scene video or interviews into a multimedia story.
- *a small digital still camera.* Again, you may find this feature is part of the video camera you carry, but, if not, a stand-alone model for stills will help you grab a few "snaps," as they're called in some newsrooms, for later inclusion with your multimedia story.
- *a cell phone or other mobile device with photo, video, access to the Internet and social media.* This is always your backup, allowing you to send elements of the story back to your news organization for fast upload to the web (especially important for breaking stories). The ability to blog or interact with your audience via various social media using your cell phone or other mobile communication device helps measure audience interest and gain audience input to your story.

Once you make crucial decisions about how you will tell your story, the tools you'll need, and how best to convey it across different media, a number of central questions remain.

- *Will the audience primarily read my story or scan elements of it?* We can't overstress that reading stories online is an entirely different behavior from reading a newspaper story from start to finish or watching a TV news story from first frame to last. Multimedia empowers the audience to choose those elements of a story they find most interesting or compelling and process those elements in the order they want, not the one you prescribe. This is a daunting prospect for many traditional journalists, precisely because it means giving up a large measure of *control* over the story. Rather than automatically thinking "First, they'll want to see this piece of video or hear that fact, or read that quote." multimedia journalists have to recognize the specific story elements may not be ordered the same way for every reader, viewer, or user. Some in your audience may want to see the exciting video of a car chase or the emotional reaction to a tragedy first, even before reading the specific details of what they're viewing. Some may only want to see the video and won't even read the story; others may skip key elements that you find vital, but they do not. It's a reality – and a challenge – for you, the multimedia storyteller.

• *Where does the whole story reside?* Is it primarily in the text? How about the visuals? What is most compelling? Where will my audience more than likely gravitate first? Most importantly, ask yourself, "Are there elements of this story that it is likely the audience knows better than I do?" If you are doing a story about parents of autistic children, it's more than highly likely your subjects – who may also be your audience – have expertise in this area that you do not have, unless you have also lived it. Reach out to your audience even as you prepare to tell your story. Use polls, reader response boxes, e-mail, social media – whatever it takes – to jump-start the process of engaging them in the process of storytelling while it's still in process. Readers and users online will help you get it right.

Now that you've learned some strategies for finding, conceiving, writing, and building a compelling story, we'll turn our attention to the specifics of multimedia storytelling, both print and on the web. In Chapter 3, you will confront the challenges faced by traditional print storytellers when adapting their stories for other media – television and the web.

A Multimedia Exercise

Take a moment and consider the following scenario:

A residence hall on the campus of a large metropolitan university has been leveled by a tornado. Several apartment complexes have also been destroyed. Early reports indicate that the tornado also tore through another area of the city, destroying numerous luxury homes. Search and rescue operations are underway at various locations.

Using everything you've learned in this chapter, especially those elements of power performance in multimedia, outline a plan for telling this story across media: print, broadcast, and online. Don't forget the audience for social media.

Works Cited and Further Reading

Barron, Jackie. "Multimedia reporting in a never ending news cycle," *Nieman Reports*, Winter, 2000. Retrieved from: http://www.nieman.harvard.edu/reportsitem.aspx?id=101795.

Dunn, Christian. "Basic HTML for journalists," Accessed March 5, 2009. Retrieved from: http://christiandunn.blogspot.com/2009/03/basic-html-for-journalists-video.html.

McIlroy, Thad. "The future of publishing," accessed May 1. 2007. Retrieved from: http://www.thefutureofpublishing.com/influences/internet_metrics.html.

Messina, Paula. "Multimedia storyboarding," part of the Knight Digital Center's Digital Media Site. Retrieved from: http://multimedia.journalism.berkeley.edu/tutorials/starttofinish/storyboarding/.

Quinn, Sara and Adam, Peggy Stark. "Eyetracking the news: what are the differences between reading news in print and on-line?" *Poynter Institute for Media Studies*, accessed April 25, 2007. Retrieved from: http://eyetrack.poynter.org/.

Rickel, Larry M., Sardella, Ed and Owen, Carol. *The Producing Strategy*. The Broadcast Image Group, 1995.

Ruel, Paula and Paul, Nora. "Multimedia storytelling: when is it worth it?" *The On-Line Journalism Review*, accessed February 12, 2007. Retrieved from: http://www.ojr.org/ojr/stories/070210ruel/.

Stevens, Jane. "What is a multimedia story?" Knight Digital Media Center, accessed May 18, 2007. Retrieved from: http://multimedia.journalism.berkeley.edu/tutorials/starttofinish/choose/.

COURTESY WFTS-TV

LINDA HURTADO

WFTS-TV

Job: Anchor, health reporter, multimedia journalist (MMJ), WFTS-TV, abcactionnews.com
Market: Tampa-St. Petersburg, FL
Hometown: Born in San Francisco, CA, grew up in Illinois and South Carolina
Education: University of Georgia, BA in Journalism, 1989
Career Path:
  Internships: Potomac News Service, Washington, DC
  Local TV internships in Athens, GA
  Worked on student newspaper and radio station
  Reporter, WECT-TV, Wilmington, NC
  Reporter, WEVU-TV, Fort Myers, FL
  Anchor-reporter, WKMG-TV, Orlando, FL
  Weekend anchor and reporter, WFTS-TV, Tampa-St. Petersburg, FL
  5 p.m. anchor and health reporter, WFTS-TV

Why did you become a journalist?
I loved acting, singing and dancing, but didn't feel that I was good enough to make it in that field. I've been a writer all my life and wrote a book in high school. I tried to think of something that would combine everything that I loved to do. I joined the high school newspaper and got addicted. By the time I graduated from high school, I knew I wanted to be a television news reporter. It just seemed to fit.

How did your college education prepare you for your career?
If you're going to be a journalist, you should look for a school that has a reputation of turning out people who actually work in the business. At the University of Georgia, we had a professor who was a former foreign correspondent for one of the networks. A few of the people who graduated from there had made it big. The professors were very hands-on. They pushed us out in the field and made us shoot. I had a job lined up in a small

market before I got my diploma. You have to go into it with a willingness to move away from your family and friends and make very little money.

WFTS-TV has a major commitment to multimedia journalism. All of the anchors and reporters have to know how to shoot video and edit. How has MMJ training changed your job?
It changed everything. I think about story ideas in terms of whether I will shoot it as an MMJ or work with a photographer. If a story can be shot in one place, I can shoot it myself and get back to the station in time to anchor at five o'clock. I keep a different set of shoes and clothes at the office so I can carry the equipment and be comfortable. I have to budget my time differently.

Are there some types of stories that are better told by one person with a camera?
I did an MMJ story on a former foster child who is now working in an emergency shelter for kids. I was in an environment with kids who have been abused. I had to tell their story without showing their faces. Being a woman and being alone helped. They weren't intimidated by me and a smaller camera. If you need an intimate bond, working alone helps you make a better connection. MMJ gear is smaller and less threatening, and people feel like they are talking to a home video camera. It's a casual conversation and less of a formal interview. On the flip side, you have to deal with technical camera issues and that can interrupt the conversation sometimes.

When you are working alone as an MMJ, does it affect the way you present the story?
I like to do the stories that deal with the most intimate details of people's lives, so I try to do interviews in a very casual setting. I might want to reach out and hug somebody. It's hard to do that when you're an MMJ because taking care of the technical details can create a barrier and pull you away from the story. I might request a photographer to shoot a series or an in-depth story where I need to interact more. But there are times when being an MMJ is just perfect for a day-of-air story. Carrying all the gear in the Florida heat can be a challenge. It's a visual business and you have to look professional. I bring a jacket, but I wear a comfortable shirt, flats or low heels, and pants or capris. When it's time to do the standup you stop and clean yourself up, brush your hair and put on makeup. No one expects you to look perfect, but you do have to brush your hair.

How do you adapt your stories for multimedia on the web?
I have a Facebook fan page. I spent two days in Orlando interviewing (TV talk show host) Ellen DeGeneres. Every day I put a story on the air, but I also posted pictures and video and interacted with her fans. I am also responsible for the health page on our station's web site. After one of my health stories airs on television, I'm not done. I post it on the web site and my fan page. Each story requires a few extra steps that weren't part of the job a few years ago.

What career accomplishment are you most proud of?
I did a story on a man who was climbing Mt. Everest and at the same time I was talking to his wife. He was worried he wasn't going to make it to the top, and she was worried he wasn't going to make it down. It turned out that he was okay. It was the kind of story that makes a difference and helps people see me as more than just a journalist, as a friend and a member of the community. To me, my greatest accomplishment is that people trust me enough to allow me into some of the most intimate moments of their lives.

I did a story on a woman who was molested for ten years and kept it a secret. She finally came out because the same man was accused of molesting kids in another neighborhood and she realized she might be the only one with the power to stop him. So she came forward, and it went to trial and he was convicted and sentenced to 25 years. Now she has written a book and goes around to schools, trying to convince kids that it's okay to tell someone. I was in the classroom watching her do this, and a young girl started crying. She stayed afterwards and told her story. It was a powerful moment, a story that made a difference. Those are the moments I am most proud of.

When you record these intimate moments on video, how do you deal with privacy issues?

I had to change the ending to the child molester story because my news director didn't feel like we were doing enough to protect the 16-year-old girl's identity. It was fine legally, but ethically we wanted to do the right thing. Sometimes it is hard. Journalists have the power to do a lot of things, but that doesn't make it right. As a health reporter, I deal a lot with patient privacy. It helps that I have been working in this market for years and people trust me. They know I'm an ethical journalist. Sometimes you just have to convince them to let you shoot the story first and make an ethical decision about whether to air it later.

What is the best career advice you ever received?

It's important to believe in yourself. A Hispanic woman news director told me I would never be an anchor. That was devastating. I'm Hispanic and I looked up to her. Her advice made me take a step back and look at what I needed to change to become better. You can be yourself. People will like you or they won't, but at least you're being real.

What's your advice to multimedia journalists?

Don't be afraid of the technology. Embrace it. It makes you a better storyteller. Ultimately, that's what we are.

CASEY CORA

http://oakpark.patch.com

Job: Local editor
Market: Oak Park and River Forest, IL
Hometown: Joliet, IL
Education: Eastern Illinois University, BA Journalism, 2004; University of South Florida, St. Petersburg, MA in Arts, Journalism and Media Studies, 2007
Career Path:
  St Petersburg Times, FL
    Freelance community news reporter for *Neighborhood Times*
    Police beat and general assignment reporter
    Reporter for Tampabay.com breaking news blog, including photography and multimedia
  Southtown Star, Chicago Sun Times Media, Tinley Park, IL
    Beat reporter for daily print and online editions
    Blog: blogs@southtownstar.com/oaklawn
  Patch.com, an AOL network of hyperlocal sites

How would you describe the job of a local editor at Patch.com?

Being a site editor is mix of reporting, decision-making, assigning stories, administrative duties and community outreach. I'm responsible for all news coverage on this site, government news, police and fire, sports, business, feature stories. I'm assembling an army of freelancers to help cover stories. It's a mix of newspaper veterans, recent college grads and people who just want to write about their neighborhood. It's different from working for a traditional newspaper that is trying to establish a presence online.

What do you expect your freelancers to contribute to the site?

We have a fantastic web platform, with a lot of smart programmers, engineers and designers behind it. It can accept anything. If someone shoots video of a block party, they can upload it, along with photos and text. It's hassle-free. I put a lot of value in good, clean web design. We have all the tools we need. For local, online journalism, the future is now.

How did you get started in the news business?

When I got my undergraduate degree, the job market was pretty tight. So I decided to go to graduate school. I got involved in the student media, but I also had to pay my own way through school. Some local reporters came to speak to our classes, so I reached out to them and found out that I could freelance for the community news insert. I did anything to get my name out there and show I was reliable, right from the outset. I covered the police beat in the evening. That opened another door. They were looking for somebody to work for the online department. I worked from 5 to 8 a.m., and then went to school. Looking back, I think it's cool to say that my first real newspaper job was on a web site. I was the first person hired exclusively for tampabay.com. You have to move fast on the web. You have to be quick, think on your feet and take advantage of opportunities for cool multimedia stuff.

You made the front page of the newspaper with your multimedia coverage of a breaking news story. How did that advance your career?

It was a tanker truck explosion. Unfortunately, someone lost their life. But it was the type of thing that is a big break for a young journalist. We heard "explosions on the highway" come over the scanner. I ran out of the newsroom and I was the first reporter on the scene, talking to people. It was old-school hustle. I had a lot of help, but the editors realized they could count on me.

Eventually, you landed a job with Chicago Sun Times Media. Describe a typical day as a municipal beat reporter.

There was an expectation every day I would have stories for the next day's paper. You're alone on the beat and the editors expect you to know what's going on at all times. You cover a lot of meetings, civic government 101. There were days when I didn't even come into the office. I'd work remotely from the village hall on my laptop. I tried to start everything on the blog and let it develop from there. I might start off on Thursday morning with a post about the story I was working on for Sunday's paper.

How has multimedia affected the way you do your job?

I'm listening for people's voices, thinking about photos and video, and looking for the best way to tell the story. At the *St. Pete Times* they gave me a pretty nice professional camera. At first I had no idea what to do with it. But I had a serious responsibility to go on the scene and get the photo and write about it. On the beat, there are always opportunities for audio or a slide show. It's a balance.

What are some of the challenges of being a beat reporter in a local community?

You are trusted to be fair, accurate, unswayable and reliable. Not everybody goes to boring village hall meetings or watches them when they're televised. You have that responsibility. I covered 60,000 people and I had to think about how a meeting might affect their lives and their money. It's important to have somebody out there who's looking at their property tax bill. To be a reporter, you have to have a measure of civic pride. After a while, if you treat people fairly, you gain respect. The visibility is scary at first. People will recognize you in the local coffee shop and give you news tips.

What attracts you to a story?

For me, it's all about the writing. I may write about a lady who's fighting an insurance company. People read it and respond. We get so bogged down in day-to-day stuff, like the park district meeting that isn't going to change anybody's life. But you find stories that do matter. Making the connection that helps someone out, and shedding light on a situation, it's still possible to change lives.

What's the best career advice you ever received?
One of the top editors at the *St. Pete Times* had this advice: read the work of other journalists you admire, learn how to read official documents, and most importantly, be polite. When you approach people and you have to ask a tough question, a little friendliness goes a long way.

What career accomplishment are you most proud of?
I'm grateful that editors saw some talent in me and molded it. They believed I could step up and be a part of a team. Now, as local editor, I have to prove myself every day.

How do you see the future of multimedia journalism?
I'm wildly optimistic, even though there are a lot of realities out there that suggest otherwise. I have no idea on the time frame, but things will be better. Younger journalists are coming into the business, while the big institutions tend to crumble or run themselves into the ground. New opportunities are springing up. There's a start-up mentality. It's only a matter of time before we can take advantage of the advertising opportunities online. We'll be able to cover all kinds of awesome stories without being limited to 12 inches in the paper. It will be you and your personal brand. It all comes back to trust and reliability. People will realize when you are doing good work.

3

Writing the Story for Print and the Web

If you haven't already heard, here's some breaking news. Newspapers are either dead or dying. Depending upon who you listen to in the traditional media universe, the blogosphere, or Wall Street, the funeral has already taken place; we're just awaiting the burial. True? Well, certainly if the "patient" is the traditional print medium that we commonly refer to as the "newspaper," its vital signs are anything but healthy. Let's examine what the so-called "experts" cite as evidence of newspapers' mortality. Most of it is undeniable and some of it is even compelling.

First, there's the nationwide shutdown of many prominent newspapers in some of our largest metropolitan areas. So many traditional papers have closed up shop that the trend has even prompted the development of a web site entitled, appropriately enough, "Newspaper Death Watch." It chronicles the demise of the following papers: the *Tucson Citizen*, *Baltimore Examiner*, *Cincinnati Post*, *Albuquerque Tribune*, *South Idaho Press*, and the venerable, 150-year old *Rocky Mountain News*, which called it quits at the end of 2009, as did the *Seattle Post-Intelligencer* earlier that year. Even more notable is the fact that this is an abbreviated list – and only began in 2007.

Second, one can argue about the causes behind newspapers' decline and demise, with reasons ranging from reduced advertising dollars being pumped into their traditional sections within papers (car dealers in the sports section; realtor listings in the classifieds), to younger readers with decreasing attention spans. The first reason is often blamed on social networking sites (craigslist is commonly cited as the biggest culprit) that give ad space away for free or at a greatly reduced cost with which traditional print media cannot compete.

There is a name for the trend toward reduced attention spans among younger readers: the "Sesame Street Effect." Studies point the finger of blame at that cultural icon Big Bird. The reasoning goes that generations have been raised on the expectation that every story, like those on the ubiquitous and cross-generational PBS program, must be told using lots of small words, short sentences, moving visuals, and fast pacing. Some studies even suggest a strong correlation between the average length of a segment on *Sesame Street* and that of

Power Performance: Multimedia Storytelling for Journalism and Public Relations, First Edition. Tony Silvia and Terry Anzur.
© 2011 Tony Silvia and Terry Anzur. Published 2011 by Blackwell Publishing Ltd.

a news story on the nightly network broadcasts. As story length fell on the "Street," the research suggests, it resulted in reduced storytelling time on the "screen" of Americans' television newscasts.

Regardless of which cause–effect relationship you believe, the scenario for traditional print media (and, by extension, those who work in it) is not a hopeful one. Notice, however, we use the term *traditional print media*. By that, we mean the way in which generations of readers (today we call them news *consumers*) received their news and generations of journalists were taught to *present* that news. Newspapers, journalism students were taught, had the advantage of *length* and, therefore, the ability to go into a story in *depth*. Radio and television, by contrast, had to be short to fit into a timeslot; therefore, depth was sacrificed. If you wanted the "real" story, the newspaper was your medium of choice. Traditional newspapers also had advantages over broadcast storytelling in terms of *permanence* and *portability*. It was no accident that the *New York Times* was for generations of Americans the "newspaper of record." Along with its local counterparts in towns and cities across America, newspapers were used as the foundation of all journalism – an enviable position to occupy and one envied most often by storytellers in other media: broadcast news, especially. The difference meant that if you were a newspaper reporter, your story would be around in perpetuity for readers to retrieve and re-read. It had real historic import. Broadcast news – radio or, later, television – was more ethereal.

For the broadcast reporter, once your story aired (and it usually aired only once in the pre-CNN media world), it was gone; viewers had no chance to go back and watch it again. Hence, the concept that broadcast storytellers had only one "shot" to tell their story, since viewers, unlike readers, couldn't access a permanent "record" of the story. Of course, beginning in the 1970s with the mass production and widespread use of the home VCR, the argument about permanence for traditional print media changed somewhat, but not much. There's little, if any, evidence that Americans used their VCRs to record local or network newscasts so they could go back and watch them again.

As for portability, the invention of the transistor radio in the 1950s and its widespread adoption in the 1960s, certainly made radio more portable for Americans. Radio, however, was not principally a news medium to the extent that newspapers were. The majority of radio's content was aimed at entertainment, first with dramas, soap operas, and comedy shows, then with pre-recorded music. There were exceptions of course; radio, in the person of Edward R. Murrow, pioneered on-the-scene reporting from the rooftops of London and the battlefields of Europe.

Still, the newspaper had an attraction that appealed to many of another generation. It was tactile. You could pick it up, carry it with you, read it when and where you wanted. It was easy to read on the bus or train, without disturbing others, as the sound of a transistor radio could easily do. It could be carried from one room to another at home and sections could be shared with family members. It became an indispensable morning or evening family ritual. The traditional newspaper was "king" and those who owned them "the royal families" of media.

So it remained for decades, despite some audience erosion due to the upstart medium of television, considered by many in the traditional print media a "fad" destined to fail over time. TV, after all, was neither permanent nor portable. Sure, it had some of the technological (for its time) "whizz bang" that had also fascinated new audiences at the advent of radio. However, both radio and TV, throughout the twentieth century, relied on the newspaper in their cities for story ideas and, sometimes, entire stories – albeit newly adapted and written for a broadcast audience.

Papers dominated, pure and simple. The audience was happy. Owners were happy. The product itself was respectable. The profits were ample and often approached margins unheard of in other industries. Legions of young people wanted to pursue a career in print journalism, a number that only swelled in post-Watergate America, when two *Washington Post* reporters, Bob Woodward and Carl Bernstein, uncovered the story that brought down an American president. Colleges and universities that had once offered only a course or two in journalism suddenly developed entire curricula in the subject. To use a phrase borrowed from the late David Halberstam, "the best and the brightest" flocked to be journalists – and they flocked to newspapers beyond all other media.

Today's Print Media: Changes and Challenges

Just as print journalism has had to change, so have those who work – or who *want* to work – in the medium of traditional newspapers or magazines. Working for a newspaper today means not only acquiring a new skill set, but also a new *mind* set. If the reason isn't obvious, think of the lyric from Bruce Springsteen's song "My Hometown," in homage to where he grew up in New Jersey, but also relevant to thousands of towns across America toward the latter part of the twentieth century, racked by unemployment, caused by a changing and deteriorating economic climate. The jobs are going away and "they ain't coming back," he sings. The same could be said of traditional print media storytelling jobs.

According to *The American Journalism Review*, an estimated 15 percent of the nation's newspaper newsroom jobs were lost in 2008. The *New York Times* reported that this occurred "as news consumers continued to gravitate to online sources and as traditional revenue streams dried up." It suggested that:

> At the same time, the shift from a print-based, scheduled world of media to a digital, on-demand world of options is changing how journalists do their jobs. "New media" doesn't mean transplanting old media to a new medium; it requires a new vocabulary, a new relationship with the audience – a massive social network that now talks back – and, sometimes, a new set of expectations about objectivity and timeliness.

Focus on those words: a *new vocabulary*, a *new relationship* with the audience, and a massive *social network* that talks back. They are the building blocks of the transformation print reporters must embrace if their medium is to survive. Much has been written and discussed about the need for a new business model to recapture revenue and, by so doing, sustain the future of newspapers in particular and journalism in general. Meeting that need depends upon knowing how best to engage the audience where they are, while using a new way of speaking and, simultaneously, listening to them. "At stake is a generation of reporters, and the continued role of journalists as the eyes, ears and questioners for the public," as the *Times* article put it.

Where do you begin? Looking at where the "best and brightest" are going and what they're doing to prepare themselves for a career as storytellers in today's news media environment is revealing. It may seem counter-intuitive, but in 2009, journalism as a major field of study saw a significant increase in student enrollment at America's colleges and universities. However, while some students still enjoy seeing their names on by-lines in traditional print media, the majority appear to be moving away from specialization in favor of learning the skills and developing the mindset to tell their stories across media. While the majority of students at Columbia University say they are "enamored by print, the percentage of applications for that track is dropping, to 49 percent for fall 2009 from 64 percent in 2007; at the same time, applications for the digital media track are up 10 percent." It's similar at many other large journalism schools nationwide.

What does this say about the challenge facing you as a so-called print journalist in today's multimedia world? Do you have a future or is the medium for which you have a passion destined to become DOA before you find your first job? For perspective, consider the words of that famous American storyteller Mark Twain. Before he followed the path of writing short stories and novels, Twain worked as a newspaper reporter across the US, at papers from Iowa to California to New York, beginning in 1853. His most famous quotation, deals with his mistaken death, reported by newspapers in 1897. A reporter had confused him with a cousin who had passed away. Twain wrote the paper a note stating that reports of his demise had "been greatly exaggerated." The same might be said of those reports detailing the death of newspapers themselves. Twain survived a good many years to tell many more stories. The same can be true of print journalists today – provided they recognize how their medium has changed.

Newspapers and Television: More Alike than Different

The changes in how newspapers tell stories didn't begin with the Internet. There was no Internet in 1982. That's the year Gannett Corporation began its experiment in publishing a national newspaper called *USA Today*. Its impact on how newspapers would begin to look more like television news – in content, writing, and design – was immeasurable. Instead of looking like the "old" stodgy print model containing long stories on "heavy" subjects, this new kind of newspaper featured stories on the front page that finished on the front page. Few stories continued inside the paper and none culminated below the front page "fold." Founded by Al Neuharth, the staff's marching orders were clear: tell it quick, tell it short, and tell it visually. Photos were encouraged, as was other visual material, including graphics of all kinds: charts, artist renderings, information boxes – anything that would capture the eye and keep the reader's attention.

Histories of the paper vary, but most agree Neuharth's vision was to cater to younger audiences of the "television generation." Given the timing of its launch – the post-Watergate, Vietnam era – the strategy was to create a paper that gave the audience "light," yet informational stories, ones that engaged readers both textually and visually. The effort was highly criticized by critics who claimed it "dumbed down" the news of the day, but readers embraced the differences between *USA Today* and traditional print publications – especially the emphasis on human interest stories and the "explainers": those graphic elements (today, we call them "infographics") that helped decipher difficult concepts (think political and economic stories) that other newspapers spent gallons of ink explaining in words instead of "pictures." While it took Gannet's venture 16 years to turn a profit, it changed newspapers' visual design, textual content, and marketing distribution. Printed at central plants or "hubs" strategically located regionally around the country, it was sent by satellite to local plants where a modicum of hometown news could be inserted. Perhaps most significantly – or one could argue symbolically – the end product was dispensed in a vending machine that looked like a television set mounted on a pedestal. The front page, featuring color photos and splashy graphics, was framed through the glass window, reminding readers that *this* newspaper was more like the TV they watched every day than the newspaper of their parents and grandparents. Few knew it at the time, but it was the beginning of the need for newspapers to become multimedia in their approach to storytelling!

Learning a New Vocabulary

Most people only take the time and make the effort to learn a new language based upon a *need* to do so. That need might be based upon a trip to a foreign country, meeting a new acquaintance who speaks that language, or a job description. Some people, of course, learn a new language solely for the sake of expanding their breadth of cultural knowledge. If you're a traditional print journalist or are in school to learn the skills traditionally associated with that career, begin by accepting the fact that you need to learn how to speak what may be, to you, a new language – the language of those who tell their stories not just for the page, but for the ear and the eye. Like learning a new language, it can be difficult and it does take time, but if you need more motivation, consider a study done early in 2010 of careers showing the best and worst career tracks.

Based on five criteria – environment, income, employment outlook, physical demands and stress – the study, done by the job site CareerCast.com, and reported widely in the *Wall Street Journal* and other media, ranked 200 jobs. "Reporter, (Newspaper)" in the traditional sense we've discussed, ranked #184, prompting the headline "Newspaper Reporter Ranks Poorly in Career Ranking" on the Huffington Post web site. To be fair, other journalism jobs don't rank much higher, with photojournalist even lower on the list; it's noteworthy that "Reporter (Multimedia)" is not included as a category. If one glances at the top of the list, however, the pattern is clear: two of the top jobs are linked to what we call digital skills, to the extent that both required computer proficiency and a third, at number 15, is specifically tagged as "web developer."

There is of course, a huge difference between knowing what makes a computer work and knowing how to use a computer to *do* work. The first is technical knowledge that you have to use to program or repair your laptop; the second makes that same laptop your *newsroom*. In learning how to use the digital skills to make better stories for a web audience, it could be argued that television reporters have an advantage, since they've been taught for years how to *think visually first*. It has become part of their journalistic DNA. But for traditional print reporters, it can indeed be like learning a new language. The best place to start is by pointing out some fundamental differences between writing for the page and storytelling for the screen – not just the television screen, but also those steadily smaller screens on various mobile information devices. But let's begin with writing for television if you're inclined to write for a newspaper or other print publication.

Visual Writing for Newspaper People

A reporter working for a large metropolitan newspaper was once overheard telling a television reporter who had covered the same story a day earlier: "I don't know how you do it. I have three times as much space as you get to tell your story and still feel like I have to leave important stuff out. I couldn't do what you do." This is a real conversation and typical of one that used to occur fairly regularly when the "wall" between print reporting and broadcast reporting was firmly established and impenetrable. Today, if you're a so-called "newspaper" reporter, you have no choice: you have to do what TV reporters do – in a whole number of ways.

First, let's look at the traditional model of how newspapers once worked. A general assignment reporter was given a story to cover by the "desk" – city desk in the case of the metro area, a regional desk in outlying areas. If the story was from that reporter's "beat," she or he may have come up with the initial idea. The reporter's job was to make the phone calls, find the facts, visit the scene, do the interviews, and write the story – pretty much in that order. Notice what's missing? Just about everything. That reporter was not expected to take photos, record his or her interviews (except for note taking purposes), record video clips, or suggest graphics to accompany her or his story.

The photos were the job of a photographer – and if the story warranted it, one would be assigned by the "desk" to shoot them. The photographer might go out on the story at the same time as the assigned reporter, but maybe not. Often reporters would go to the story alone to get the "print" side of the story and the photographer would either show up earlier or come later to get the "visual" side of the story. In this scenario, it's easy to see how so-called "print" reporters never learned to *think visually* on the job. Traditionally, they were the "wordsmiths," and how those words aligned (or didn't) with the photographs; graphics – what newspaper people commonly referred to as the "art" – was someone else's problem. So words became king and photographs were either an afterthought or "window dressing" for the "real" story as told in prose.

Few contemporary newsrooms work this way. Increasingly, print storytellers are mandated to think first about how the words of their story have a corresponding visual element, either for on-air or online. That brings us to Rule 1: *Every word should produce a picture in your head.* That's the way television reporters have been conditioned to think since the medium's inception. It's a part of the lexicon or language today's successful newspaper reporters know – or learn. Notice the differences between the following two versions of the same story:

Example 1

Toyota Corporation executives promised the millions of consumers affected by a recall of a majority of their automotive models across the United States that errant accelerators will be replaced at designated intervals within the next 28 days, even if that means Toyota franchises must remain open 24 hours a day until the situation is finally brought to a conclusion. To date, the recall action has cost Toyota a total of 120 million dollars and left consumers like Mary Day with shaken faith in a corporation she once believed to be above reproach, the pinnacle of reliability and trust. In a letter to her local dealer, Day, 65, admonished the company for its slow response time. "I feel as if you, as a representative of the world's largest carmaker, should stand up for us who have bought your cars and been loyal to your brand – in my case, since I was 18 years old and bought my first used Corolla."

Example 2

Mary Day is not slowing down on her trip to the local Toyota dealer. Usually, it would be for an oil change. Today, it's about changing her 2007 Toyota Camry's faulty gas pedal. Mary is like Toyota owners nationwide who have a car on the recall list. She's not happy with Toyota's response – and plans to let the dealer know it:

> (Sound bite) THEY WERE FAST ENOUGH TO TAKE MY MONEY WHEN I BOUGHT THE CAR THREE YEARS AGO. I WANT THEM TO BE JUST AS FAST TO FIX IT OR TAKE IT BACK.

This dealership will stay open round the clock until the problem is fixed. Repairing the cars may be hard, but restoring customer confidence could be harder.

The most obvious difference between the two versions is that the writer of the second version kept the potential for *visualizing the story* firmly in mind. Walk through the story and take it one sentence at a time. Can you see a picture produced in your head? "Mary Day is not slowing down on her trip to the local Toyota dealer." Is there a corresponding visual? How about Mary driving her car and turning into the dealership's lot? That would work. So would a shot of her putting her foot on the gas pedal for the next sentence. Before the sound bite, you could envision Mary talking with the dealership's service manager or handing him the keys to her car. Following the sound bite, how about shots of technicians fixing Mary's car? Next could be a graphic of the cars on Toyota's recall list. You could also envision Mary driving her repaired car out of the dealership and heading home, bringing the story full-circle from where we first saw her and ending on a resolution of her problem. The story follows the structure of Crisis, Conflict and Resolution (CCR) as described in Chapter 2.

There are, of course, different ways of visualizing the same story, but these are some plausible suggestions. Notice that if you try to do the same exercise with the story's first version, you won't get far before running out of *tangible, attainable visuals* to accompany the text. Not surprisingly, the first version corresponds more to a traditional newspaper story and the second more closely conforms to the way good television stories are written. It follows the principle of, "say dog, see dog." In other words we *see* what the story *tells* us at the same instant when we *hear* what we're being told.

KISS (Keep It Short and Simple)

Another major difference between the two versions of the same story above is their length. The print story contains 159 words; the television version, exclusive of the sound bite, has only 86 words. Even with the sound bite, the word count is 117 words. Why is length important? Because the audience for television storytelling is notorious for being distracted. The kids could be screaming for dinner. The pan could be boiling over on the stove. The dog could be begging to be taken out for a walk. The spouse could be calling on the phone. All of the above could be happening simultaneously. Your story is competing for the viewer's attention. Newspaper reporters, traditionally, believed audiences sat down on the sofa and read their stories in a relaxed, nearly serene environment. Maybe they did. Contemporary audiences, however, live hurried lives and seldom sit down long enough to absorb your story fully – unless you maximize the chances for them to do so. That's where the visual element comes in and where the brevity becomes central. Together, they optimize the opportunity you have to get your good writing noticed. Television reporters have always known this; print reporters need to learn it.

Together with brevity comes simplicity. Not only do contemporary audiences not have the time to hang on every word of a long story, they also won't take the time to decipher complex language. The Toyota recall story written for print contains a lot of formal language that everyday people never use. Have you ever used the words "errant accelerator?" Of course not. Does anyone you know use those words? Doubtful. Most of us would say "faulty gas pedal." That's the *language of conversation* – the way real people talk (notice we didn't say "speak," on purpose). By comparing the two stories along these lines, you may notice that the television version uses simple, not formal language – and that's its strength. "24 hours a day" in the print story becomes "round the clock" for the TV version. *It's the way people talk.*

Who talks in this story, besides the reporter who wrote and narrates it? Mary, of course. Notice that we see the broader issues associated with the recall through the eyes of one person affected, not the millions whom we can neither visualize, nor with whom can we empathize. What's better?: the quote from the letter Mary wrote to the dealership contained in the print version or Mary herself expressing frustration first-hand in a very human way, easily understood by a sympathetic audience? Clearly, it's the second. We can't visualize what millions of Toyota owners are going through, but we can identify with one owner – and to the extent that she's representative of the multitudes of others, we can even sympathize with her. *It's the human element.* Most of us can't relate to the problems of millions, but we can *connect* with the troubles of one. In Chapter 4, we'll consider other variations on this "diamond" story structure, using the concerns of one person to symbolize a much larger group. To put a turn on a well-worn phrase, *it takes one to make a village.*

Relating to the Audience

Nothing turns off a television audience more than complexity. It can take many forms. We've already discussed complex language, but there are also complex subjects that may be important to society, but have little intrinsic interest to an individual. Often, print reporters like to take on big issues that take a long time to explain. They're the products of the days when newspapers invested heavily in complex, long-form stories that found a home in Sunday sections with names like "Perspective." The worth of these kinds of stories to an audience inclined to invest the time it takes to read them is inarguable. However, such audiences *self-select*. They can choose whether to read or skip over these kinds of stories, based on knowing what they're going to get and their willingness to make the effort. Television audiences, in general, are not so inclined.

The surest way to alienate an audience is to sprinkle a story for television with what is commonly referred to as jargon – specialized language used by experts and seldom understood by the rest of us. It makes viewers feel left out, much like someone who is on the sidelines of a conversation they would like to join, but cannot understand. Relating to a television audience means stripping your language of words that set up a barrier between them and you. If a storyteller for television is perceived as being the only person in the room who knows what the conversation is about, a breakdown with the audience occurs. Examples of jargon are terms related to science, medicine, politics, and economics. In print, an often used term is the consumer price index. Does anyone know exactly what that term means? Maybe economists, but they're expected to know its meaning. For most of us who are not economists, it's one of the more common examples of jargon. And yet, newspaper reporters use it all the time.

If you're a traditional print reporter trying to tell the story of the latest increase or decrease in the consumer price index, relating to the audience means expressing the concept free of complexity and jargon. That does not mean abandoning the term entirely; it just means helping the broadcast audience relate to the concept by making it tangible. Here's one way:

Marty Smith bought all the same groceries this week as he did last month – bread, milk, eggs, tomato sauce, pasta, ground sirloin, sugar, and fresh vegetables, among them. What isn't the same as last month is what Marty paid. The same full basket of groceries today cost Marty $107.63. Same time last month, it was only $93.16. That extra 14 bucks out of his pocket and Marty is just one person feeling the latest consumer price increases at the cash register.

Marty is a far better spokesman for the actual impact of a complex issue than any economist or government spokesperson. To him, the consumer price index isn't a mathematical equation; it's real money. The story could certainly go on to give the audience facts and figures, either through graphics on television or online, but the concept has been simplified, the complexity removed.

This example also brings up another aspect of relating to the audience. *Choose your interview subjects wisely.* In contemporary television news, they are often referred to as *characters* in your story. The audience will relate to you and your story to the extent that they find those whom you include interesting and involved. They must be *relatable.* In Chapter 2, we referred to compelling characters as "people like us." Most are people who remind us of ourselves, our family members, our neighbors, or our colleagues at work. Few occupy the sphere of what we call "officialdom." The term refers to law enforcement officers, government officials, politicians, and bureaucrats. All of them may be fine people, but the interviews they give and the information they impart are often not relatable to a TV audience. For one, they fall into a group that audiences are already inclined to "tune out." For another, they often don't come across well on camera. Consider the two sound bites below. Which would be better to include in a TV story?

Sound bite 1

We apprehended the suspect, male, Caucasian, age 24, seen making his escape over a rear enclosure, heading in the direction of Interstate Route 95 and creating a situation in which a large number of motorists became involved in a multi-vehicle collision when they were attempting to avoid coming into contact with him.

Sound bite 2

I saw this young guy jumping over the fence and running down the highway. From what I could see, he ran between a lot of cars. A couple of them almost hit him, but then they crashed into each other.

If you're accustomed to writing for a newspaper, your choice was probably #1. It's from an investigator who speaks with authority and has all the facts. But it lacks opinion or emotion. For multimedia, the better choice is #2. It contains essentially the same information, but is conveyed in the first person through a direct observer of the action. The person speaking *was there.* He is an "eyewitness" to what occurred. He has credibility with the audience and is more relatable to them than the somewhat stilted police spokesperson of sound bite 1 using "police speak." An entire format in television news is based upon this approach; in many markets, it is called "Eyewitness News." Its philosophy is that those who know the story best are those who have seen it, lived it, and can, therefore, best express it. It is okay to quote the cop if he avoids jargon and speaks from his own personal experience: "I've been doing this job for 20 years and it was the craziest chase I've ever seen."

Initiating Interaction

Those at newspapers have long been accustomed to feedback from their readers. "Letters to the Editor" have a long tradition in print news media. Some papers even have the position of ombudsman to address reader concerns and complaints. Television news people are acclimated to a more personal form of audience interaction; their high visibility makes many well known to their viewers, who recognize them on sight in the local market or surrounding community. Newspaper reporters have traditionally been fairly anonymous physically; other than a handful of columnists whose photos run alongside their columns, print media storytellers don't create instant recognition with their audience.

Working at a newspaper used to mean mostly one-way communication with readers – you to them, most of the time, and them to you only infrequently. The traditional mindset was that if you heard from readers and they had something good to say, great. If they had something not so good to say, you might chalk it up to the old adage "you can't please everyone." In neither instance did the print reporter invite, let alone actively *initiate* two-way interaction. The multimedia environment demands two-way interaction with the audience. Examples of how the definition of interaction has changed are all around us. Former New York City mayor Ed Koch became known for asking his constituents on the street "So, how am I doing?" Presumably, he really wanted to know. It helped him do a better job as mayor. The same could be said of print media reporters. Interaction with the news audience serves the identical purpose.

That interaction can take many forms. When a major story breaks, savvy newspaper editors recognize that they can't possibly cover every angle of a story. One solution is to invite the audience to help. Increasingly, newspapers ask their readers to contribute to the story. That contribution could involve asking readers to share their experiences as they relate to the story. Consider the following scenario.

Seven and a Half Million Cases of Beer May Build a New Brewery

The Narragansett Brewery in Cranston, R.I. was, for generations of New Englanders, a part of their heritage, a marker of coming of age, and a welcome place to work. The brewery opened its doors in 1890, but closed in 1981, falling victim to a stagnant economy and increased competition from regional breweries. At the time, it was among the state's biggest employers. Its signature slogan "Hi neighbor, have a Gansett" made it a household brand. Now, a group of young entrepreneurs want to bring the brew back to the place that made it famous. Having brewed Narragansett outside of R.I. for the last five years, the current owners have a campaign ongoing to restore and reopen the original Cranston brewery and say they will do so if Narragansett lovers buy 7.5 million cases this year.

A story like this one is ripe for inviting interaction from the audience. How you go about building that interaction is an indicator of how good a multimedia storyteller you can become. Take a moment to think about what role your audience could play in bringing this story alive. Would you: (1) ask your readers to relay their memories related to the original brewery?; (2) invite former workers to share with you what it was like to work there?; (3) initiate a request to readers for photos or film of the old brewery that they might have in their homes?; (4) determine if readers have memorabilia, such as original Narragansett bottles or other souvenirs of the "old days?" or (5) do all of the above?

Clearly, the answer is (5), "do all of the above." How would readers reach you? If your story is running in the print edition, most newspapers now supply the reporter's phone number and e-mail address at the bottom of the story. In the web version, that information might also be supplied, but so would a comment box where readers could directly respond to the requests. A story like this one is perfect in other ways for inviting interaction. It's a goldmine of memories. A community landmark like a brewery creates a social bond between workers and families over long periods of time. As such, it provides a great opportunity to tell a compelling story by using various forms of social media.

Social Media for Print Storytellers

Is there a Facebook page for fans of Narragansett beer or groups who want to see the brewery returned to its home state? How about for beer aficionados in general? What do they have to say about this particular brew? Are any blogs devoted to the topic? These are among the first questions today's print storyteller needs to ask her or himself. Facebook is just the beginning. How about Twitter? MySpace? All of these fall under the category of social media, and while they are sometimes perceived as competition for traditional – especially print – media, they can also be a strong ally to your storytelling. Let's briefly discuss them individually and consider their potential for broadening your story's scope and perspective.

Early in 2004, a Harvard student named Mark Zuckerberg, along with his college friends, founded Facebook (FB), a free social media site connecting people with their current friends, to help them find people from their past, invite people with similar interests to attend events and share media like personal photos, audio or video. To give some context to how fast this phenomenon has grown, by 2009, five years after its launch, Facebook reached 350 million users. The following year, that number was half a billion! By contrast, it took television three decades to reach a similar plateau of reaching about half America's population. Myspace is a social networking site operating similarly to Facebook, but it doesn't have nearly the same reach; also, where Facebook users are both young and old, Myspace has mainly a youth audience.

Facebook has grown significantly as an information source for millions of users. Literally moments after a killer whale attacked and drowned its trainer at Sea World in Orlando, Florida, in 2010, the story was posted with links to the first accounts on newspaper and television news sites – some users' pages even contained photos from observers' cell phone cameras or small video cams. Reporters, including Ted Daniel of Boston's Fox affiliate, used his Facebook page to solicit eyewitness accounts of the incident.

When Sarah Palin was selected as Republican presidential candidate John McCain's vice-presidential running mate in 2008, many Facebook users got the news first through updates posted by their online "friends." Facebook was considered to be such a force that CNN successfully partnered with the site to cover the election, garnering more visitors to their combined site than the network's television coverage drew that year. Newspapers have begun to establish their own Facebook sites, the *Atlanta Journal-Constitution* being one of the most recent and active.

Social networking sites are another way for print storytellers to connect with their audiences, getting to know readers' interests, ideas, and insights. Whether you use your paper's FB site or link readers to your own, social media help measure the audience's pulse while creating a dialogue. In the process, you may find interview sources, photos or video relevant to your story, or leads to a new related story. Encouraging readers to join your paper's FB site also creates the opportunity to link them to stories on your main webpage. In other words, Facebook can be part of an overall synergy between the story you're seeking to tell and other stories you've already written or ones you're considering writing. It can be a marvelous tool in this respect, as well as functioning as a news distribution vehicle in itself.

Twitter, another free social networking web site, started in 2006. Its users send their messages to each other via a "tweet," a compressed form of text that contains no more than 140 characters. Its advantage is *immediacy*: allowing "followers," as they're called to get instant updates on where people are, what they're doing, and what they're thinking in real time. Tweets are sent and received either on the Twitter web site or on a follower's cell phone equipped with the needed application. While social networking messages may seem superficial, especially those expressed in 140 characters or less, they can be powerful.

In the earliest hours and days of the 2010 earthquake in Haiti, cell phone signals failed and traditional news media – both print and television – weren't yet in place to get information out of the island nation to concerned parties around the globe. Anxious relatives of the 45,000 US citizens living in Haiti are just one group who would have been left in the dark about their loved ones' fate had it not been for social networking. Soon after the quake hit, the only news coming out of Haiti didn't come from newspapers or TV; it didn't even originate from the major news web sites. It did come from Facebook users and Twitter followers: another example of how social networking can assist in our news gathering and storytelling.

Make the Reader a Partner in Your Story

A major lesson for all storytellers in the twenty-first century, but perhaps most applicable to traditional print reporters is the following: you are more than likely not the expert on the story you are writing; even if you think you are, you're not the *only* expert. That doesn't mean the search for so-called *experts* of the ilk often referred to as "the usual suspects": those professionals who clutter cable news with their predictable views. Readers today most value stories where *their* voice is heard. We've already briefly touched above on how best to reach those readers using social media. Now, we'll elaborate on some specific means you can use to contact readers for information they have that you need.

That information could relate to a specific story or idea for a story or about their interests in general.

Today's savvy print reporters, like their counterparts in traditional broadcast media and public relations, recognize that a large part of their job as storytellers is *outreach* – engaging the audience in a conversation about their stories. One of the simplest and yet most effective ways to accomplish this is by writing a blog, giving your own perspective on the story while getting valuable audience feedback. Readers like to know the person behind the byline. Most enjoy being part of the *process* behind the story. That could mean either contributing to the story as it develops or commenting on its future course.

This goes against the grain of many traditional print reporters, since it appears to threaten the time-honored standard of journalistic objectivity. It's a problem that many newspapers (and television stations, for that matter) confronted in the earliest days of journalist blogging. Some news managers were originally wary of allowing their reporters to step outside the story and interact more directly with the audience. The fears of most have been calmed by accepting that contemporary audiences are sophisticated enough to distinguish between your role as a journalist reporting the story, and your role as a blogger sharing a more personal view of the story.

Writing a Blog

Perhaps not surprisingly, today's college journalism students are far more versed in the mechanics of blog writing than many professional journalists. A 2010 e-mail to about 50 industry professionals – many in journalism, some in other communication fields – asked for them to join and comment on a classroom blog created for journalism and media students at the University of South Florida St. Petersburg. The topics ranged from change in the media workplace to journalism's fight for economic survival. The instructor's postings were on subjects any media professional would know about and have views on. Despite that, only about a half dozen responded and joined as "followers" of the blog. Were the rest too busy? That's certainly possible. But a fair number confessed confusion over what a blog was, how it worked, and how to join and comment.

In many ways, contemporary blogs share a lot in common with the traditional editorial page in a newspaper. However, while there are only a few editorial writers, a newspaper can have many bloggers. It's even possible that some newsroom managers are unaware of the fact that their reporters write blogs in their "spare" time. Others, though, have not only encouraged blog writing (and this applies both to traditional print and broadcast newsrooms), but *require* it, as part of a staffer's job duties and description. Increasingly, this is the more common model.

Blogs can help a reporter – especially a print media reporter who lacks the visual recognition of his/her television counterpart – put a "face" to the written word, replicating what good storytellers in any genre strive to do in their writing. They also help create or reinforce the writer's *brand*, an increasingly important aspect of being a storyteller across media platforms. It helps you relate to many "ordinary" citizens, who may write their own blogs on topics like movies or gardening, sports or parenting. Here's how to get started.

Depending upon the newsroom where you work or *want* to work, there may already be a system in place for you to locate your blog on the paper's main web site. Many newspapers now centrally locate their reporters' blogs on a single link using a pull-down menu from which to select. If you go to work for one of these papers, experiment with the institutional software that already exists to create your blog, which, in the beginning at least, needs to be nothing more than your thoughts on any one or a combination of the following questions below.

The Blog Behind the Story

- Who did you find to be the most interesting character in your story?
- What led you to the topic in the first place?
- Where did the trail lead you?
- When did you find out how good a story you really had?
- Why is it so important?
- How might you follow up on a "universal truth" contained within your story?

This is, of course, only one approach to a blog and it presupposes you're blogging about a story you've already done. It could be your blog focuses on a community problem or a national social, political, or economic issue. You may not have done a story on the specific problem or the general issue yet, but your blog may "test the waters" with your readers to see where they stand and why. It can be a way of gaining information for the eventual story through the network of readers you develop. For that reason, perhaps the most important element on your blog is the "comment" feature, where the audience can react directly to what you've written by contributing to the storyline, offering an alternative point-of-view, or registering outright disagreement.

Keep in mind that blogs are hardly the domain of professional journalists. Many college newspapers have web sites where student reporters often blog about their stories, their individual interests, or opinions on campus issues. In fact, if you are currently in a journalism class and looking for a way to distinguish yourself with professional journalists, writing a blog can be indispensable. Rob King, editor of ESPN.com, once told a student audience not to send him traditional story "clips" when applying for a job. He advised: "Send me the address of your blog and if I'm interested I'll check it out to see how you write and tell a story."

The best part is that blogging is a free activity for students. Where professional reporters are well advised to stick to blogging software approved by their employers, students can use any one of a number of no-cost blog software programs. The most popular and easiest to use are Wordpress (http://wordpress.org/) and Blogger (https://www.blogger.com). The process is self-guiding and intuitive. In addition to text, links to other stories or sites can be included, as can photo images or video. Remember that blogs *invite interaction* by posing a question or suggesting a solution.

Cell Phones as Storytelling Tools

In June, 2009, over a quarter billion Americans – about 89 percent of the total US population – possessed a cell phone; globally, that figure rises to over 4 billion users or about 61 percent of the world's population. What do these figures have to do with storytelling? Just about everything. Besides affording the ability to make and receive phone calls, the latest generation of cellular phones has features ranging from text messaging to still and video capability. In many ways, the cell phone is a mobile news center, enabling radio reporters to file voice stories with audio sound bites, television reporters to transmit cell camera video, and print reporters to text a first story on a breaking news event with accompanying still photos. Journalists across all platforms can send and receive e-mail and access their Facebook pages and Twitter accounts via their cell phones. And, if journalists can do all of the above, so can any average reader/viewer/user who has a cell phone.

Consider the day after Superbowl XLIV, February 8, 2010. The cable news network HLN (formerly known as CNN Headline News) did a segment indicative of how social media intersects with hand-held cellular technology to tell a better story. Besides football, the Superbowl is best known for its commercials – perhaps it's the sole media event where advertisements demand as much, if not more, attention than the event itself. A traditional "day after" story brings together advertising executives and other media types to critique the previous night's commercials using criteria like "best" and "worst." That's the way NBC's *Today Show* handled the story that morning. HLN's treatment, however, made full use of both social media and mobile cellular technology.

Starting with anchor Christi Paul's invitation for viewers to let her know which Superbowl commercials they liked most and least, she listed on-screen a menu of options. First came her personal Facebook page to use for comments, followed by a phone number to call for verbal feedback (presumably using your cell phone). Next were numbers for texting: one corresponded to "liking" a given commercial from the night before and another to "disliking" the same commercial. Viewers could also use their phones to transmit a video question in to the network. The only thing missing was cell phone-generated still photos or video of viewers enjoying the big game with friends and family. That, no doubt, became part of another coverage plan that day somewhere in the world, whether in a newspaper, on television, or online.

We seldom think of it as such, but a cell phone really is a multimedia device, empowering journalists and citizens alike. When covering breaking news, some of the earliest information originates as text messages from reporters and eyewitnesses at the scene. Some of the initial and often most compelling photos and video of a news story *as it happens* result from someone with a cell phone – professional or amateur.

Web Writing

The multimedia storytelling approach is actually closer to a strategy for the web than it is for television or newspapers alone. Writing is only one part of the process. Assembling the additional elements needed to tell a story online is paramount. Writing in and around those elements is the essence of good web storytelling. Here are two examples of the same story, the first written in traditional newspaper style, the second for the web:

The Washington, D.C. metropolitan area received 15 inches of snow yesterday, adding to the 20 inches already on the ground and complicating the problems of thousands throughout the region who are without heat and power. Meteorologists say that this second major winter storm in two weeks resulted in both airports in the nation's capital, Dulles and Reagan National, being closed in anticipation of more inclement weather later in the week. The storm is also predicted to bring heavy downfalls from New York City, spared last weekend, and other major cities up the east coast as far as Boston. There is a possibility, according to record keepers, that this latest storm could break all records in terms of accumulation. Paul Cocin, National Weather Service severe weather expert, has written a book on the worst winter storms of the last century and said that "this one is likely going to be historic, especially in the Maryland–Washington, D.C. area." Meanwhile, frustration built among area residents. Offices were closed on Tuesday and the federal government was shut down for the second straight day.

Major Winter Storm Adds Insult to Injury

For second straight week, D.C. hammered by snowfall

If you live in the middle of the US or anywhere near the east coast, bundle up and hunker down. It's only February and wintry conditions, meteorologists say, are threatening to shatter all snowfall records. Many are still reeling from last week's 20-inch snowfall in Washington, D.C. Concerns about losing heat and power are mounting. Some residents have been without either since last weekend's storm. It's not business as usual at many businesses and federal government offices. Most were closed on Tuesday. So are the area's two major airports today.

What are some of the major differences between these two versions of the story? They might be summarized this way:

Print story: longer sentences, uses past tense, gives more detail, contains direct quote.
Web story: shorter sentences, uses present tense, less detail given, quote paraphrased.

There are certainly many other differences. How about which version is more *conversational*? The web story, obviously. It gets to the point quickly, sparing the reader a long, detailed lead that attempts to answer the "who, what, when, where, why, and how" in a single sentence. One way in which web writing shares a lot in common with television news writing is the way it adopts a familiar tone with the reader. Notice the use of the pronoun "you" in the first sentence. Web writers and editors generally embrace this kind of *inclusive tone* established early in a story. It invites the reader to *share* the story, rather than read it.

The print story talks about what *went on,* using past-tense verbs; the web story tells us what *is going on,* using present-tense verbs that suggest *action.* It focuses on *immediacy,* what the reader can expect now or soon. Where the print version includes a complete, direct quote from a meteorologist, the web story paraphrases his major point. It's one more way in which stories for the web are kept *shorter.*

Another is *punctuation.* Notice how many commas are used in the newspaper story. Can you find a single one in the web version? Not a single one. The writer has consciously eliminated them, using a period instead wherever she/he might be tempted to place a comma. This has two purposes: (1) it ensures sentences are kept short; (2) it ensures that each sentence contains a single thought. To put it succinctly: complex punctuation leads to complex sentences. Don't misinterpret this to mean you shouldn't use correct punctuation in a web story. Do remember that your choice of punctuation either speeds a story up for the reader or slows it down. Finding ways to tell your story with a minimum of interruptions is what effective web writing is all about.

Elements of a web story

As part of the title of his book on broadcast news writing, former network TV news writer Mervin Block used these three words: "shorter, sharper, stronger." Nothing could better describe what a web story must be in order to capture attention and retain the reader. Research from the Poynter Institute, in its Eyetrack studies, indicates that once they click on a web story, readers will finish reading it about 60 per cent of the time. The rest of the time, they move on to another story or another web site. The decision to read a web news story – or not – is largely based on an initial scan of that story's major elements. Putting extra effort into writing those elements first noticed by readers is time well spent.

Using the "winter storm" story in its web version above helps us illustrate the strategic placement of elements that will attract readers' attention and make them *want* to read your story – instead of moving on. On initial scan, what jumps out to you first about the winter storm story? Does it sound "urgent?" What key words make it sound that way? *Insult* and *injury* are both powerful words. They prompt us to ask ourselves "Who's insulted?" "How are they injured?" "Is it anyone I know?" "Am I at risk?" Those three simple words, "Insult to Injury," combined with "Major Winter Storm" create interest and galvanize attention. They're short, sharp, and strong.

Similarly, if you simply glance at the story, your eyes are likely to alight on other words that provoke curiosity. "Hammered," "bundle," "hunker," "reeling," "closed" are all good choices for words to place at intervals in the web story. As the eye scans the screen for meaning, the probability increases that some of these "key words" will register with the online reader. It's the reason why so much attention in web writing is placed upon what we will call "*frontloading*" the story: putting special emphasis on what the reader sees at his/her point of entry into that story.

Each section of a web news story has a name, along with a purpose. While their order may vary somewhat depending upon a story's subject, in general, web writing follows this formula:

Order of Elements in a Web Story

Headline   *Captures attention, much like a newspaper headline*
Blurb   *Summarizes story's major action*
Lead   *Draws the reader into the story*
Brief   *Gives major details of the story*

Compare how our winter storm story conforms to this format:

Headline: *Major Winter Storm Adds Insult to Injury*
Blurb: **For second straight week, D.C. hammered by snowfall**
Lead: If you live in the middle of the US or anywhere near the east coast, bundle up and hunker down.
Brief: It's only February and wintry conditions, meteorologists say, are threatening to shatter all snowfall records. Many are still reeling from last week's 20-inch snowfall in Washington, D.C. Concerns about losing heat and power are mounting. Some residents have been without either since last weekend's storm. It's not business as usual at many businesses and federal government offices. Most were closed on Tuesday. So are the area's two major airports today.

If you think back to your classes in traditional newspaper reporting, the headline serves exactly the same function as it might in a newspaper, although it contains perhaps more action words. The most effective headlines have a six to ten word count. The blurb corresponds to what you may have called the "subhead (line)" in your print journalism courses. The lead is the same as you've learned about in the past, although it's more *personalized* for the web. The brief is what you may have learned to call the story's "nut graph." It gives the "nut" or essence of the story.

Returning to the two versions of the winter storm story, a fair question to ask is "Which story is more complete?" Clearly, it's the print story. It contains more detail, valued by some readers, but considered "information overkill" by many others. Keep in mind, however, that the web story you just re-read would invariably contain far more than just words on the screen. Including additional elements would ultimately make it more "complete" than its traditional newspaper counterpart.

Writing with Additional Elements

In the earliest days of newspapers, one of the primary means of distribution was street sales and the main vendors were called "newsboys." Starting in Britain, these young "hawkers" of the daily news developed a loud chant: "EXTRA, EXTRA, read all about it!" As newspapers gained a foothold in America during the nineteenth century, in large cities and small towns, the "EXTRA EXTRA" tradition followed. In both countries, it indicated that the paper had published an "extra" edition that day in order to accommodate the latest developments on a big story; some stories were deemed too important to have all the details, all of their essential elements, contained in a single version on the front page. So, new front pages were published, containing material not included in the original version.

Today, the storytelling equivalent of that "extra" edition exists not in print, but on the web. It's useful to think of the web not as an extension of the newspaper, but an integral storytelling medium that creates additional opportunities to tell parts of a story that, for a number of reasons, can't be told – or can't be told as well – in the traditional print medium. Even good web storytellers sometimes lose sight of the fact that "extras" on the web aren't "leftovers" from their print or television stories.

Effective web stories contain elements that add value to the reader/user experience of the story; they don't simply include textual or visual elements that didn't "fit" in an earlier story. That could mean adding graphics, audio or video clips of entire interviews done for the original story, perhaps a reader poll or hyperlinks to additional resources for under-standing the story. Each of these will be discussed in detail, but first, ask yourself a number of questions as you consider how best to tell your print or television story on the web. Remember, the goal is to *illuminate, not duplicate*.

Extras on the Web: Questions to Ask Yourself

What does the reader/user still want to know about my story?
Will everyone be interested in this additional information or just some readers/users?
Why are these parts of the story better told on the web than in print?
How can I best add that content to my web version?
What's the best way to make that content interactive?
Will the reader/user's understanding and experience of my story benefit from additional visual elements?
Which elements are best for that purpose – graphics, audio or video clips, links to additional resources?
Will my story benefit from a reader/user poll that gauges interest in the general subject and gathers ideas for future stories?

As a practical exercise in the thought process involved with web storytelling, let's return to the "major winter storm" story considered above in both its print and web versions. How might you make this a more effective web story by using additional elements beyond those included in either the original newspaper version or the rewritten web version? There's no right or wrong way, but there are *better* ways, using resources readily available to you. Think about the interviews you may have done for the story. Did you record them, either on audio or video? *You should.* Keep track of quotes or clips that you didn't use in your print story. What elements do they contain that might interest at least *some* of the audience for your story, if not everyone in your audience? What elements of the story did you have to sacrifice because they slowed down the pace for a print audience? This could be either because (1) they contained highly technical information or (2) they weren't compelling using text alone.

A web story about the winter storm using the "extras" might contain some or all of the following:

An interactive map showing where the heaviest snow fell, hour by hour.

A graphic displaying record snowfall in the region over the past 50 years.

A graphic explaining how meteorological conditions can lead to this level of extraordinary snowfall.

Video clips from readers/users personalizing the storm's impact on them and their neighborhoods.

Audio or video of the meteorologist named in the print story, giving more details of your interview with him.

A slideshow, with or without sound (music or otherwise), containing compelling still photos taken by you, your photographer, or submitted by your audience.

A live webcam feed from various areas especially hard hit, perhaps including links to webcams at the major airports.

Hyperlinks to resources needed by the audience, as in emergency phone numbers, social agencies, transportation officials, etc.

This list is by no means exhaustive. You should spend some time composing your own list of those elements that show promise for creating more interest, adding more value, and making a more compelling story. If you are sitting in a college classroom right now, this process is no doubt intuitive to you. Those accustomed to getting their news and information from the web are comfortable and conversant with those elements that, for older generations of readers, seem to be "extras." For today's younger media consumers, they are "essentials." Let's briefly consider each individually.

Slideshows

For whatever reason, web audiences love slideshows. Good slideshows are, in essence, photo essays. Some contain "natural sound" that reinforces the slideshow's overall theme. For the snowstorm example, that might mean the sound of snowplows scraping roadways down to pavement. It might also be the sounds associated with falling snowfall – stillness interrupted by an occasional bird vocalizing or wind blowing the snow about. It might also carry a musical soundtrack – a song with snow in its title or lyric (so long as the copyright is cleared for usage). Slideshows are successful to the extent that they are self-paced and, therefore, interactive. In other words, the user should have control over how fast or slow the images change, whether they dissolve from one to another or simply "switch" to the next photo.

Television stations like KNSD in San Diego began using slideshows on their web site in 2003. The audience response was overwhelming and, after tracking where their viewers spent the most time online, the station prioritized slideshows as the most important element of their web storytelling. Some of the photos were station-generated, others aggregated from elsewhere on the web (especially other NBC-owned stations and affiliates), and still others were submitted by viewers.

Maps and graphics

Ask any fifth grade geography student if he or she finds maps, filled with latitude and longitude markers, interesting and you'll probably get the response: "not so much." For some reason, it's the opposite response when maps are put online as part of web news stories; audiences show a predisposition toward wanting them – especially if, like slideshows, they can be manipulated and personalized to the user's needs.

The snowstorm story is a perfect example. Ask yourself, "Do I really care how much snow a town 100 miles from me got?" The answer is probably not. But I (and by extension, *the reader*) may care a lot about how much snow that town got *compared* to where I live. An interactive map that allows me to put my cursor over that town, my town, and any or every town between the two creates a high level of interactivity with the story. It surely beats any flat, static map on a traditional newspaper's pages.

Graphics are no stranger to most newspapers' daily format. Many contain computer-generated images to illustrate a writer's story. Most are straightforward, factual, and, unfortunately, dull. Even with color, few engage the reader's imagination. Online, graphics for web stories can engage the reader through a variety of means. One is *animation*. Visualize telling our snowstorm story using a graphic where piles of snow can be put in motion, creating the sensation of a dynamic storm with inches of snowfall accumulating. What's called a "timeline" – displaying the storm's progress from, say, 3 a.m. right up to the present moment, complete with updated accumulation totals – could be built around just such a graphic.

Audio and video clips

There's something *empowering* about listening to what *you* consider interesting or important – or, better yet, *watching and listening* to it. When print reporters decide which quotes to use in a story and television reporters settle on the sound bites they will use in their packages, the selection process is up to them. Who's to say that what a reporter finds most interesting in the interview she/he has done is what the individual reader thinks is most interesting? By posting the entirety of an interview – audio or video or both – as part of your web story, you give readers a *choice* to explore more or less of what a person in your story had to say.

Placing the audience in the same environment where the storyteller gained his or her information helps web users measure its credibility. So often, journalists are accused (sometimes with good reason) of taking quotes or sound bites "out of context." By providing the whole interview, the reader can assess that context for her or himself. There's another, perhaps more practical, reason for posting your unedited audio and video as part of your web story. You can't possibly use it all on other platforms. Every traditional medium has its space or time limitations – traditional print, radio, and TV certainly do. But the online world has neither. The only limitation is the user's willingness or inclination to read more, hear more, or see more. As a storyteller in this new media environment, making the audience's experience limitless is a challenge – and an opportunity.

Returning to our snowstorm story, some of the online audience would want more insight from the meteorologist quoted in the original print version, especially if, as in the actual instance, he was an expert who literally wrote the book on historic snowstorms across America. His perspective might be important to weather and history buffs alike. They might not get that element anywhere else, so why not make it part of your web story?

When it comes to video, especially, why not "use" YouTube as part of your story? There's a reason that the video sharing site has become so captivating to so many "ordinary" people. It's a virtual treasure trove of material, some serious, some of it silly, a lot of it historic. It can help beef up your story by linking the reader to relevant video. A simple search for "Blizzard of '78" can produce valuable clips. Seeing a monster storm from another time can help provide perspective on the current one.

Links to other resources

We are a "Google" culture; by that, we mean that almost anyone can find anything they want to know online. But how many find good, reliable information there? Any number of sites – Google, ask.com, yahoo, to name a few – can direct readers to resources related to your story. Your job as a web storyteller, however, is to cut that step out for your reader. Provide her or him with links to the most credible, most important, and most relevant resources. *Do the research for them.* Vet the sites with the best information. And make it easy to get there by providing the hyperlinks to these sites as an integral part of your story. Eliminate the reader's need for a "second party" search site and you maximize the chances that reader will stick with you – not only for this one story, but others in the future.

For the snowstorm example, there are infinite resources available to the online audience. Successful storytelling – power storytelling – involves paring those resources down. It's especially true today that anyone with the technology, the time, and the will has access to anything to which journalists have access. There's a school of thought that suggests not everyone has the skills to *organize and prioritize information* for a given audience. It's a skill sometimes referred to as news *processing.* There are those in the journalism field who dislike that term, but the task is what's important here. Help direct your audience to the resources they most want or need as part of your web story. That's where your judgment counts. Use it!

Putting the Pieces Together

Today's technology makes the process of adding elements to your web story amazingly simple. Digital audio recorders, as well as small, hand-held video cameras, now contain the hardware and software necessary to upload sound and images directly to your story, web site, or blog. Most can be linked to your cellular phone or laptop computer, enabling audio and video to be inserted either from the newsroom or a remote location. The key is to use a digital recorder or video camera containing a USB output. It is not at all uncommon today to have audio and video devices contained in one unit.

After completing your interviews, it's an easy matter to plug the USB output from your audio/video device(s) into your laptop's USB input. The device then functions exactly like another one with which you are no doubt familiar – the small, portable "flash" or "thumb" drive. By using a program like Windows Media Player or Real Audio, it takes very little time to download your interviews in whole or in part. The exact process, of course, depends on your specific computer, its programs, and features. But you're well on the way if you use a digital recording device as opposed to older tape or camcorders. The entire transfer process from interview to story can literally take minutes.

Ask Al Tompkins of the Poynter Institute for Media Studies, writer of a daily online column called "Al's Morning Meeting." Tompkins, a former television news photographer and news director, files his column from wherever he finds himself – down the street, across the nation or around the world. He uses a multimedia device to capture stills, audio, and video that cost under $100 at a local drugstore chain. By linking it via the built-in USB to his laptop, he has sent sound and pictures for his column while riding in a taxicab!

Similarly, slideshows and graphics can be created on most laptops using programs already available to you that you may not know you have – or you never use. Just about everyone is familiar with PowerPoint. It can be used to design simple slideshows on a PC. Those slides can then be ordered, arranged, and a soundtrack can be added. It may be the most basic way of building a slideshow, but it works. This points to the advice of many professionals: Don't be afraid to experiment.

While the current expectation is that journalists can work alone across multiple media platforms (hence the advent of the term "sojo" – for solo journalists), most of us are better at some things than others. Begin by using what you already know and expand your knowledge through talking to the experts: those who have specialized knowledge and are all around you, in your classroom or your newsroom.

Maximizing the Web Experience

As previously discussed, storytelling on the web presupposes a very different set of expectations – and demands. It's not as simple as transferring your print or TV story to another medium. One major reason is how the web audience consumes information. Newspaper readers, for the most part, read stories one at a time. It's not exactly a linear process, since some may skip from the front page to the fourth page or from one section to another; still, it could be argued that print readers operate in a more or less linear manner, concentrating on a single task in a defined order (for instance, front to back of the newspaper or section to section).

Television viewers are more or less forced to be linear in their consumption of stories; they have to sit through some stories, regardless of whether they're of interest, in order to get to the stories they want to see. Web readers, it has long been known, can multi-task: that is, while online they can do many other things, including watching TV, doing e-mail, engaging in social media sites, bill pay, any one of scores of activities. Their attention is divided.

A 2010 PBS documentary, *Digital Nation*, focused on the different ways in which our media-drenched culture stimulates the human brain. The work of researchers at Boston's Tufts University identified, to put it most simply, "the brain on newspaper reading" as opposed to "the brain on Google." Using brain scans, the researchers were able to visually identify high stimulation patterns through bright colors reflecting activity. When reading a newspaper story, they found that the brain functions in a passive manner; there were few "bright" spots evident. However, when engaged in a Google search, those parts of the brain most closely associated with interactivity lit up like a pinball machine.

While we don't pretend to be neurosurgeons, it does seem that this research could have practical applications for storytelling on the web. For one, interactivity – *controlling* part of the storytelling experience by *selecting* what *you* want to read, see, or hear – is an antidote to the passivity of reading a print news story or watching a TV story. In traditional media, we *absorb* information from others; on the web, we *discover* it for ourselves. What does this mean for you, the storyteller, in this most interactive of all media? It could mean one of two things: adapting content from another medium (print or broadcast) to the web or creating content specifically for the web.

Unfortunately, most web storytelling falls under the first category: adapting content from another medium. But think of the possibilities for the second: creating content specifically for the web. That means creating stories that scream for and thrive on interactivity. Like we said, consider the possibilities. Dream large. Here are two scenarios to get you started.

Scenario 1

San Francisco Police are cracking down on what are called "shooting galleries," usually abandoned houses where drug users share needles to inject heroin or cocaine. Along with "crack houses" – places where addicts smoke a form of cocaine known as "crack" – they have provoked an outcry from neighbors and outrage from city officials. Authorities say they plan to raid the houses at all hours to help put an end to the nuisance in many neighborhoods.

Scenario 2

An accident involving a rollercoaster ride at the State Fair has left three people in a critical condition and 15 others with minor injuries. Officials said the Saturday night mishap involved the malfunction of a device called an "over-speed governor." That device is intended to slow down a ride once it reaches a certain speed. In this instance, the ride's operators said, it failed to engage, leading to speeds of up to 75 miles an hour. Those injured were thrown from the coaster and landed among other fairgoers.

Both scenarios involve pretty basic stories: a drug bust and an accident scene. They're easy to tell for a newspaper or television audience. For television, especially, they present many visual possibilities. How about for the web? Question 1: how do you add to each of these stories through interactivity? Let's begin with the "Shooting Gallery" narrative. All the facts are there, but what's missing? How about the *experience* of what it's like to be on the police raid of a drug house? Many journalists have followed police on such raids and already know that experience; few in the audience have or will have such "inside" access. Why not take them there?

Use your imagination. Which of the following interactive multimedia tools would help tell the story best?

1. Graphics
2. Animation
3. Audio
4. Video
5. Blogs
6. Slideshows
7. None of the above
8. All of the above

If you replied "all of the above," you're really in a multimedia state of mind! However, to a greater or lesser extent, each of the individual responses from 1–6 is also correct. Any of the tools listed could be used individually to enhance the web story's impact on your audience. Combined, they help create a powerful narrative – one that immerses the user in your story. Think about it. If you have never been in a house where illegal drugs are being used, what would your expectation be? What would you see and hear? What would be most interesting? What would be most surprising? This thought process is natural to most journalists and those studying journalism. What comes less naturally to some is how to create an online environment in which the audience becomes engaged and informed simultaneously.

One way is to apply all the visual elements listed above: graphics, animation, video, and slideshows. While the text of your story might focus on a specific neighborhood where drug houses have taken over, it might be accompanied by a graphic showing how the problem has risen over a number of years. Graphics, as discussed earlier in this chapter, are a reliable way of conveying complex information in an interesting manner. One step higher than a static graphic, though, is one with *motion*. That could involve a specialized category of graphics we have not yet considered: *animation*.

Think for a moment about the sophisticated computer-generated animation that consumes movie audiences. From Disney to Dreamworks, from *Toy Story* to *Avatar*, some of our culture's most compelling and memorable films rely heavily on animation techniques. Contemporary animation techniques, on a much smaller scale, can be used to illustrate stories for the web. Computer programs like Flash, while difficult to master at first, can have a powerful, lasting impact on your web storytelling.

What's better than being told in words what it's like to be inside a place where addicts are sharing needles to "shoot" their drugs? How about simulating the experience for the online audience? It's possible to do so using animation. By using technology already in place on many news web sites, a short "tour" of the drug house can be under the web user's control. Doors to different rooms open, revealing the activities inside. By putting your mouse's cursor over buttons on the screen, the web user can choose to hear the story of one addict's life in her/his own words. Placing the cursor elsewhere on the screen results in a law enforcement officer discussing how and why drug dealers and users bring on the decay of a neighborhood. You get the idea. The possibilities are both infinite and intriguing.

All of this, of course, presupposes that everything on your "tour" is based on fact – either from interviews you've done with the story's principles or research gained from exhaustive research. In fact, both could be part of the story's final treatment for the web. We envision a story that has it all: text, graphics, animation, audio clips of the full interviews you do with those involved in the drug trade and those who arrest and prosecute them. Audio and *video* clips include it all, especially the views of those neighbors whose families, property, and safety are at stake. You may find that those in the neighborhood have photos of the house in question in better days; they could be put into a slideshow showing the contrast between then and now.

How about writing a blog about your own, first-person experience in going along on a drug raid with police? If they're permitted, why not have someone from law enforcement or, if not, the head of the neighborhood crime watch group write a blog about their experiences? Maybe an attorney who has dealt with defendants in these cases would detail his/her experiences or a drug counselor who treats addicts like the ones in your story could be tapped for a blog entry. All of these perspectives could have their separate place on the page where your story is posted. Each of these elements leads to interactivity between many different stakeholders in this story. Best of all is that this can lead to a community discussion about a serious issue, with feedback from those commenting on the story's individual elements by e-mail or through one of the included blogs.

User Polls

One way to consolidate the audience feedback, beyond blog comments or e-mail responses, is to include a "poll" in your web story. The poll need not be complex – in fact, the simpler, the better. Questions can range from the audience's opinion on the story to what action they believe should be taken. Polls that are easy to collate involve what are called "closed" responses – that is, the user has a limited number of choices when replying to your question.

For the "Shooting Gallery" story, here are some possibilities.

Question: *Do you believe the police are doing enough to fight drug abuse in your neighborhood?*

- Yes, definitely
- No, not at all
- Could do more
- Not sure

Question: *How would you characterize illegal drug activity in your neighborhood?*

- Very heavy drug activity
- Very light drug activity
- Non-existent
- More during the day
- More at night
- Don't know

Question: *What more could law enforcement do to help rid your neighborhood of drugs?*

- Put more police patrols on the street
- Be more visible in the neighborhood
- Step up arrests of known drug users and dealers
- Have longer jail sentences for those convicted

These are just a few of the kinds of questions you might ask relative to this specific story. You might also include a question asking your readers how useful they felt your story was to them, or how it either confirmed what they already thought about the prevalence of illegal drugs in their neighborhood or, perhaps, changed their preconceptions surrounding a drug user's profile (as in her/his gender, age, race, ethnicity, social/economic status, and so on). For an individual in your audience, answering the questions brings the opportunity to view (after responding) how others felt about the same issue. Again, interactivity is encouraged and ensured.

It need not be difficult to make sense of all the "data" you gather through these polls. There are many online resources for automatically putting your responses into a comprehensible form; some are even free of charge. Survey Monkey is one of the more popular. The key is in the survey's design and, again, there are numerous self-guiding sites on the web to help you right from the start.

Thinking it Through

Can you apply the same approach used in the "Shooting Gallery" story to the scenario involving the rollercoaster accident at the state fair? You should be able to do so. First, they share much in common. Both have potential for involving the audience through interactivity. In the first scenario, graphics, audio, video, slideshows, animation, blogs, and polls each played an appropriate role in putting the web audience into the story. Each helped them experience the story from a perspective ordinarily outside their realm of access. Think about this when considering how best to enrich the rollercoaster story for the web. Most people have been on a rollercoaster ride; few (fortunately) have been involved in a rollercoaster accident. Ask yourself the same questions you asked about the "Shooting Gallery" story. Each question should prompt you toward at least one multimedia "extra" to enrich your web story; they follow the sample questions below.

What must it be like to feel like you're going 75 miles an hour and stopping or slowing down isn't under your control? *Animation.* How often does this happen with rollercoaster rides or amusement rides in general? *Graphic.* How did the accident sound? *Audio.* Is there an expert who can describe what went wrong with the device in question? *Video.* Did anyone take still photos with their digital or cell phone camera? *Slideshow.* How likely are safety concerns to prevent the public from riding the fair's rides in the future? *Poll.* Using this as a starting point, work through the process of implementing each of these "tools" into the rollercoaster accident story. In other words, what kind of animation is possible? What will your graphics look like? Which piece of sound will you post as part of the web version? How can you make the video interview work in tandem with the story's major points? What photos should be emphasized as part of the slideshow? In general, what value does each and every element add to this story?

Next comes the hard part. Once you've conditioned yourself to think beyond the words you write, it's time to begin taking inventory of all the storytelling elements you have. That includes considering the most logical way in which to arrange and present those elements in and around your story on the web. There are practical considerations to keep in mind, as well as a few relating to matters of design. As we've stressed throughout this chapter, understanding *how* readers consume stories on the web is often as important as creating *what* they consume.

Web Considerations

A colleague of ours who teaches visual journalism courses constantly tells his students that the most important aspect of a web story involves *simplicity*. The term applies to everything about the story, from navigation to the overlook design scheme. Navigation should be easy to grasp – in other words, the audience is not inclined to search around a cluttered screen to find specific elements of the story that most interest them. As stated previously in this chapter, web readers will read and stick with your story if a quick scan of its major components helps reveal its story line in a compelling manner. A general rule of thumb: *Don't make me search for what are the most important parts of your story*. That means putting links to audio/video, graphs, slideshows, polls, etc. in obvious spots on the page around your main text story. If the eye can grasp the overall scheme, navigation from one element of the story to the next becomes a pleasure, not a burden.

Add to simplicity the concept of keeping the visual look of your story *clean*. Think of clean as the opposite of clutter on the story's page. Too much competing information in a confined screen space leaves the web reader overwhelmed. So do "fancy" fonts or overly clever images. Strive for clear, sharp design elements that assist your story's meaning. Fight the temptation to "fill the page" with material; as the old adage goes, *often less is more*. Web readers won't sift through myriad postings to reach what they want. Make links clear. Put them where they make sense.

In a newspaper, the eye is drawn initially to a headline or graphic; on the web, the eye goes directly to the text. Most web readers scan stories from top to bottom, not left to right. Keeping this in mind can help you position strong sentences accordingly, as well as using bold characters for major points. Here are some other tips:

- Keep sentences short.
- Limit paragraphs to one thought.
- Create lists of major points.
- Use bullets to draw the eye.
- Index the resources in your story.
- Look for places for the reader to "enter" your story.
- Liberally use subheads (short for sub-headings)

The first four tips are pretty self-explanatory. The fifth refers to structuring the "extra" elements around your text story into a clearly defined index, as in "Full Court Decision," with a link to the verdict in a trial or "Complete Judge Interview," containing audio of your full interview with the judge in that trial. You might index other items, such as "Jurors Speak Video" linking to videotaped interviews with jurors outside the courthouse or "Path to the Verdict," another link consisting of a timeline to illustrate the trial's progress from jury selection through closing arguments and culminating in the verdict.

The term "points of entry" refers to building multiple opportunities for the reader to "enter" your story. How? First, create strong subheadings and sprinkle them liberally throughout your writing. Doing so allows the web reader to "pick and choose" from among the story's major points. Once past the headline and lead, web audiences search for details that interest them. The headline and lead should do their job and create reader interest, but if a web reader isn't drawn in by either, the idea is to increase the chance something else will capture his/her eye.

In web parlance, the concept called "stickiness" applies to every story you write. The goal is not only for readers to "stop" and pay attention to your story; it's to keep them on your newsroom's page. "Stickiness" is a measure of how long, in seconds and minutes, that readers remain on the page before moving on to another story or another web site. The longer they stay, the more "sticky" the site. On a stickiness scale, anywhere up to a minute is considered good; any time spent in multiple minutes is, in web terms, almost an eternity. Strive for the longest time spent with your story and on your site possible. Following the above suggestions helps maximize stickiness and minimize the chance your readers will navigate to another page.

One proven way to drive readers away from your story is making them have to scroll down the page. *Scrolling* works against scanning. In other words, it makes web stories harder to absorb at a glance. Every time you force a web reader to scroll, the probability increases that you will lose that reader. Therefore, work at keeping the major parts of your story high on the upper half of the reader's screen, minimizing the necessity to scroll down. Readers may scroll for additional information; they won't scroll to get the basic story. They expect to see it up high, much in the way newspaper readers have always been more likely to read the front page stories above the paper's "fold" than those below it.

Another thing: size matters. When it comes to the video you post on the web, it matters a lot. There's a major difference between how a video looks on a computer screen compared to how it appears on a 42-inch high definition television in your living room. As good as today's computer monitors have become, in general, they are still smaller and of lower resolution than contemporary HD television sets. So, save the video that shows the most detail for TV; wide angle shots are often "lost" on a laptop. They're even more ineffective on an iPhone or other mobile communication tool. As more and more people are expected to access their news via the web through such hand-held devices, video that is shot in close-ups is probably a better bet for the web.

Space matters, too, as in the space in which your story is read, heard, or watched. The environment surrounding the audience is a major determinant of how well it will be understood. It shouldn't come as a surprise that sitting on a comfortable sofa in your home's living room creates a very different experience from pulling up a story on your cellular phone while driving to work or sitting at your son's hockey game. That brings up another point. As you consider how to write your stories for the web, keep in mind that for the web audience "on the move," some stories might include "news you can use" as part of the overall package.

For example, if you're writing the web version of a story involving a major oil spill on a local bridge, think about the person who drives across that bridge every day to work – and who might be in her/his car while reading your story. Can you instantly provide maps or alternate routes? How about estimates of time delays? Condition yourself to think not only about the "at home" audience, but the "mobile" one. Doing so helps you conceptualize your story across media platforms. It also creates opportunities to promote your story using those platforms.

Promoting Print Stories in Other Media

So, you've written a great print story and now a television station wants to interview you about it on camera. Or, you may be asked to do a short version of your newspaper story for TV to promote the print version. This is not an uncommon scenario, given how many newspapers and television stations are co-owned. At the *Tampa Tribune*, the paper's reporters often appear on camera during sister-station WFLA-TV's newscasts – sometimes to talk about their stories appearing in the following day's paper. Media sharing the same ownership are not alone in promoting stories across platforms. WJAR-TV in Providence has long had reporters for the *Providence Journal* appear on their late evening news to promote stories in the next day's paper. The two do not share ownership, but they do have a partnership – an increasing trend in the media marketplace.

Many traditional print journalists have real trouble going on camera to promote their stories. One reason may be that print journalists often consider themselves to be "writers" rather than "talkers." Overcome your reticence. Think of it this way: any story, no matter how well you write it, is of little worth if no one reads it. Promotion is part of the storytelling process. It's like "telling the story of your story." Done well, that story gains an entirely new, expanded audience. Tell the story of your story well.

An on-camera interview may involve a questioner who is next to you, or you may be looking straight into a camera while hearing the questions from another studio through an earpiece. You'll want to read the full performance tips in Chapter 5, but here are some starting points:

- *Posture.* Make sure you are sitting or standing comfortably in front of the camera. If you are in an awkward position, your unease will be visible to the viewer. On the other hand if you are too laid-back, you'll seem uninterested.
- *Volume.* Don't shout. Many beginners are tempted to talk to the camera, or even the operator behind the camera, which can be halfway across the studio. In fact, the microphone is much closer, only six inches from your mouth. Speak as if you were talking to your best friend who is standing six inches away.
- *Speed.* An interview is an enhanced conversation. Keep up a normal, conversational pace, and slow down when there is a word or phrase you want to emphasize. It's better to be a little too fast and animated than too slow and monotone. Don't be afraid to show your natural energy and enthusiasm for the topic.
- *Enunciation.* As you keep up the pace, be conscious of moving your lips to enunciate every word.
- *Eye contact.* Just as in any normal conversation, you will want to make the appropriate connection with the interviewer or the listener. Imagine that you are talking to your best friend. Maintain normal eye contact with the interviewer and let the camera find you. Don't stare into the camera. Imagine the interviewer on the other side of the lens if you are on a remote. Ideally, you'll forget the camera is there.
- *Gestures.* Use natural gestures to animate your conversation, but avoid distracting mannerisms like tapping your fingers or playing with your hair. The usual framing of an interview is a "head and shoulders" shot, so most of your gestures won't be seen anyway, unless you bring your hands up in front of your face. Avoid distracting body movements like rocking or swiveling in your chair.
- *Hair and make-up:* Avoid anything that distracts from your message. Your hair should be neatly combed and provide an attractive frame for your face. Never let your hair invade the crucial communication zone around your eyes.
- *Wardrobe.* Wear solid, bold colors and avoid chunky jewelry, distracting fabric patterns or extremes of black and white. For most topics, business attire or business casual is appropriate. An exception can be made if you are wearing some type of "special purpose" clothing that relates to the story (a parka outdoors in a snowstorm, for example). Obviously, anything too skimpy or sexy will detract from your message and may even be offensive in some cultures.
- *Simple language.* In normal conversation, people don't refer to the person in the next car as a "motorist." That person is a "driver." No one ever celebrates "receiving an increment in wages." They do celebrate "getting a raise." This is a natural extension of using conversational language when writing a story for TV or the web. Keep it short and simple. Use the "mom" rule: how would I tell this story to my mother?
- *Get to the point:* Organize your thoughts. The important points of your story will get lost if you ramble on. Think of your answers as possible "sound bites" and try to plan at least one clever or quotable thing to say.

Now it's time to put these tips to work. Below is a classroom exercise that can also be easily adapted to the newsroom. It requires only that you be prepared and that the person with whom you collaborate is observant and honest.

Step 1: Select a story that you've written recently. It's important that it be *your* story, not one written by someone else. It can be something that appeared in the student newspaper or online.

Step 2: Spend about 10–15 minutes thinking about how you would tell this story on camera. Keep in mind the tips above.

Step 3: Pick one person in the class to whom you will tell the story. Think of this person as someone watching you on television in her/his living room.

Step 4: Set up a video camera in the room. Position the person working with you just to either side of the camera's lens.

Step 5: Start the camera. Begin telling your story. You have 1 minute (which in television is a lot of time). While you are speaking, the person observing you, grades you on these criteria, with "5" being the highest, "1" the lowest.

Posture	1	2	3	4	5
Volume	1	2	3	4	5
Energy speed	1	2	3	4	5
Enunciation	1	2	3	4	5
Eye contact	1	2	3	4	5
Gestures	1	2	3	4	5
Appearance	1	2	3	4	5
Conversational language	1	2	3	4	5
Organization	1	2	3	4	5

Step 6: Have the other person share with you his/her scores in each area and, as importantly, any comments she/he may have. Have her/him focus on specific reasons why you were evaluated high in some areas and low or moderate in others.

Step 7: Watch the video of your storytelling. First, ask yourself: "Do I agree with what others (in this case, the person observing you) see?" Second, if so, spend 15 minutes planning how to modify each of the areas where you need improvement.

Step 8: Repeat the exercise and determine if there is progress in the areas you needed to strengthen. To get a different perspective, you might try repeating the same exercise using another person as your "viewer."

A variation of the above training exercise can be done for an interview situation, by introducing a third person as the TV interviewer and having you respond to his/her questions. Both approaches give you practice in putting your on camera skills to work. If you're a student who has been spent much of your college career working on your writing, this may be the most useful new skills set you can develop.

Professionals long accustomed to telling their stories for a print audience can also benefit from this approach. Practice with others in the newsroom who share your desire to expand their verbal and interpersonal skills to another medium. An advantage to learning effective promotion of your story in other media is the opportunity it affords to show off your versatility – a prime advantage toward landing your first job right out of school or moving up the career ladder. Those who can tell a story on one platform while promoting it on another become valuable players to news organizations. To the extent they are comfortable with social media, they provide a service to their newsroom by creating a one-to-one bond with the audience. They understand what's become known as "synergy."

Synergized Storytelling

So, let's say you've finished your day's story for the newspaper. In most instances, your job is far from over. In fact, it has just begun. Not everyone will read your story in the paper; some may read it online; still others may watch it on television. How do you connect with each of these audiences and make them want to read, watch, or click? To start, you promote your story in each medium.

Since at least the last decade of the twentieth century, newspapers have promoted their web sites on their pages. Web sites, in turn, have promoted longer versions of their stories in the print medium. Those media corporations that also own television stations (and there are many of them) promote the story's "extra" elements by moving the audience over to the newsroom's web page. In turn, the web page refers users back to television for another version. And round it goes. It's called *cross-promotion*.

For the "Major Winter Storm" story above, that might include the following reminders of how/where to find more information on the developing story in each co-owned medium:

- In the newspaper: "To track the storm, go to our web site, tbt.com, for up-to-the-minute reports."
- On the web: "Read about one family's extraordinary efforts to help their elderly neighbors in today's *Tribune*."
- On TV: "For live radar of the approaching storm and a look at how the snow is affecting people in your neighborhood."

Synergized storytelling not only means writing, but parceling information across each media platform. It means thinking ahead – realizing what you can "save" (some might say "hold back") from a story in each medium – to create a fresh and appealing story in another medium. It also means recognizing which elements of the story have the most potential for promotion in each medium.

In the twenty-first century, media corporations most value those who can "do it all" – write for their newspaper, report for their television station, and create content for their web site. They even have a name for this particular kind of storyteller: "backpack journalist."

The Backpack Journalist

Anyone who is or has been a student, at least in the United States, has carried a backpack. Backpacks are most often associated with the young, so the term "backpack journalist" is appropriate for this new breed of storytellers who carry everything they need with them wherever they go – a continuation of their classroom days. In their backpack's pockets, ready to use at a moment's notice, are a digital camera, digital audio recorder, hand-held video cam, microphones and stands, tripod, cell phone, laptop, flash drives – anything needed to cover a story from front to back.

They can write, photograph, videotape, podcast, Facebook, text, and tweet. And they can do it all from anywhere. They can send it anywhere. Completely finished stories, in print, audio, video, and on social media – their "beat" is less about covering specialized kinds of stories and more about covering *any* kind of story. Technology may give them the advantage as storytellers over journalists with more traditional experience. At their finger-tips they have the ability and the inclination to do alone what it once took four or five people to do. They are backpack journalists. And *they* could be *you*.

If you're studying journalism or communication right now, you are a valuable com-modity to those running newsrooms – print or broadcast. Why? For one thing, you have never lived in a time when you didn't have in your home a computer, a video camera, a cellular phone, and digital camera. You've tinkered with, taught yourself, and learned from your peers the operation of all these "gadgets." You used them in high school to create stories and programs for your student radio or TV station. You're at ease with technology precisely because it comes easily to you.

When news staffs are cut, those who are hired in the place of former writers, editors, photographers, and producers are those who can "do it all." In 2010, ABC News cut 350 staffers due to "changes in the news business in the digital age." Network executives said their "restructuring plan" included "more digital journalists who both produce and shoot their own stories" – in other words, "backpack journalists." They're comfortable with tech-nology, work across media platforms, are efficient, and, yes – compared to those who preceded them – they're less expensive. That also probably means they're young.

For journalism students, this is the time to gain the skill set we've discussed and dem-onstrated throughout this chapter. To quote the great New Yankees icon Yogi Berra, "If you don't have it, that's why you need it." Start with your strength. Is it print journalism? Great. Now, make a check-list, based on the skills in this chapter, of those you don't have and those you *need* to become a multimedia reporter in today's newsrooms. Similarly, if televi-sion news is your strength, ask yourself "what else do I need to know in order to function effectively?" That's the focus of Chapter 4, designed to help strengthen your video storytell-ing skills on the web. Before moving on, take a moment to consider the question and exercise below; by doing so, you will be better prepared to take on those social media skills that contribute to *power performance*.

A Multimedia Exercise

One of our students wrote the following as her class blog entry: "I've always wondered, in the midst of this crazy transformation in journalism and the hype of social networking sites such as Facebook and Twitter, how can journalists embrace those sites and utilize them for their work, or should they not look to FB and Twitter at all? I ask because I constantly hear about Twitter on ESPN, various athletes using it, and the reporters quoting their 'tweets' and I was just wondering if that is considered good journalism or just pure laziness."

There's no clear answer, but it does present an intriguing issue. Do you think social media contributes to better storytelling? What's the counter-argument? Can it also lead to lazy storytelling? Discuss this issue in class or with your friends.

Next, from your local newspaper, select stories that you believe would benefit from a social media component. Which of your choices lend themselves to research via Facebook or another social media site? Why? Which are most suitable for a blog? Why?

Works Cited and Further Reading

Associated Press. "ABC news plans major cutbacks," *CBC News*, February 24, 2010. Retrieved from: http://www.cbc.ca/arts/media/story/2010/02/24/abc-news-cuts.html?ref=rss.

"Newspaper reporter ranks poorly in career job rating," *Huffington Post*, January 6, 2010. Retrieved from: http://www.huffingtonpost.com/2010/01/06/newspaper-reporter-ranks_n_413514.html. The full rankings are from a study done by the research firm Careercast and are published in "Best and worst jobs, 2010," *Wall Street Journal*, January 5, 2010. Retrieved from: http://online.wsj.com/public/resources/documents/st_BESTJOBS2010_20100105.html.

O'Brien, Timothy L. "The newspaper of the future," *New York Times*. June 26, 2005. Retrieved from: http://www.nytimes.com/2005/06/26/business/yourmoney/26kansas.html.

Rich, Carole and Harper, Christopher. *Writing and Reporting News: A Coaching Method*. Belmont, CA: Wadsworth. 2007.

Rubel, Steve. "The newspaper reporter of the future is here today," February 16, 2009. Retrieved from: http://www.micropersuasion.com/2009/02/the-newspaper-reporter-of-the-future-is-here-today.html.

Sachoff, Mike. "More journalists using Facebook and Twitter," *Web Pro News*. April 5, 2010. Retrieved from: http://www.webpronews.com/topnews/2010/04/02/more-journalists-using-facebook-and-twitter.

Stelter, Brian. "J schools play catchup," *New York Times*, April 14, 2010. Retrieved from: http://www.nytimes.com/2009/04/19/education/edlife/journ-t.html?_r=1.

"Stop the presses: another newspaper shuts down," February 27, 2009. Retrieved from: http://www.psfk.com/2009/02/stop-the-presses-another-newspaper-shuts-down.html.

Wenger, Debora Halpern and Potter, Deborah. *Advancing the Story: Broadcast Journalism in a Multimedia World*. Washington, D.C.: CQ Press, 2007.

COURTESY J.R. RAPHAEL

J.R. RAPHAEL

Contributing Editor, *PC World*

Job: Technology journalist
Hometown: Springfield, MO
Market: National, based in Jacksonville, FL
Education: University of Southern California, BA Psychology, 2003
Career Path:

   Internships: KYTV, Springfield, MO
       Extra, Telepictures Productions, Los Angeles, CA
       The Late Late Show, CBS, Los Angeles, CA
   Summer producer, KYTV, Springfield, MO
   TV News Producer, WTLV-TV and WJXX-TV (*First Coast News*), Jacksonville, FL
   Freelance writer, Jacksonville, FL

On majoring in psychology instead of journalism.
I would not write off a journalism degree as something no one needs. But there are certain circumstances where it might not be absolutely vital. From my perspective, it can provide a solid foundation of skills and ethical decision-making that all journalists should have. But if you are actively learning a lot of things on your own, the argument can be made that you can broaden your perspective with another area of study.

I knew I would go into some form of broadcast journalism, but being on-air wasn't what I wanted to do. What I was learning in the classroom was overlapping with what I was doing in the real world. I left the scholastic world of journalism behind and focused on another path that would give me more breadth of knowledge. Through experience, like my summer job producing newscasts in my home town, I got the skills needed to do the job.

Why his early interest in technology paid off.
I started doing web sites and a computer bulletin board system in high school.

That gave way to working in more traditional multimedia. The web was just starting to blossom and I jumped on the opportunity. When I went to work as a full-time TV news producer, the web was just starting to become a priority and I was able to take a leadership role developing some of the online services and think of creative ways to tie in the broadcast product with the online product. This thing has evolved so quickly that now it's a given, but five years ago it wasn't.

On his first full-time job as a TV news producer in Jacksonville, FL.

I realized my passion was creating a product, being at the control panel and putting the pieces of the puzzle together, seeing how they fit. After spending some time in the news room it became apparent to me very quickly that the producer's chair was the place for me. I started out on WTLV and WJXX, ABC and NBC affiliates. The brand is *First Coast News*. I started on overnights and worked my way through just about every show. By the time I left, my title was news/special projects producer, one of the lead evening show producers but also spending time on specials. The internet was always a part of it, especially on the special projects. With any special I do, I try to come up with some web angle to add value and give people a reason to get engaged in the broadcast. News producers have so many responsibilities that it's easy to push the web aside because there is so much on your plate. But soon it's going to be the main thing.

Why he left TV news for multimedia freelance journalism.

I still loved what I was doing, but everybody was doing more with less. To me, the fun of it was the creativity, and when it became a high production factory, I didn't feel I was getting anything out of it. I was losing sleep, my health, the stress was tremendous and it wasn't paying off for me anymore. When I plunged into the free-lance writing world, I wasn't quite sure where I would go. I had nothing to lose. I started out small, writing for online tech blogs and publications. Little by little, things built up, and within two or three months it was a full-time deal for me against all odds. A year later, it had blossomed into something I could call a career.

What went through his mind when ABC News asked him to appear on camera to talk about one of his tech stories?

It was rather daunting, no doubt. You're used to expressing yourself in one medium and then a whole different set of parameters is thrust in front of you. Coming from a TV background, I'm comfortable around cameras. But it was still very far out of my comfort zone and definitely scary. It's easy to say you can just sit down and talk. The truth is: if you don't know how to present yourself on camera, the power of your words will be lost in the awkwardness of your presentation. You look at print web sites that do video and there's a clear difference seeing some guy in front of the camera versus someone who knows what they're doing.

I had done a story for *PC World* on email addiction. A new study had come out about the number of people suffering from the compulsion to check their email. Quite honestly, it was a simple story, interviewing a psychologist about the symptoms, how serious it is and what you should do to curb your email sending habits. It did fairly well in the social media world and gained a lot of attention. Somewhere along the line it caught the attention of a producer at ABC News who worked on their World News Webcast, an internet companion to the nightly broadcast. He wanted to know if I'd go down to the local affiliate and do an on-camera interview with him. I'd be lying if I didn't say it was a little terrifying. A phone interview is one thing, or writing your thoughts out, but in front of a camera there are so many other dimensions: how you speak, how you sound, how you look. You turn your head a certain way and it makes you look silly, or if you smile too much or don't smile enough, what you wear and how it fits. There's so much to think about on top of thinking about what you're going to say, and when you're not used to doing that it IS a little scary. Looking back at the first time I did that, I see things I didn't do well. In this context it was even more strange because it was a remote interview and so I was sitting there looking into a camera lens with one other guy in the room, talking to a guy on speaker phone who was across the country. I wasn't used to looking into a camera lens, seeing my reflection and those moving parts in the camera as the photographer was focusing. When you first see that, even if you've been around cameras a long time, it's a different experience.

How he improved his on-camera skills.

One thing that made a big difference was learning how to use make-up. As a guy, that's something that you want to shy away from. But when you look at yourself on camera, it makes a difference. I have a fairly pale complexion to begin with so you really can see the difference. I had to talk myself into going down to a local make-up shop for a color match. That alone made a world of difference.

I consulted with Terry Anzur, one of my professors from USC. We talked about punching up my energy a little more. A lot of it comes down to nerves. You're talking into a lens. I had to work on having the right energy, rehearsing and practicing to deliver what I was saying in a more emphatic and enthusiastic way. Another big thing was wardrobe, not necessarily my strength. I wear shorts, a t-shirt and sandals seven days a week. Figuring out the way to complement myself with colors, how a jacket fits and how I was sitting made a big difference in how I appeared.

You can't rely on the person asking the questions to lead you in the right direction. You have to think in advance about what the major points are, and how *you* want to craft it. I'm used to working on paper or a computer screen where you can go back and edit. When you're speaking out loud in front of a camera, you can't do that. You have to develop a way of thinking a step ahead while you're speaking.

The second time ABC called, the story was about Facebook scams, different security threats, viruses and programs that might take more information than you realize, putting you more at risk on a social network without realizing it. I was, without question, far more comfortable and confident. Having that confidence allowed me to focus much more on the content and on the storytelling. I was feeling more comfortable that the performance part of it was becoming a more natural thing, having taken the time to rehearse it. I could be in the moment and I could certainly see the difference when I went back and watched the segment. Just going in and sitting down, I was a lot more certain of what I was doing and not overwhelmed.

Why web journalists need presentation skills.

There's no such thing as a strictly print or broadcast journalist anymore. It's all converging. You really have to put yourself in a mindset that you're not strictly a writer. You are basically a multimedia journalist and being prepared for that mentally will not only help you, but it also will help you sell yourself. When you're looking for a job or a freelance opportunity, you have more value if they know that the next time a major webcast needs one of our people, that this person is really good. Since I started doing on-camera interviews I've been getting a pretty steady stream of requests.

Most memorable stories.

There was a series of devastating tornadoes in northeast Florida. We had our share of hurricanes and bad weather and all sorts of natural scares. But this was the first time it hit this close to home in such a big way. It happened in the early morning hours and I was producing the 6 p.m. news. Entire communities in our viewing area were flattened. From the beginning of the day, I was thinking about how we would tell the story. It's easy to fall into a patterns of "what we always do" for weather coverage when a bad storm strikes. I didn't want this to be a generic cookie-cutter thing. I wanted to harness the emotion. It stands out for me personally that on that day I came forward and took charge of how we were doing it. I wasn't the boss but I went in with a vision for telling the story, and really conveyed the magnitude of it. In five years of producing it's the one piece of television that I'm most proud of. There are a lot of days where you do cool stuff in TV news, but on this day we pulled back on the bells and whistles and went back to the basics of storytelling, no crazy video effects, only slow dissolves and straight cuts. The fact that we were able to put aside the cool toys and still have more impact than anything I've ever done, really made that significant to me. Later, we won awards, but that only reinforced my belief that we really made a difference.

As a web journalist dealing in technology news, we're typically not dealing in life and death issues. But there are days when I feel like I can make a small difference. Facebook changed its governing documents without notice and by changing a few little words they took a lot of control out of the users' hands. No longer were you in ownership of your content, your photos you uploaded, the company was. Even if you deleted your account altogether, they retained the right to use an image you uploaded in an ad months or years later. Facebook in the end allowed users to vote on a revised privacy policy. But there was one small change in the revised policy that wasn't getting any media attention. There was a clause that stated you could not use Facebook if you were in a country embargoed by the United States. This meant that a lot of people who relied on Facebook for communications, people in Cuba and the Sudan, were no longer going to be able to access the network. In America it didn't affect anyone directly, but I ended up doing a pretty detailed feature story and talked to people from Iran, the Sudan and Cuba who said that Facebook was the one place where they could keep in touch with their families. It was their lifeline to the outside world, and that lifeline was being pulled and they weren't getting any answers. I got through the wall at Facebook and talked to a person who was surprised to hear about it. All the emails weren't getting through to the person who had a say in the matter. The company ended up clarifying that clause to put people's worries at ease. They adjusted the code so that these people would still have access. The fact that it had an impact on so many people globally, it was very memorable to me.

His advice to multimedia journalists.

Go in with your ego in check. Be willing to take on anything. By starting out small, you will build up to bigger and better things. In the new media world a lot of the barriers that used to be up aren't there anymore. Ten years ago to get a byline in a major magazine would take years of dedication. Now, with the internet, you can make a name for yourself as a writer very quickly, even if it's for smaller publications.

Now more than ever, it's crucial to develop yourself as a brand. There are millions of writers and reporters out there – what makes you unique? Decide what you represent as a professional, and then reinforce it with everything you do. Every little thing down to how you present yourself in social media or what tone you take in your bio affects how people perceive you. In the modern media world, you have the opportunity to develop your own following. Having a recognizable identity can make you stand out from the pack.

ERIC DEGGANS

St. Petersburg Times and tampabay.com

Job: TV and media critic
Market: A local audience that is interested in Tampa-St. Petersburg media and a national audience on the web for major media stories
Hometown: Gary, IN
Education: Indiana University, BA in political science and journalism, 1990
Career Path:
  Suburban news reporter, Pittsburgh Press, Pittsburgh, PA
  Music critic, Asbury Park Press, NJ
  Music critic, *St. Petersburg Times*, FL
  TV critic, *St. Petersburg Times*

How do you describe your job?

I have always viewed myself as a print journalist who works on other platforms. If you look at my output over the last six months, you could say I do more material online than what gets in the paper. It depends on whether the story is evolving and whether it's important enough to file several updates. Being a critic, you can take your time and write feature stories. Rarely am I working a news story that is evolving minute by minute, but the blog has made that more possible. It is easier for me to find out what's going on, file an initial report to the blog and then file an update later. By the time you get to the end of the day and you know everything, you can write a story that pulls it all together and it goes in the newspaper the next day. We're not like a lot of institutions where there is a line between the web site and the paper product. Our web site has a separate staff, but editorially the material has always been very mixed and we've always been in the same building. I can put my criticism on any platform.

Will people who read your blog get a sense that there's still something fresh for them in the next day's paper?

I really get a sense that those audiences are separate. I don't think there's a lot of cross-pollination between people reading the blog and then picking up the newspaper the next day.

How did you get into journalism?

My dad was a newspaper columnist in town. Newspapers in cities with big minority populations would sometimes hire people to write about that segment of the community. My dad wrote a column that was updating people on the young black social circles, the clubs, the jazz, the jams, the parties, people's birthdays and what the black politicians were doing. He also worked as a deejay, a city official and as a bailiff. Part of it was seeing him do his thing. Mostly it was me realizing I had a talent for writing and wanting to find a way to make that a career. I started writing a column when I was in high school for a community newspaper and it followed from there to my college newspaper. I also wrote for the yearbook and an independent local newspaper and the professional daily newspaper in town, the *Bloomington Herald-Telephone*.

How did college prepare you for a career in journalism?

Indiana University always encouraged a lot of outside writing and internships. I was in a band that got a record deal in Motown when I was in college, so I took two and half years off. I finished my degree by correspondence while playing in a club in Japan. I had done an internship with the Pittsburgh Press and when I got back from Japan, they offered me a job as a suburban news reporter. My job was to cover nine or ten school districts in the northern suburbs of Pittsburgh. My internship had been in the entertainment department, and the editor of the section wanted to make me the music critic. The editor of the paper was wary of (giving that job to) someone right out of college. They put me in a job where I would get a little bit of seasoning.

From there, you went on to be a music critic and a media critic. What is your job like now on a typical day?

I usually try to start the day with a good blog post. Today, for example, I looked at two new conservative blogs that got started, seemingly, as an answer to the Huffington Post. I put up a piece taking a quick look at what is on those sites and analyzing what it means. I like something substantive to start the day out. There are a lot of other media blogs that might link to my stuff, but they tend to put those links up early. You don't want to be so early that it feels like old news, but you want to have it up there when they start trawling for the morning links. I try to get something online before I take my daughter to school at 8:15. I'm in the office by nine, and I figure out what I'm going to do that day. I have a standing column in the metro section every Sunday. It's basically a print version of my blog, The Feed. There's a main (story), and then I might have a fun list, and a couple of capsule reviews of TV shows coming out that week. Sometimes I write a Sunday feature story. This week I did a piece on *American Idol*, but I would be researching throughout the week and write it on Thursday or Friday. I may find out newsy things that are happening (in the local media) and put together a story for the next day's paper.

What is the best advice you ever received?

One of the things that bums me out about journalism is that you don't get a lot of direct training once you ascend to a certain level. It's hard for editors to find time to do evaluations and they tend to only do it when someone is having a problem. You should try to be somebody who solves problems for your boss instead of somebody who creates them. In today's environment, editors have more power than ever. We have less space to tell stories, there's more competition for the front page and the metro section front. If you can get an editor in your corner who is advocating for you as a person who can tell a story well, that relationship is more important than ever. You want that editor going into a meeting and fighting for your story. Having your boss on your side is very important. The constellation of jobs is changing. You might be an entrepreneur. But somebody is going to control the outlet you are publishing in. You may be freelancing or contributing to a bunch of different places. When you are a freelancer, and not on staff, you are easy to overlook. But if you are the person who is solving their problems, they come to rely on you and use you more. That's when you can really thrive.

How has multimedia changed your job?

The news cycle has speeded up tremendously. For example, word started leaking out that Simon Cowell might leave *American Idol*. Other TV writers were twittering about it. My value as a critic is that I can take that raw information and contextualize it, tell people why it's important. I can vacuum up the information from Twitter and put it on my blog. When I first started, I might see something like that on the wires, make a couple of calls and write a piece that would run the next day. Now it's to the point where I might do that piece in an hour or two.

Is it more important for you to put information out on Twitter, or to listen and monitor what others are saying?

I think it's important to do both. What you find is a lot of columnists and news sources put out tweets on their biggest stories. I can follow David Carr or Bill Carter from the *New York Times* and all the top entertainment sites. Whenever they break a story, they tweet about it, and I get a snapshot of what the entertainment world is thinking. When I contribute to that with a blog or a piece in the paper I can float a tweet on it, and possibly more than 1600 people will see it and retweet it to the people who follow them. Plus, my Twitter account changes the status update on my Facebook account. I have over 3000 followers there, too. I also occasionally blog for the Huffington Post, and put a version of my blog post there. That invites people to check out my blog, and I also get a boost in my Twitter followers.

At the moment, sites like the Huffington Post don't pay writers. What advice do you have for students who hope to make a living doing journalism?

You have to divide your work into the things you do to spread your brand, and the things you do to make money off your brand. In my case, it helps me to position myself as a national authority on media by having access to national outlets. The Huffington Post will often put me on their home page, so I get a lot of views. I appear on CNN regularly, on NPR, on the (PBS) News Hour. I don't get paid for any of that. It's spreading my brand to a bunch of people who will never read the *St. Pete Times*. There are two reasons why I do that. Frankly, I want (the newspaper) to think twice about laying me off if there are staff reductions. My goal is to make myself as valuable to my news organization as possible. If they look at me, they can say, "He's a nationally known expert on media and goes on all the outlets and spreads the name of the *St. Petersburg Times*. We don't want to lose that." Also, it helps me personally. If I want to try other things, freelancing, another project, or if I want to move on from this job, my reputation precedes me.

As a print journalist, how do you feel about doing television and radio?

When I took over this job, I had to do a spot on one of the local morning radio shows every Monday, to talk about what was going to be on TV that week. I did that every Monday for seven years. Now it's to the point where I have figured out how to present myself in a way that's professional and makes me look good. It's fun to do that stuff.

What's your advice for print journalists who have to appear on camera?

Talk to the camera as if you are talking to a person. You have to visualize that you are talking to the host of the show. Because I appear by satellite, and not in the studio, I have to remind myself that I'm talking to a person. You have to figure out the points you want to make before the segment starts. If it's a typical cable segment, that's anywhere from five to six minutes. If you're on that segment with a couple of other people, you're going to get a chance to make three points. You should figure out what those points are and talk it through in your head how you want to say them. Often you'll know who is going to be on the panel with you. Try to anticipate what they might say and be prepared for that.

I make sure to watch the clips, read what other people have written, and I might write a blog post myself, just to think through the issue. There are techniques that hosts and other panelists use to try and win arguments. They try to break in when you are talking and try to get you to answer a different point than the one you are speaking on. Most people are inclined to stop what they were saying and answer the question they've been asked. But really what you need to do is finish the point that you were making. When you are on these adversarial shows and you are making points about ideas, you have to be prepared for how they try to dominate the conversation and trip you up.

What career accomplishment are you most proud of?
Sometimes you learn more from your mistakes than from things that go well. I'm not the guy who writes the big story that fills the front page. I'm more of a columnist and a commentator. What I'm most proud of is that I've built up a body of work and a reputation in the community. I'll be in the grocery store and someone will come up and say, "Man, I really like your stuff." That is the ultimate compliment for me. That's the kind of race I'm running. It's a marathon.

4

Video Storytelling on the Air and on the Web

Video storytelling was once considered to be a team sport. It wasn't unusual for a TV news crew in the late 1970s to consist of a camera operator, a sound technician, a lighting specialist and a field producer, as well as the reporter who would "front" the story. For a live report, an engineer and a truck driver might be needed to operate the microwave or satellite transmitting equipment. Back in the newsroom, people on the assignment desk might contribute to the story research, a newsroom-based "writer" might take in the video feed from the field and order on-screen graphics, and a video editor would assemble the package to be fed to the control room crew for air. Today, all of these functions can be performed by one person. The job has various names: digital correspondent (DC), one-man band, video journalist (VJ), multimedia journalist (MMJ) or backpack reporter. Regardless of the label, a video storyteller in multimedia must be prepared to take responsibility for the entire process, from the initial story idea to uploading the finished presentation.

At the same time, there are new ways for your video story to reach its intended audience. A 2010 survey by the Pew Research Center for the People and the Press found that television remains the dominant source of international and national news for 66 percent of Americans, regardless of age. But the internet is gaining fast, rising 17 percent since 2007 while newspapers declined. The internet was the top news source for those under 30 and was on track to surpass television with the 30–49 age group in a few years. Radio remains a significant choice for about 16 percent of the US audience (Table 4.1).

The overwhelming trend is the rapid growth of online video. The Nielsen Online Video Census recorded a whopping 41 percent increase in total video streams from 2008 to 2009, with the leading video site, YouTube, racking up millions of views as 20 *hours* of video were added to the site every *minute*. Overall, Nielsen said that 72 percent of internet users watched online videos, but this could include anything from silly pet tricks to serious documentary footage. Nielsen also found that people were spending more time watching

Power Performance: Multimedia Storytelling for Journalism and Public Relations, First Edition. Tony Silvia and Terry Anzur.

Table 4.1   Sources of local and national news

	National/international news (%)
Television	66
Internet	41
Newspapers	31
Radio	16

Note: Figures add up to more than 100% because of multiple responses.

internet videos, another trend that is expected to continue. However, some 85 percent of these viewers tend to be "snackers" who prefer videos that are short and to the point. They don't have time to sit down for the equivalent of a lengthy video banquet, and will click away if they are bored or uninterested. What all this means for you, the video storyteller, is that the techniques developed over the past half-century for concise reporting on television newscasts are even more important for new media delivery platforms. You will still have a sizable audience in front of the television set, while users are searching for your video content online. Your audience can grow over time because your storytelling can be archived and accessed on the web, and shared through social media indefinitely, instead of disappearing into thin air when the real-time broadcast is over. However, you also face the challenge of standing out among millions of possible video sources. It is imperative that you master the skills that will enable you to establish your personal brand as a trustworthy video storyteller and searched-for source of information. Your audience is counting on you to deliver what YouTube news manager Olivia Ma has described as "a snapshot of real life."

Public relations practitioners are producing and posting their clients' video stories online, often bypassing traditional journalism filters and speaking directly to the audience. Traditional media lines are being blurred as more newspaper-affiliated web sites offer online video, and broadcast-affiliated web sites offer more text and graphics. Networks not only embrace online video as a way to reach workers who do not have access to a TV during the day, they also see it as a guaranteed revenue stream because of the advertisements a viewer must watch before seeing the story. *ABC World News* executive producer Jon Banner told *Broadcasting and Cable Magazine*, "We need to do more. I am not going to be satisfied until [we] probably double, triple, quadruple the amount of content that is able to be read, watched and listened to online."

Video Story Formats

Video storytelling may involve an announcer or anchor in the studio, and a reporter or videographer in the field. Due to the demands of fast-breaking news in a multimedia world, there is often no time to write a script; the storyteller must improvise, or ad-lib. However, you will be able to improvise more effectively if you have learned the basic concepts of scripted video storytelling. Think of it as learning the rules of the road. Once you know the basic rules and terminology, you will be able to effectively "drive" your story.

Let's begin by looking at the most common formats for video storytelling on the air and on the web:

- *Reader*: The storyteller appears on the screen and speaks directly to the audience. This is most often used to announce breaking news when pictures and sound are not yet available. It allows the reporter to give background information, share analysis or opinion, explain a concept that is not visual, or discuss what is likely to happen in the future. This is the simplest form of on-camera storytelling, and has the advantage of immediacy. It also allows the presenter to make a personal connection with the audience through eye contact, facial expression, and body language. However, unless the information is extremely compelling, a "talking head" can be boring. It also fails to take advantage of the audio-visual possibilities of multimedia. In television news, it is also called an "on camera read," a "copy story," or a "tell" story. Script abbreviation: OC.
- *Raw video*: This is the simplest way to quickly share images of breaking news or sound from a newsworthy interview. Live video has the advantage of immediacy, and when unedited video is broadcast or shared on the web, the audience has the feeling of "being there." However, the viewers are on their own to decipher the meaning and context of the images. Interviews may be too long to hold the viewers' attention. And, without filtering the material through the editing process, there is always the risk that something distasteful or misleading may be seen or heard. During a highly competitive breaking news story, raw video may be your best option. In the aftermath of an event, viewers may appreciate the option of clicking on the raw footage and judging it for themselves. "Raw video does very well on our site," says YouTube's Olivia Ma. "There's a cycle. People will hear about a story on the news and then they will search for more information. Unfiltered, raw, unedited. That's the real source material."
- *VO*: The abbreviation for voiceover, when the storyteller's voice is heard while pictures are shown to the audience. The video may be raw or edited. The voiceover and footage may be live or recorded. There may be natural background sound that can be heard under the voice track. You may also voice over still photographs in a slide show. In any case, the narration, or VO, adds context and meaning to the visuals, and nearly always includes the five Ws and one H: who, what, when, where, why and how. Script abbreviation: VO or VO/NAT to indicate there is natural sound on the video.
- *SOT*: This refers to an interview or natural sound track that is cut down to its most essential content. A sound bite may stand alone, or be part of a longer story with narration and pictures. Although today's recordings are likely to be digital, the script abbreviation is SOT, which stands for "sound on tape" and usually refers to a recorded interview. You can say "sot" or say the letters S-O-T. NAT or NATSOT may refer to natural sound that is amplified so the user can hear it.
- *VO/SOT*: This script abbreviation refers to a combination of narrated video and one or more sound bites. In a VO/SOT/VO the sound bite is followed by additional video and voiceover material, so that the audience does not see a jarring transition from the talking head of a newsmaker to the talking head of the storyteller, and there is a definite "end" to the story, which may be a voiceover or on camera. The storyteller, not the newsmaker, should have the last word.

- *Package*: This format combines narration, pictures, sound bites and natural sound to produce a finished story that can stand on its own with a beginning, middle and end. A package may be aired as part of a broadcast, or posted on the web. The storyteller may be seen on camera as part of the package. Script abbreviation: PKG.
- *Toss* and *Tag*: On television, a package generally begins with a studio toss or intro, a reader in which an announcer introduces the story and the reporter. It also may end with an additional on-camera tag, a reader that may add new information or refer to what may happen in the future. Unlike a reader, however, these two elements are tied to the package and do NOT stand alone. News organizations may post the intro and tag on the web as part of the package, or introduce the video link with text.

Story slug

Each story is identified by a one- or two-word description called a slug. Choose your slug with care, because it is often the word or phrase that is used to archive your story for later access. If your slug is too generic, it will be more difficult to find the story months later when you need to access the video from the file. The slug generally appears on the upper left corner of your script page. In the following example we will use the slug "House Fire." Each script element for the story will contain the slug, whether it is a toss, tag, package or VO/SOT.

You should not repeat slugs within the same news program. For example, if a political leader is visiting your city, you cannot slug every story as "president." However, you can identify the different elements of the story as "president arrival," "president security," "president speech," and so on.

Video Script Forms

Video scripts are written in split-page format (see Table 4.2 for an example). The left side of the page tells what you will SEE: an announcer on camera, a reporter in the field, an interview sound bite, or pictures from the scene. On-screen graphics, if any, are listed on the left side along with the times for displaying them to match the video. The right side of the page is for the actual script of what we will SAY. Most newsrooms have a computer system to generate scripts in split page format. You choose the format from a menu that may include reader, VO, VO/SOT or PKG and then fill in the required fields. If you must generate a script by hand or on a simple word processing program, divide your page into two columns or create a two-column table (Table 4.2).

Choosing the right format

Keep in mind that viewers never say something like, "Wow! That was a great VO/SOT." They are watching or searching for content that will meet their needs, not a particular format. When planning your coverage, consider how the viewers' needs may change as the story unfolds. Let's use a very simple example to explore the different uses of story forms.

Table 4.2 Split–page format

STORY SLUG	
Left side of page – VIDEO	Right side of page – AUDIO
What we SEE	What we SAY
Video sources: Anchor OC, VO/video, SOT	Audio sources: OC, VO, SOT, NATSOT
On-screen graphics and display times	Actual script
Length of VO, SOT or PKG in seconds	Sound bite transcript, or in and out cues

Table 4.3 House fire reader

HOUSE FIRE	
ANCHOR ON CAMERA	(ANCHOR)
	Breaking news … a house fire burning right now on Hill Street. City firefighters are battling intense flames and trying to determine if anyone is trapped inside. We have a crew on the way to bring you pictures and more information.

Imagine that you are working the night shift for a TV station and its web site, and you've just learned that a house is on fire. A breaking news alert would go out to web users, and a TV news anchor might break the story with a reader (Table 4.3).

Even though this is just a short reader, it draws the viewer's attention with crisis, conflict and resolution:

- *Crisis*: A house is on fire.
- *Conflict*: Will the firefighters be able to save everyone?
- *Resolution*: No final resolution yet, but stay tuned for more developments.

As you read this series of scripts, remember that each update of the story must keep the viewers engaged with CCR. Always include as many of the Ws as possible.

When a video journalist reaches the location, you want to share the dramatic pictures as quickly as possible, by broadcasting live or airing and posting raw video. To help the

Table 4.4 House fire raw video

HOUSE FIRE RAW	
ANCHOR ON CAMERA	(ANCHOR) We have more now on our breaking story … a house fire on Hill Street.
VO/RAW VIDEO FEED	(ANCHOR VO) These pictures are just in to our newsroom. Right now, as you can see here, city firefighters are working to put out the flames and determine if anyone is still trapped inside. This is in the 500 block of Hill Street near Pinewood Elementary School. A neighbor saw the flames and called for help … fire crews arrived on the scene about 20 minutes ago. Officials say the family who lives here was sleeping when the fire broke out. We're told that two adults and two children got out safely. We don't know the cause of the fire, but we're working to bring you more details
Video Out	as soon as we get them.

viewer understand the images, there may also be a scripted or improvised VO, or text to explain what the viewer is seeing (Table 4.4).

Notice that the VO is adding value to the raw video, with new information that gives the viewer a reason to care about the flames and the efforts of the firefighters, because of the impact on the people who live there. The storyteller also encourages the viewer to stay engaged with the story by referring to the fact that it is still developing. We have crisis and conflict, but we don't know what the resolution will be.

Later, a fire official holds a news conference. Your next update will include airing or posting SOT of the fire captain explaining that all occupants of the home are safe, but that rescuers were unable to save the family's cat (Table 4.5).

Notice that the left side of the page will include the on-camera graphic that will be shown on the lower third of the TV screen to identify the person who is speaking. Depending on how the graphic is generated, it can have different names such as a "chyron" or "CG," which stands for "character generator," or "super" to indicate it is superimposed over the video. For TV, you will also include the length of the SOT in seconds on the left side. When posting the interview on the web, the graphic may not be visible; you will need to identify

Table 4.5   House fire SOT

HOUSE FIRE SOT	
ANCHOR ON CAM	(ANCHOR) We have new information about the fire that destroyed a home on Hill Street tonight. Firefighters are still on the scene, and just moments ago, fire officials held a news conference with more details about the rescue efforts:
Take SOT Graphic: Capt. Tony Silvia/City Fire Dept. Tape out: :12	(SOT) "One of the neighbors was outside walking his dog and saw the flames. He's the real hero tonight because he called for the help, and then rang the doorbell to wake up the family. We have two adults and two children accounted for, and one of our firefighters was overcome with smoke when he went inside to search for the family's cat, Lucy. Unfortunately, he was not able to locate the animal."
ANCHOR ON CAM	(ANCHOR) That was city fire captain Tony Silvia. We just learned that the firefighter who tried to rescue the cat has been released from the hospital in good condition. Meanwhile, the home is a total loss and the family is staying with neighbors tonight. Investigators will be on the scene first thing in the morning to determine the cause of the fire.

the speaker in the text that accompanies the video. Of course, the web gives you the flexibility to post additional sound bites or a longer version of this one. Unless a sound bite is extremely compelling, it should run no longer than 12 seconds on TV. In a news program, every SOT should be followed by some kind of tag or transition, either a VO or a reader. Playing a SOT and then moving on to another topic leaves the viewer with the feeling that the story is not complete.

The web is different. Sound bites can stand alone, and you have the option of running a longer bite to include more detail, since the user has the option to listen or click out. Be sure to link with a descriptive line like "hear what fire officials are saying," or "watch video of house fire rescue."

The sample script in Table 4.5 contains the transcript of the SOT. This may cause confusion because the right side of the page is usually what the studio announcer sees in the teleprompter. There is no reason to include the text of what another person is saying in the teleprompter script, although you may need the quote later for a text version of the story on the web. In the TV version, use only the In Cue and the Out Cue. This refers to the first few words and the last few words of the sound bite. Let's make this version a little more visually interesting by including an edited VO before and after the SOT, or a VO/SOT/VO (Table 4.6). The direction "VO/NAT" on the left side indicates that the natural background sound on the video should be heard under the VO as the video is shown.

Table 4.6 House fire VO/SOT/VO

HOUSE FIRE VO/SOT/VO	
ANCHOR ON CAM	(ANCHOR) We have new information about the fire that destroyed a home on Hill Street. (VO)
VO/NAT Graphic: 505 Hill Street/ Pleasant City	Here's how it looked earlier tonight when firefighters arrived at the home to fight the flames. A man and a woman and their two small children got out safely. Fire officials say the family can thank a neighbor for saving their lives.
Take SOT Graphic: Capt. Tony Silvia/City Fire Dept.	(SOT) IN: One of the neighbors …
SOT out at:19	OUT: … not able to locate the animal.
VO/NAT	(VO) Firefighters say the home is a total loss and the family is staying with neighbors tonight.
Tape out Runs: :30 (ANCHOR ON CAM)	(ANCHOR) We just learned that the firefighter who tried to rescue the cat was taken to the hospital. Right now he's in good condition. Investigators will be on the scene first thing in the morning to determine the cause of the fire.

Notice that we have included the exact length of the SOT on the left side of the page. In addition, we have indicated a "runs" time for the last piece of video. It is important to understand the difference. We know exactly how long the sound bite is, but the video includes a bit of wiggle room so that the announcer can ad lib without running out of pictures. By putting in a "runs" time we are indicating the length of the video "pad" so that the control room knows when to punch out of the video before the screen goes black.

Meanwhile, our video journalist has been busy on the scene, getting additional video as well as interviewing rescuers and the family who escaped the fire that just destroyed their home. She is preparing a package that will run on the next day's morning news program and on the web. It will include the most dramatic video, and emotional sound bites from family members and the neighbor who saved their lives. The storyteller may also appear on camera in a standup to explain the parts of the story that are NOT on video. For example, the reporter could talk about the firefighter who risked his life in an unsuccessful effort to save a pet, or preview what is likely to happen when the investigation begins.

Of course, there is also the possibility of a live report from the scene of the fire, with the studio anchor tossing to the reporter in the field. We'll discuss packages and live reports in more detail later in this chapter. But first, let's explore the basic ingredients for effective video storytelling in any script format: video, sound, interviews and writing.

Story Focus

You should approach every story with some idea of the main focus. Although most video stories are mini-movies, you don't have the luxury of working from a script or a story board. It is more like performing an experiment, in which a scientist begins with a basic research question or a hypothesis of what the end results may show. Similarly, a video storyteller begins by mentally visualizing an outline of the elements that will be needed for the finished story.

Avoid the common beginner mistake of trying to "shoot everything that moves." For example, you are telling a story about the first day of school. Will your focus be on the experience of a child, a teacher or a parent? If your story focuses on an issue, like overcrowded classrooms, concentrate on getting the pictures and sound that will illustrate the problem in terms of crisis, conflict and resolution. If a reporter and photographer are working as a team, they should discuss the story focus on the way to the location and continue the conversation as the story unfolds. Ideally, you will have done some background research before going out into the field. If the situation permits, you might want to approach the story without the camera and spend some time talking to the participants in order to sharpen your focus before you begin the actual shooting process.

Keep in mind that you may have to change your focus as the story develops, especially if your initial concept turns out to be wrong or uninteresting. In the house fire example, upon learning that the entire family is safe, you might decide to shift your focus to the heroic firefighter who risked his life to save a pet. By being flexible, you can stay focused on the most compelling elements of the real-life situation. Never distort actual events to conform to your preconceived notion of the story, but always have a plan to get all the video and sound you will need for the finished product. Don't waste time recording images and interviews you won't use. One experienced videographer talks of "making the movie in your head" and then gathering what is needed to make your theoretical story come to life on the screen.

As an exercise, try to reduce your story focus to a simple subject–verb–object sentence explaining "who did what." The most obvious sentence isn't always the best story. At the house fire, for example, you could write:

- Fire destroys house.
- Family escapes flames.
- Neighbor saves family.
- Firefighter risks life.

The video storyteller must choose the *one* focus that will result in the most compelling story and then make sure to gather all the necessary elements to tell the tale.

Story Length

As early as 2008, a survey by the Magid consulting firm found that "short, professional videos are among those most regularly watched online." Eight of the ten most-watched types of online video were short-form, with news stories among the most popular. The average duration of an online video was 2 minutes. The bottom line for video journalists: Keep it short, get straight to the point, and don't waste the viewer's time.

Compelling Video

Video storytelling has its own visual language. Most people can easily tell the difference between professional and amateur video because of the way it is shot and edited. A video storyteller must know how to use a camera to capture images that are technically acceptable and pleasing to the eye. Many cameras have automated features, but you should be familiar with the manual settings as well. Knowing how to operate your equipment will help you avoid common beginner mistakes such as forgetting to "white balance," which can result in off-color or "blue" video. Take the time to practice using all the features of your camera before you find yourself in a newsgathering situation where there is little room for trial and error. Before going on a story assignment, check to see that all of your equipment is in working order, with batteries fully charged. Carry spare batteries, just in case.

Follow these guidelines to gather compelling video:

- Avoid zooms and pans, unless you have a specific reason for a camera move.

The camera should work like the human eye. Imagine that you have just arrived in a crowded stadium where a championship game is about to be played. You would first take in the immensity of the location, but you wouldn't spend the entire game with your gaze wandering aimlessly around the arena. You would begin to focus on the field, the players, the action of the game and the reaction of the fans. In gathering video of the event, you would want some wide shots, medium action shots, closer shots of individuals and extremely tight shots to show details. Like pieces of a puzzle, each of these shots is an important part of the "bigger picture." It is also easier to follow action, or to pay attention to what someone is saying, when the camera is NOT moving.

There may be a reason to zoom in on an object, such as a face in a crowd, if you are trying to call the viewers' attention to it. Alternatively, you may wish to pull out from a specific object to a wider shot in order to show a relationship between an object and its surroundings. You may pan or tilt, moving the camera horizontally or vertically, to show a relationship between objects, or the camera may naturally follow action. These camera moves should be done on a tripod and should not take so much time that you will have to edit in the middle of a camera move. If you must make a camera move, be sure to roll for a few seconds before and after the move. You can often make the same point by cutting together two or more static shots. For example, you might cut from the wide shot of the packed stadium to a close-up of the good luck charm that the team captain is holding in his hand. This would be much more effective than a slow camera move from the extremely wide to the extremely tight shot.

- Hold each shot steady for at least 10 seconds.

As a general rule, use a tripod. In situations where you must hand-hold the camera, look for a way to brace yourself and/or the camera for a steady shot. Until you get into the habit of holding your shots, count to ten slowly to yourself before changing the shot. It is easier to shoot steady shots when the camera lens is set on a wide focal length. If you are on telephoto, it will be very difficult to hold a long-distance shot steady. Close-ups should be shot on a tripod.

- Shoot sequences, including establishing shots and cutaways.

In the language of video storytelling, the shots are the words. A sequence of shots is a complete sentence. Instead of nouns and verbs, your video sentence may consist of:

- Wide (long) shot: To establish the location, set the scene for the story.
- Medium shot: To introduce the characters in your story, bring viewers closer to the action.
- Close up: To show details, may suggest emotions.
- Master shot: A complete shot of an action taking place.
- Cutaways: Shots required in the editing process to show reactions or different angles on the action being performed.

A basic video sequence will include:

- video of the person
- video of the thing
- video of the person *and* the thing.

Let's walk through a simple sequence for a common situation: an official is holding a news conference. In this case, the news conference is the "thing." Your raw video might include:

1. A medium shot of the official entering the room.
2. A wide shot of the official speaking in the front of the room.
3. Medium shots of the official speaking or performing an action.
4. A closer shot of the official's "talking head" during the possible sound bites.
5. Close-ups of any visual items used during the news conference, such as a chart, a printed report or a prop.
6. Cutaways, including individual shots of reporters listening, taking pictures or notes.
7. An extreme wide shot from the back of the room, showing the official and the crowd of reporters.
8. Relationship shots:
   (a) a reverse angle from the front of the room behind the speaker;
   (b) a side angle, possibly panning from the official to the reporters and back. If you are at the scene of a breaking story, such as the house fire, you could show the relationship between the captain's news briefing and the damaged home behind him.

You may not be able to get all of these shots every time, and you may not use every shot that you take. Choose a camera position that will allow you to get as many different kinds of shots as possible from one place. You may need to make a decision that you have recorded the necessary sound bites before turning the camera away from the speaker to get cutaways, or moving the camera to the back, side or front of the room while the event is still in progress. However, it is important to shoot as much of a complete sequence as possible, so that you will have options for putting your story together. A common complaint heard in the editing room is, "There aren't enough cutaways!" Don't limit yourself to the talking head at the microphone and shoot more than you think you will need. Don't worry about disrupting the event by moving around the room to get your shots. Unless there are security concerns that prevent you from moving, the people staging the news conference understand that you have a job to do. Just be sure to move as quietly and efficiently as possible.

• Frame your shots, using the rule of thirds (Figures 4.1–4.3).

All great pictures, from classic art to high-tech videos, follow this basic rule of composition. Mentally divide your screen into thirds, both horizontally and vertically. Place the key elements of your picture along the lines. This is called the rule of thirds (Figures 4.1–4.3)

Let's imagine that you are shooting a picture of a lake with mountains in the background. Placing the far edge of the lake on the 1–2 line would emphasize the lake in the foreground. But placing it along the 3–4 line would emphasize the mountains in the background. When shooting people or other key vertical objects, you should avoid placing them squarely in

Figure 4.1 Generic photo with grid using rule of thirds.

Figure 4.2 Using the rule of thirds to direct the viewer's attention: In Figure 4.2 a we have placed the pond along line 1–2, emphasizing the muddy foreground. In Figure 4.2 b we have placed the pond along line 3–4, to emphasize the threatening clouds in the background.

Figure 4.3 Using the rule of thirds to convey action: Figure 4.3 a is incorrect and static because it places the subject in the center. Figure 4.3 b conveys action because the child is on line 1–3 and the ducks are on line 2–4. The composition becomes more intimate in Figure 4.3 c because the camera is closer to the action.

the center of your shot. It will look better if you put the person along the vertical line 1–3 or 2–4 (Figure 4.3). Unless you are shooting a person who is speaking directly to the viewer, placing your key object in the center of the shot will make the viewer uncomfortable. Even then, notice that most reporter standups are shot with the reporter along one of the vertical lines.

When composing your shots, be aware that you are working in a horizontal medium. Even on the web, video screens have a 4/3 ratio, four parts wide to three parts high. Wider HDTV screens are more than five parts wide to three parts high. You must compose your shots with this in mind, placing vertical objects on the appropriate lines, using the rule of thirds and filling in the rest of the horizontal picture. Unlike using a still camera, you cannot rotate the lens to capture something vertical. The audience is not going to tilt their video screen sideways to view a vertical image.

- Shoot at or near eye level unless you have a reason to choose an extreme angle.

Viewers expect your camera to be a neutral observer. If you choose to shoot from an extreme angle, you are making a visual statement. For example, you might shoot from a high angle to look down on the helplessness of a small child. Shooting up from a low angle will make your subject appear dominant, such as an authority figure lecturing to an underling. Occasionally you will want to take a high wide shot for perspective on a scene, or you might shoot from a low angle to show a specific point of view.

- Pay attention to lighting and take your own lights if necessary.

You can't take great pictures in the dark. Make sure your subject is not "backlit" by a bright source of light from behind. When you are shooting outdoors, pay attention to the position of the sun. If you have the option to move your subject or move the camera, make sure that the sun is lighting the front of the key object. At high noon, you may need to use a fill light or reflector to compensate for the strong lighting overhead. Of course, breaking news often happens after dark. Many professional cameras can be equipped with a small, battery-powered light. It's better than nothing and may be your only choice if you are not near any other power sources. When you are in control of a situation, such as a scheduled interview, compensate for any lighting problems by taking your own lights and light stands.

- Do not "stage" video.

If something is done for the camera, disclose it. Let's say you have arrived at the fire too late to get the live action footage of the firefighter going into the burning house to look for a missing cat. The next day, you revisit the scene to interview the firefighter about his rescue attempt. You might ask him to show you how he put on his safety equipment, and then disclose in your script that "we asked him to demonstrate how he got ready to enter the burning house." If you are getting video of a routine action, such as an official working at her desk, tell the person, "Do what you would do if the camera were not here."

• Overlap action sequences.

Always keep the editing process in mind, especially when shooting action. If you are shooting video of someone riding a bicycle, you'll want to have some shots in which the person rides into or out of your frame so that you can cut to or from a different shot in the sequence. Tight shots, such as the rider's face, or her feet on the pedals, will give you more editing options. Make sure that your action shots overlap each other so that you can avoid abrupt, non-sequential shot changes called "jump cuts." If possible, you may need to ask the subject to perform the action more than once. You might ask the bicycle rider to pedal down the street twice, taking your wide shots the first time and your tight cutaways the second time. This is NOT staging, as long as it is an action the person would reasonably perform if the camera were not present.

Shoot 5 to 1

Video technology makes it easy to shoot a great sequence because you don't have to use everything you shoot. Always shoot more than you think you will need, but don't take so long that you waste time or miss your deadline. As a general guideline, plan to shoot five seconds of video for every one second you will use. You don't want to find out in the editing process that you don't have enough to complete the story. And you don't want to approach the editing process with so much extra video that you can't quickly locate the best shots and sound bites.

Permission to shoot

The vast majority of subjects welcome the opportunity to participate in video storytelling. But there are also situations where you and your camera will not be greeted warmly. Be sure you have the legal right to take pictures. Generally, this right is assumed if you are in a public place where there is no expectation of privacy. If you are standing on a public sidewalk taking pictures of something that is happening on private property, you are usually entitled to the same view as any other bystander in the area.

The moment you step on to private property, the rules are more complicated and can vary based on the laws of the country where you are working. Generally, if a business is open to the public and there is no expectation of privacy for the customers, such as a grocery store parking lot, you theoretically have the right to shoot. But the person in charge of the property also has the right to ask you to turn off the camera and/or leave. You should comply if you are asked to do so, although videographers will often continue rolling on the dramatic footage while the reporter is being escorted from the premises. Many times, the situation can be remedied simply by making a phone call and explaining the purpose of your story to a public relations person. However, if someone tries to harm you or your equipment, withdraw from the confrontation as quickly as possible. No video is worth risking your life.

In some emergency or military situations, authorities may restrict your movement in an area that is usually public. You should comply with all instructions from law enforcement and do your best to get the story anyway. If your ability to do your job is seriously compromised, or you simply disagree with an order, don't try to hash it out on your own. Get in touch with the management of your news organization for assistance and advice.

There are situations where privacy is assumed and you may not shoot any video until you have permission. A hospital or doctor's office, for example, has an obligation to respect the privacy of its patients. A public school may be public property, but school officials have an obligation to safeguard their students. Schools and hospitals may ask the people you are interviewing to sign a release. You may have to agree to show the faces of only the children whose parents have signed a media release. A private business or government agency may allow interviews only with certain employees who are trained to speak to the media. Public relations practitioners should be aware of the need to set ground rules and have a spokesperson available.

A journalist can legally shoot an exterior of a school, hospital, home or private business from the public sidewalk, but you may not shoot anything or interview anyone on the property without permission. The best practice is to call in advance to arrange a video opportunity, or approach without the camera to work out the details of your shoot. Public relations should have a procedure for dealing with media requests. If you cannot get permission to shoot, you can ask a source to leave the private property and meet you for an interview in a place where you have permission to shoot or in a public area.

Compelling Sound

Sound quality in your video story is just as important as the pictures. Research has shown that viewers will tolerate less than perfect video, but they are more likely to click away if they can't hear what's going on. Silent video lacks the "real" quality that users crave. Begin by choosing the right microphone for the situation:

- *Shotgun*: Named for its resemblance to the barrel of a shotgun, this microphone is very "directional." You must point the mike directly at the sound you are trying to record. You often see a shotgun mike mounted on top of a professional video camera, or it can be attached with a longer cord to allow greater flexibility. Compose your shot to avoid showing the microphone.
- *Hand-held*: This is the standard microphone for most video journalists. It can be placed on a stand to record a speaker at a news conference, or hand-held in a standup or an interview. It is omni-directional and will record whatever sounds are in the general area, including background noise, like a passing truck, that will interfere with what the speaker is saying. The closest sound will be the loudest. As a general rule, position the mike about six inches from the person's mouth. News organizations frequently identify their microphones with a mike flag showing a channel number or logo because they know the microphone may be seen in the shot. However, if you are getting in close with

the microphone to record natural sound, such as footsteps, do not show the mike in your shot.

- *Clip-on*: A peanut-sized microphone that clips on to the speaker's clothing is a good choice for the video journalist because both hands are free. A reporter wearing a clip-on mike in a standup is free to gesture or hold a prop. A clip-on is also a good choice if the subject is using his or her hands to demonstrate something. It also has the advantage of being less visible, giving the feeling of a real conversation as opposed to a staged interview with a hand-held microphone. It is easy for your subjects to forget that they are wearing the clip-on, and they may be more at ease if you are not sticking a hand-held mike in their face.
- *Wireless*: Each of the above microphones can be wireless, meaning that there is a small transmitter sending the sound to a receiver on your camera. Going wireless is your best option when you need to move around while shooting the story, or it is not possible to run a cord from the mike to your camera. You can also do some very creative things with a wireless mike, such as attaching it to a person to get the natural sound as they go about their business. Make sure you have fresh batteries and always use headphones to verify that your wireless is working without interference.
- *Built-in*: The simplest video cameras have built-in mikes and may not have a port for plugging in sound equipment. You may need to get up close to your subject to get decent quality sound.

Always use headphones to monitor the quality of the sound and fix problems. If you are recording yourself on camera, you will use the headphones to check your sound first, and then put them aside while doing your standup.

The importance of natural sound

Wearing headphones will also help you pay attention to the natural sound that makes your video seem real. Users want to hear the birds singing in the forest, or the wind rustling through the trees. If there is crowd noise or a musical performance, we want to hear it. Look for opportunities to enhance the natural sound by placing a microphone closer to it. And while this may seem obvious, shut up while you are shooting! The audience wants to hear the natural sound of the sirens as the fire engines race to the burning home. But you won't have a clean recording if you are cracking a joke about what took them so long.

Interviews

One-on-one interviews are often key building blocks in your video story. They are, by definition, staged events. There are some guidelines to help this somewhat artificial situation seem more "real."

Getting it on the record

When preparing to conduct an interview, be clear about topic you would like to discuss and how the comments will be used. Always begin by clearly identifying yourself and your news organization. State clearly that you are working on a story. Never say your story is "just for a school project" or "just between you and me" if there's any possibility that the interview will be eventually broadcast or posted online. When you arrive for the interview with your camera, a tripod, a microphone and a notebook, it is pretty obvious that you are doing a story for broadcast, print or web publication. A person who talks to you under these conditions is giving their "implied" consent.

Example 1

Reporter Paul Wang is at the scene of the house fire. A neighbor points out the man who saw the flames, called for help and woke up the family. The reporter might approach the man and say something like this: "Hi, I'm Paul Wang from Channel 3 News and I'm working on a story about the fire. I understand you did a very brave thing tonight. Can I ask you a few questions?" If the neighbor modestly says that he doesn't want any publicity, Paul might try some gentle persuasion, such as mentioning the possibility that the interview might save more lives by educating people about what to do in an emergency. If the neighbor still says no and walks away, Paul may have to respect the man's privacy. Unlike a public official, a private citizen has no duty to talk to the press. Paul could interview some of the other bystanders who think the camera-shy neighbor is a hero.

Example 2

Sports reporter Terry Anzur is trying to arrange an interview with the mother of a local athlete who is going to the Olympics. Their phone conversation might go something like this: "Hi, Mrs. Jones. I'm Terry Anzur with localsports.com and I'm working on a story about your son's accomplishments. Would it be possible for me to come to your house for a video interview for our web site, and perhaps a look at some of your family photos?" At this point, the reporter has been clear about the purpose of the interview and the subject is more than likely to consent.

Do you need a release?

News reporters almost never have to ask for a release, which is a signed legal document giving you permission to publish the interview. It is unrealistic to expect someone in the midst of a breaking news story to review a legal document for "informed" consent. If you are doing an interview in a restricted setting, such as a school or hospital, officials on the scene may ask the subject to sign a release to meet the privacy and consent requirements of their organization, not yours. If your interview will be used for entertainment or public relations, instead of a news program, you may need to get the subject to sign a release required by your company. Check with a manager to learn the specific policies of your organization. It is better to get the release signed *before* the interview, if one is required.

Don't submit questions in advance

What if the subject wants a list of your questions in advance? Just say NO! Providing a list of questions allows the subject to prepare rehearsed answers instead of responding spontaneously and naturally. In order to do your job, you must be free to ask follow-up questions that may not be on the list. An interview that is based on pre-arranged questions usually comes across to the audience as rehearsed and phony. It is reasonable, however, to discuss the possible topics in general terms so the subject will have some idea of what to expect. You won't get very good answers if the mayor is prepared to talk about crime and you want to ask about the city budget.

Keep your interview request as general as possible. In the example involving the mother of the Olympic athlete, you might mention that you'd like to know what advice she has for other parents, or whether she feels nervous when her child is competing.

If you are also planning to ask a tough question that fits within the general topic of her son's accomplishments, such as how the mother feels about the rumors that her son might have used performance-enhancing drugs, you don't want to be tied down to an approved list. Of course, if the subject says she'll do the interview on the condition that you don't ask about the drug rumors and you agree, you have to keep your word. Just disclose to your audience that you agreed in advance not to ask the question as a condition of getting the interview.

Do your homework

Before any interview, you should do enough research to understand the story. You should have some general knowledge of each subject's point of view and background. Again, think of it as forming a hypothesis for your experiment; you want to approach the interview with a general idea of what you expect the person to say. Although you won't share your questions with the subject in advance, it's okay to have a list of questions and possible follow-ups for your own reference. However, you must *really listen* to the answers and react if the responses take off in an entirely new direction. You should be prepared to press for complete and clear answers with follow-up questions.

Ask open-ended questions to encourage storytelling, opinions or emotions

Prepare questions that allow your subjects to speak in sound bites. Avoid questions that can be answered with a simple "yes" or "no." For example, you are asking the firefighter if he was afraid to enter the burning house. A yes or no answer won't shed much light on his frame of mind. Better to ask: "As you were going into the flames to look for the missing cat, what were you thinking?" Don't ask the Olympic athlete's mom, "Are you proud of his accomplishments?" The answer is obvious. Better to ask: "What will it mean for you if your son wins the gold medal?" Remember: feelings are more powerful than facts. You can always write the facts of the story in your narration, but it is best to allow the participants to express opinions or emotions. Encourage storytelling, and allow the person to tell their own story in their own words. A good practice is to end the interview by asking if there is anything they would like to add, and then follow up if it's something of interest.

Choose an appropriate location

The right background will give the viewer important visual clues to the context of your interview. Avoid putting your subject up against a blank wall. Try to frame the shot with background items that will help to identify the role of person who is speaking. Lawyers, for example, are often framed with a background of legal reference books. Don't be shy about slightly rearranging the knickknacks and furniture in the room for a more pleasing composition. Close blinds or drapes to eliminate backlighting and use your own lights if necessary. Just be sure to ask permission and return the room to its original condition when you are done.

If the indoor lighting is poor and the weather conditions permit, take the subject outside. A lawyer could stand outside with the courthouse in the background. Be sure to eliminate any visual distractions in the background, such as bystanders waving at the camera. Choose a quiet location and try to turn off or minimize any background noise, such as a loud air conditioner or recorded music. Use a wind screen, a foam cover that fits over the microphone, to reduce wind noise. If it's a noisy situation, such as fans celebrating their team's latest victory, hold the microphone closer to the subject's mouth.

Shooting the Interview

Let's walk through a typical one-on-one interview situation for a video journalist working alone. You will want to get your subject to stand or sit on a mark while you lock down the camera on the "talking head." Avoid having the person look straight into the camera. The subject should look slightly off to the side of the lens, where you will be during the interview, but we should be able to see both eyes in the shot. Observe the rule of thirds, and allow for some "lead room" or "looking room" between the person's nose and the edge of the screen (see Figure 4.4). Don't allow the subject to turn sideways to the camera and become a "talking ear."

If you don't have a clip-on mike, try to avoid showing the microphone in your "talking head" shot. A common beginner's mistake is to frame the interview so wide that we see not only the microphone, but the interviewer's arm as well! Proper framing of an interview should eliminate such distractions and showcase the facial expression of the person speaking. Once you have locked down the shot and checked the audio, start recording, move into your position next to the camera lens and begin asking questions. Try to keep an eye on the viewfinder, if possible, by angling it towards you. You will need to adjust the shot if the subject moves.

After you have finished asking questions, remember to shoot the interview as a complete sequence, which may include a wider, establishing shot of the person speaking, and some cutaways for editing purposes. You may also want to include a reverse angle shot from behind the subject, showing the interviewer listening. These can be tricky: the reporter

Figure 4.4 The importance of "looking room:" Figure 4.4 a is incorrect. Although the subject is placed on vertical line 2–4, she is looking at the edge of the screen. Figure 4.4 b, placing the subject on line 13, allows "looking room" and draws the viewer into the conversation and the setting.

should not nod, as if in agreement. While shooting a reverse cutaway, ask the subject an additional question and then listen to the answer with an interested but neutral expression on your face. While we're on the subject, get in the habit of using your facial expression to encourage people to talk without saying "uh-huh." Such vocal distractions will interfere with the sound track.

Some reporters use "reverse questions." Be careful here. If you are taking a reverse angle shot to show yourself re-asking a question, be sure to ask exactly the same question in the same manner as the first time you asked it, so you won't mislead the viewer about the context of the answer. The movie *Broadcast News* showed a reporter who manufactured a tear in a reverse cutaway shot, damaging his career when someone realized he had faked it. Never forget that the purpose of video journalism is "keeping it real." If it is absolutely

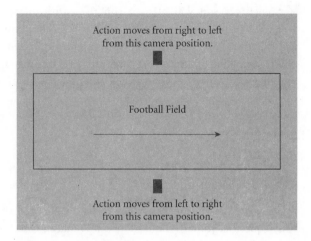

Figure 4.5 Crossing the line

necessary to show the interviewer's questions and reactions, the best practice is to shoot the interview with two cameras.

Don't "cross the line" when shooting cutaways. This concept is easy to understand if you think of shooting a video of a sporting event. The photographer must decide to stand on one side of the field so that the direction of the action will be consistent (see Figure 4.5). Skipping to a shot taken from the opposite side of the field disorients the viewer because suddenly everything looks backwards. When shooting an interview, there is an imaginary line between you and the subject. The camera should not cross that line when you are shooting wide shots or cutaways.

If you are including more than one interview in the story, plan your shots so that they are not all facing in the same direction. This is especially effective if you have two subjects with opposing viewpoints; one will face screen right, the other will face screen left. This provides visual reinforcement of the conflict in the story.

Know how your interview will be used

When preparing for an interview, you should have some idea of how the material will be used. If you are planning to use only sound bites from the interview, you need to prepare questions that will encourage the subject to deliver the memorable quotes that you need for your package. Ask a question more than once, or re-ask with slightly different phrasing if you don't get a usable sound bite the first time. With practice, you will learn to listen for bites that you can use. There is no need to let an interview drag on if you got the quotes you needed in the first two or three questions. On the other hand, don't stop until you are sure you have a usable sound bite.

Don't be afraid of silence. Sometimes the most memorable sound will occur when you give subjects a moment to collect their thoughts. Don't cut off a potentially interesting answer by jumping in with the next question too soon.

Sometimes you will plan to run the entire interview as a story. In that case, you will want to plan your questions with a beginning, middle and end. In the example of the Olympic athlete's mother, you might begin with her earliest memories of her child competing in the sport and progress through the current rumors of drug use, and then end with a question anticipating the emotions she will feel during the upcoming Olympics. Again, plan open-ended questions that will allow the subject to speak in sound bites, really listen to the answers, and do your homework to be prepared for follow-ups.

Get exact names and titles

Spelling counts! Be sure to ask the person how to spell and pronounce their name. Making this request as your first question can sometimes be a good way to break the ice for a recorded interview because it puts the person at ease; everyone knows their own name. Write it in your notebook or get it on video so that you can refer to it later when writing a web version of your story, or when ordering on-screen graphics. Also double check the person's exact title within their organization. Asking for a business card can help you get it right. However, lengthy titles don't fit within the constraints of multimedia journalism. "Vice president of public relations and marketing manager for North America" will probably be shortened to "company spokesman." Learn the various jurisdictions for law enforcement and public safety in the area you are covering. There's a big difference between a police officer working for a city, a sheriff's deputy working for a county and an agent working for federal drug enforcement. If you're not sure, ask.

Man (or woman) on the street

Your story may include the opinions of real people you approach at random. This is called "MOS" (man on street) or "vox pop" (based on the Latin for "voice of the people"). The Pew Center for Civic Journalism recommends finding places where citizens gather to talk about the issues of the day, such as a coffee house or a barber shop. If you need to talk to parents, you might find moms and dads taking their kids to school or the park. If you must approach people on the street, be polite and always identify yourself before asking questions. Prepare a simple, open-ended question that a normal person can answer. Leave it to the officials to answer institutional questions like, "How can the government improve the health care system?" Relate to the man or woman on the street by using the word "you" and asking the question on a more personal level, as in: "How satisfied are you with the health care that's available to you and your family?" If you have to launch into a complicated explanation in order to ask the question, it's probably not a good topic for MOS. "Vox pops" work best when you are asking about an issue on which everyone has an opinion. When you are selecting people to approach, try to reflect the diversity in your community. Include a mix of genders, age groups, economic status, and racial or ethnic backgrounds. Shoot some interviews facing screen right, others screen left, so that you can cut more easily between sound bites.

What if a key person in the story won't talk to me?

It's not unusual for someone to refuse to do an on-camera interview. He or she may be busy or camera-shy. Or they may actually have something to hide. You should be polite but persistent, making every effort to schedule the interview at a convenient time, or putting the person at ease. However, the refusal may be nothing more than an attempt to stop you from doing the story. In that case, you need to be very clear that you intend to do the story with or without the interview. Encourage the subject to take advantage of the opportunity to tell his or her side. If you have made a reasonable request and you are turned down anyway, you should plan to disclose in your story that person declined to be interviewed on camera. You might also ask questions via e-mail or over the phone, and use graphics to include those responses in your story.

Avoid "ambush" interviews, in which the journalist stakes out a subject and approaches him or her to ask a question with the camera rolling. This technique should only be used as a last resort after you have made a good-faith effort to set up a conventional interview, and you have failed to obtain any kind of response. Yes, it makes for great drama, but subjects tend to look guilty if they are avoiding your camera or engaging in some kind of confrontation with you. Your ambush may also have an unintended effect; the audience may sympathize with someone who appears to be harassed by a rude reporter. The nature of the interview will help you decide if an ambush is appropriate: a public official has an obligation to respond to public concerns, while a private citizen may not.

Public relations practitioners should note that refusing to do an on-camera interview is rarely a good idea. The journalist is likely to pursue the story anyway, and the finished product will, at the very least, fail to reflect your client's point of view. Saying "no comment" could put your client in a bad light. The best practice is to prepare responses to the questions you are likely to be asked, making sure to deliver quotes and/or sound bites that will make it easy for the reporter to include your client's intended message in the story. As an alternative, you could issue a text statement that may be quoted.

The Reporter "Standup"

When the video storyteller appears on camera, it is often referred to as a "standup," even if the performer is not standing. Use your standup to fill in the missing parts of your story:

- to describe something that happened in the past when you don't have pictures;
- to create a "bridge" between two elements of your story, for example, you could change locations, or make a transition to an opposing viewpoint;
- to demonstrate something;
- to explain what is likely to happen next, because you can't take pictures of events that have not yet occurred;
- to fill in any other gaps in your story for which there is no video;
- to establish your presence at the scene;
- to interact with story participants and/or the environment.

As a general rule, you should outline your story, identify any gaps, and decide where the standup should go while you are still in the field shooting the story. It is a good practice to shoot a standup in each location for your story, if there is more than one location. You won't use them all, but it's nice to have options in the editing process.

It's understandable to be nervous about appearing on camera. Keep your standup short and focused. It should not be much longer than a sound bite, typically 12–20 seconds, and no more than two sentences long. A demonstration standup may be longer if there is enough movement to sustain the viewer's interest. You will be less nervous and more natural if you give yourself something to do. A clip-on mike will free both hands for natural gestures. If you are holding a microphone, make natural gestures with your free hand. Speak to the camera as if it were a person. Don't shout. Even if you are in a noisy location, the microphone will pick up your voice.

If you are a one-person crew, flip the viewfinder so that you can properly frame your standup. You can use an object such as a light stand to focus on the place where you will stand. Pay attention to lighting and make sure you are not backlit. Talk to the viewer at eye level unless you have a specific reason for a high or low angle.

If you move during a standup, have a reason. The rule is: "Take me somewhere and show me something." Don't stroll aimlessly toward the camera. Begin walking before you talk, and stop on a pre-arranged "mark" to deliver your closing words for maximum impact. Move smoothly and deliberately. You may wish to step in or out of the frame to call attention to the scene in the background. Don't move for the sake of movement. Sometimes it is best to simply stand on your mark and transmit important information to the audience.

Finally, play back and check your standup before you leave the location. You can always do another "take" if you are not satisfied. It's a good practice to spot check all of your video before you leave the location, in case something has gone wrong and you need to re-shoot something. Just make sure you don't accidently re-record over video that you need.

Writing the Script

You are ready to begin organizing and writing your script when you have assembled the basic building blocks of your story:

- research or background information;
- video of the event or location with natural sound;
- graphics;
- on-camera interviews;
- reporter standups.

Remember that you don't need to use all of the elements in every story. Perhaps graphics would be enough to do a VO on the latest stock market numbers, or a strong sound bite might stand on its own. You may wish to show a compelling clip with or without narration.

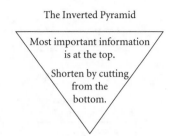

Figure 4.6a The inverted pyramid

Or, you may put together some or all of the elements in a package. The nature of the story will dictate the most appropriate way of relating that story to the audience.

Making a shot list

When you have time, it is a good practice to work from a shot list. Screen all of your video and note the time code for each wide shot (WS), tight shot (TS), close-up (CU), and so on. Mark the best shots that could be used to open or close the story, and shots that you know you will mention in the script. There's usually no need to transcribe entire interviews, but you'll want to write down the exact text of the sound bites you are likely to use. This will help you write transitions in and out of the sound bite, and then generate a text version of the story on the web..

Story structure: inverted pyramid vs. the "pregnant" I

This is a key difference between print and video stories. A print story will often be structured as an "inverted pyramid," with the 5 Ws at the top, followed by the supporting facts in order of their importance with the most important first (Figure 4.6a). A newspaper reader can decide whether to read on, or skip to the next story. If an editor is short on space, he or she may cut from the bottom of the story without eliminating the most essential facts.

The structure of a video story encourages the viewer to watch the entire clip. It consists of a strong beginning and a strong ending, and is designed to be shorter or longer in the middle to fit the available time. Think of this structure as the capital letter "I" with definite strokes at the top and bottom, and an expandable pouch in the middle. If you have more time, you can fill the pouch – making the "I" more "pregnant" – by including more material in the middle of the story (Figure 4.6b). The strong beginning grabs the viewer's attention. The strong ending provides resolution, allowing the viewer to move on to the next news item.

Variations on the "pregnant I" include:

- Telling the story in chronological order. This works best when you are describing a complex series of events that have a strong beginning and a strong ending. It is the best choice when it would be too confusing to show the events out of sequence.

The "Pregnant" I

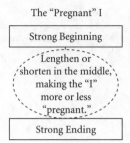

Figure 4.6b   The pregnant I

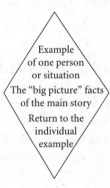

Figure 4.6c   The diamond structure

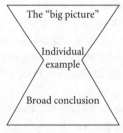

Figure 4.6d   The hourglass structure

- Using a personal example of a larger issue. This is also called a "diamond" structure because the story begins with an individual who illustrates the conflict (Figure 4.6c). Then, the reporter broadens the story to include the "bigger picture," showing the widespread scope of the problem in society and what authorities are doing about it. The story concludes by returning to the individual example. A variation on this structure is the hourglass, which features the individual example in the middle of the story (Figure 4.6d).

What is the lead?

A good practice is to write your lead first. This is how your story will be introduced by an anchor on TV or a webcast. Or it may be a text that invites the user to click on your video. Think of the lead as a promise you make to the viewer. You will fulfill this promise in your story. You should promise and deliver a reason to watch, or WIIFM as discussed in Chapter 2.

Build bridges, not walls   Your lead should provide a smooth transition to the first shot in your story. For example, let's say you are introducing a package about some heroic firefighters. If the first video in your package will show firefighters pouring water on a burning building, don't end your lead with a statement like, "Paul Wang reports." It is better to write something like: "Paul Wang shows us how the firefighters risked their lives to save a family's home." This will prepare the viewer what's next: video and natural sound of the fire crews in action.

Best video first

If you have great video, what are you saving it for? When viewers lose interest in your story, they will click away without seeing your best shots. The "old school" of visual storytelling, dating back to the film days, required reporters to begin with a location-establishing shot. Thus, every story about a political issue would begin with a wide shot of a government building. This is predictable, boring and totally inappropriate for multimedia's short attention span. As a general rule, begin your story with your best video and natural sound. We know what the Capitol building looks like; instead, show us a lawmaker banging a gavel to quiet a rowdy debate, or let us hear the applause as an official signs an important piece of legislation.

Your opening shot should have natural sound. Open with a "talking head" sound bite only when the statement is exceptionally newsworthy or memorable. And, unless you are reporting live or doing something that is truly astounding, never open a package with a standup. The best video is rarely the reporter's face! This mistake is commonly seen when a novice reporter gets a big opportunity, like covering the red carpet at a Hollywood event. The reporter may think it's cool to begin the story with a standup: "I'm Nellie Beginner on the red carpet with the biggest stars in Hollywood." This is only interesting to Nellie and her closest friends because the story isn't really about Nellie. Viewers want to see their favorite stars on the red carpet, so put the best video first!

There is an exception to the rule of "best video first": when the story has a surprise twist and your best video is part of the surprise. Obviously, you don't want to give away your secret at the top. In that case, use another compelling shot to start your package. Finally, we should point out that there is nothing wrong with setting the scene for your story, as long as you do it with attention-grabbing video and not a boring shot of an institutional building. If you are reporting from an unusual or exotic location and you want to establish a place or a mood in the viewer's mind, take the time to get some truly eye-catching, creative shots and interesting natural sound. Then, put the best video first!

Say dog, see dog

The best video stories are a perfect balance of words and pictures. That doesn't mean you should state the obvious. The viewer can recognize a picture of a dog. Your narration should add value to the image. Is this the animal that won the top prize in a dog show? Is it the hero dog who rescued its owner from danger? Is this the pampered pet whose silly trick became a viral video?

You should never write a sentence in a video script without knowing what pictures you will use to "cover" the narration. If you want to report on the dog's amazing feats, but you only have pictures of him taking a nap, reference the video before you make your point: "As you watch Fluffy snoozing on the porch, it's hard to believe that this is the dog that sprang into action yesterday to save a child's life."

Always write to the video you have, not the video you wish you had. The viewer should feel that there is a connection between the image on the screen and your narration:

- Reference first video.
- Reference compelling video.
- Avoid "show and tell" or stating the obvious.

Identify the source of video

If your story includes video that you did not shoot, identify the source. For example, if you have obtained a home video of an Olympic athlete as a toddler, write, "This home video shows that he was always a tough competitor, even at the age of three."

If you are using video from an image library, identify the date and context of the pictures. Again, let's use our sports story as an example: "This winning play from last year's world championship shows an athlete at the top of his game." If you are using a clip of copyrighted material, make sure you have permission and be sure to credit the owner of the footage, with graphics or in your narration. If you are using material from a VNR or video news release, inform the viewer of the source. User-generated images can be an important element of your story, but be sure to say who took the pictures.

Avoid wallpaper video and BOPSA

Generic video makes your story an instant snoozer. How many times have you seen a story about obesity with random shots of anonymous bulging bellies? Even worse, any story about any problem facing the general population can begin with random shots of people walking on a city sidewalk. This generic video is about as interesting as looking at wallpaper. Avoid such clichés by finding a more specific way to tell the story, such as profiling someone who is struggling to make sense of the latest weight-loss study.

BOPSA is the acronym for "Bunch Of People Standing (or Sitting) Around." It's a specific type of wallpaper video that occurs at official meetings. The participants are shown, mostly looking bored, while the reporter talks about what they are talking about. Avoid BOPSA! If the school board is discussing school bus safety, for example, don't talk about school buses while you are showing pictures of the board members in a conference room. Once you have established the fact that a meeting took place, and you have recorded the sound bites from the meeting, use video of children on school buses to illustrate the safety issue. Talk with safety experts, bus drivers, police, parents and kids about the program that is being discussed. There are times when the BOPSA is a legitimate story, if the meeting itself has historic significance. Most of the time, however, the meeting is only the starting point of a more visually interesting story in your community.

Use simple, everyday language

Although we've mentioned the importance of plain language in Chapter 3, it is just as important in video storytelling. Consider this definition, used by international media consultant Bob Andresen:

> Broadcast style is used in television to communicate the greatest amount of information, in the shortest possible time, in a manner that enables the audience to understand it upon hearing it *for the first and only time.*

The same definition applies to web video. You generally have *one* chance to transmit your message to the user. As more viewers access video online, many of them will be multitasking as they watch your story. They don't want to rewind the video to decipher what you are saying. Keep it simple.

One thought per sentence   A cub reporter was trying to impress an editor with her flowery prose. Frustrated, the editor challenged her to give him an example of a simple sentence. The reporter shrugged and said, "The black cat crossed the street."

"No!" snapped the editor. "That's two sentences. The cat is black. It crossed the street."

While this example may be a bit extreme, it illustrates an easy way to simplify your video script writing: observe the rule of "one thought per sentence." Avoid dependent clauses and compound sentences. This is a tough habit to change if you are used to more complex, scholarly writing. It may feel as if you have regressed to writing a "see Spot run" story for children. However, short sentences can pack a powerful punch. One of the most memorable sentences in the Bible is also the shortest: "Jesus wept."

Sentence fragments can be effective   When writing to video, it is not always necessary to write in complete sentences. For example, you are doing a story on someone who is trying to quit smoking: "Jack usually begins his day with a cigarette. Not today." The sentence fragment has caught the viewers' interest, making them want to know what Jack is doing differently and why. This technique can also be effective when compressing time to show repetitive action: "The home team scored again (natsot cheering). And again (more natsot). And finally, the goal that clinched the championship" (natsot crowd celebrating victory).

Use the active voice

The preferred sentence structure for video narration is "subject-verb-object."

Use the active voice to focus on the action in your story. Don't write: "A national sales tax is being proposed by the president." Better: "The president is proposing a national sales tax."

There are some exceptions to this rule. You may use the passive voice when the object is more important than the subject, or when you don't know who performed the action: "The school was vandalized." (We don't know who did it.) "The president was shot by a gunman posing as a reporter." (The president is more important than the shooter.)

Use the proper tense

*   Use present tense or present-perfect tense wherever possible.
*   Use the past tense only when you are giving background information.
*   Avoid the use of "today" or "tonight."

Write: "The government is working on a new anti-piracy program." Or: "The government has begun working on a new anti-piracy program." Not: "The government began working today on a new anti-piracy program."

If you see the words "has been" in your copy, and especially in your lead, stop and ask yourself if you have chosen the newest and most compelling angle on the story. Broadcast writers have a saying, based on an American slang term, "has-been," for someone who is completely out of touch: "When you write 'has been,' you *are* a 'has-been.'" In other words, if your story is written in the past tense, is it really the latest news? It sounds like old news if you write: "The government's new anti-piracy program has been released." Better to write: "The government has a new strategy for catching video pirates." There is no need to add the word "today" or "tonight" because it is implied. In the fast-moving world of multimedia, users want to know what is happening *right now* and what is likely to happen next. And because your online audience can be in any time zone, you don't know what time of day it is for them.

Use adjectives and adverbs sparingly

Allow your video to speak for itself. There is no need to point out that it's a "brutal" murder. Is it possible to have a murder that isn't brutal? The audience can decide for itself if something is tragic or inspiring. Users don't need a reporter to tell them what to think about a survival story or an accident in which someone is killed. Consultant Bob Andresen advises, "Don't tell the audience what to think. Tell them what to think *about*."

Avoid making value judgments about the impact of a news development. For example, if the stock market goes up, it isn't good news for everyone. Some people may have planned their investment strategy on the assumption that the market would drop. Lower food prices might be great news for shoppers, but not so great for the farmers. Some people love sunny weather, others may be praying for rain. Just stick to the facts and let the viewers decide if it's good or bad news for them.

More Style Rules for Narration

Because your script is meant to be read out loud, there are a few more style points to keep in mind:

- Place attribution at the beginning of the sentence. This helps the audience to judge the credibility of the information that follows. Write: "Police say the demonstration was peaceful." Not: "The demonstration was peaceful, according to police."
- Use names only when the speaker is well known or a central character in the story. If fire captain Tony Silvia is a well-known authority on local fires, it may help to put his name before the sound bite. If he is not well known, you might simply write: "Fire officials say…"
- Only use acronyms that are familiar to the audience:
  - NATO, UNESCO
- Use abbreviations only on second reference.
  - Example: The United Nations is sending more U-N peacekeeping troops to the conflict zone.
- Put dashes between letters that should be read out loud.
  - FIRST REFERENCE: United Nations
  - SECOND REFERENCE: U-N
  - FIRST REFERENCE: World Trade Organization
  - SECOND REFERENCE: W-T-O. (Exception: when the abbreviation is well known to your audience such as U-S or F-B-I.)
- Paraphrase most quotes: Don't write: The president says, "I will veto the bill." Better: "The President says he will veto the bill." Use direct quotes sparingly and only for extraordinary statements when you must use the speaker's exact words. It's better to play the actual sound bite of the controversial statement, or read it with a graphic showing the exact quote.
- Avoid symbols and abbreviations. Write out percent instead of %. Instead of $25, write out 25 dollars.
- Break up complicated titles. In print style, you might refer to Sen. John Jones, D-New York. For narration, you would write "Senator John Jones" and on second reference you could mention that he is a Democrat from New York.
- Write numbers so they are easy to understand.
  - Round off numbers wherever possible.
  - Use only one number per sentence.
  - When possible, do the math so the viewer doesn't have to.
- Don't write: "The poll shows 19-point-six percent of teenagers spend 49 and a half percent of their leisure time online." Better: "The poll shows that one of every five teenagers spends nearly half of his or her leisure time online."

- Follow the 10–999 rule to avoid stumbling over numbers when reading your narration.
    - Spell out numbers from one to nine (and sometimes ten, eleven and twelve).
    - Use numerals for numbers from 10–999, except at the beginning of a sentence.
    - Spell out words like "percent," "hundred," "thousand" and "million."
    - Spell out short numbers at the beginning of a sentence.

Examples

Twenty percent of the users account for 80 percent of the activity on the site.
The top five web sites attract more than 100 million page views each year.
Teenagers under 17 can be admitted to a movie that is rated P-G 13.
A movie ticket costs eight dollars and 50 cents.
During the nine-eleven attacks, there were thousands of calls to 9-1-1.

Use of Graphics

Some stories are "video poor," meaning that there is no video to explain an abstract concept such as a tax increase, the results of a survey, or a scientific principle. You may need to include graphics to explain your story. Bold and simple graphics are best, especially if your story will be viewed on a small screen. They may include:

- still photographs
- maps and drawings
- charts and graphs
- electronic titles and text.

Charts and graphs:

- reveal segments in sequence;
- animate trend lines.

Observe the principle of "say dog, see dog" when writing to graphics. Read the exact words the viewer sees on the screen, and don't change the shot too soon. A good rule of thumb is to leave graphics on screen long enough to read the text out loud.

"Lower thirds" are graphics that appear in the bottom one-third of the screen to identify the speaker. Keep them simple.

- Use a maximum of two lines:
    - LINE 1: First name, last name
    - LINE 2: Identification (Eyewitness, Neighbor, Committee Chairman).
- Avoid characterizations such as "concerned" parent or "angry" citizen.

Strive for a Balance of Narration and Recorded Sound

Make your story flow in a logical order from one fact to the next, and avoid long blocks of track or sound. To achieve this balance, first select your sound bites and decide the order in which you will use them. Then, write the narration to match your video and connect the bites as efficiently as possible. If you have a long section of voice track, try to break it up with a pause for natural sound, and mix the natural sound so that it can be heard as a presence under all of your narration.

Writing in and Out of Sound Bites

Pay special attention to the sentences before and after each sound bite. You don't want to say exactly what the speaker is about to say in the bite. A good practice is to write down the exact text of the bites you have chosen to use in your story so that your narration will flow in and out of the sound. Repetition can be a good thing at the end of the bite, if you play off of the exact quote for your next line of track.

Example

> *Narration*: Fire officials say a man who was walking his dog saw the flames, woke up the family, and called for help.
> *Fire captain SOT*: "The neighbor who called 9-1-1 is the real hero tonight."
> *Narration*: A hero, who says he only did what any good neighbor would do.

In this case we have "set up" the fire captain's opinion of the neighbor's lifesaving actions, and have emphasized the word "hero" in our transition to the line about the man's modesty.

Deliver a Memorable Ending

End the story with:

- an interesting fact
- compelling video
- a standup close.

When a reporter signs off after a sound bite, and there is no live tag, it often seems as if the reporter forgot to finish the story or has simply run out of things to say. The only exception would be natural sound that is so moving that it is beyond words, and even then you should try to add an appropriate thought before you sign off or "sig out" with your name, your news organization and your location. For example, if the Olympic athlete's victory moves his mother to weep with joy, you might seem insensitive to the drama if you use the sound bite and then say your name and sign off. Better to add something like: "A mother's tears, more precious than Olympic gold. Terry Anzur for local sports dot com, at the Olympic Games."

Beware of the "huh?" factor

When you spend a lot of time on a story, it is easy to forget that the viewer is absorbing the information for the first time. Try to explain the story as if you were talking to a friend who's new in town and may not know the local references or have all of the background leading up to the events. If there is something in your story that would make a newcomer say, "Huh?" rewrite it. Try not to leave any unanswered questions in the viewer's mind.

When in doubt, leave it out

Your edited video story should include only facts that you have been able to verify. Avoid dating your recorded narration with information that is likely to change. For example, if you are covering an earthquake and authorities have not been able to determine the number of people who have been killed, plan to put that information in your intro, live open, live close, or web site text, where it can be easily updated as necessary. Edit your package to focus on elements that will not change, such as the suffering of the disaster victims.

Editing your video

In a web or broadcast news story, the best practice to cut between the shots in a sequence without using any special effects. Use video transition effects only for a specific purpose:

• Dissolve to denote the passage of time.
• Wipe or other effect to indicate transitions between major story segments.
• Avoid breaking up the human form or face with a fancy effect.

A package script

Let's take a look at a complete script for a video story package with a live open and close. WJLA-TV reporter Kris Van Cleave was assigned to check out a report of a murder in a Southwest Washington neighborhood. There was no murder, but there was a story. Kris could see that the area was flooded with bright light from the nearby military base, making it difficult for residents to watch TV or sleep at night. He learned that people had complained, but were unable to get the lights turned off. Here is the script of his report (Figure 4.7).

Video	Audio	Comments
BRIGHT LIGHT INTRO ANCHOR ON CAM	(MAUREEN) THOSE LOOKING OUT FOR OUR DEFENSE MAY *NOT* BE LOOKING OUT FOR THEIR NEIGHBORS.	The reporter has scripted the anchor intro to set up the story, but not give away the whole story.
(**MAP**)	WE'RE TALKING ABOUT A PROBLEM THAT'S ALMOST IMPOSSIBLE TO MISS FOR A FEW SOUTHWEST D-C RESIDENTS WHO LIVE AT SECOND AND "P" STREETS BY FORT MC NAIR.	The map establishes the location of the story.
(TAKE LIVE SHOT FULL)	OUR KRIS VAN CLEAVE IS SHINING A LIGHT ON THE ISSUE. KRIS, NEIGHBORS ARE CLEARLY UPSET.	The reporter is seen on camera, actively listening to the anchor.
(KRIS LIVE STANDUP INTRO) (KRIS TOUCHES TV LIGHT STAND) (KRIS TURNS OFF LIGHTS) (KRIS HOLDS UP NEWSPAPER, CAMERA PUSHES IN)	(KRIS) MAUREEN, WHEN WE DO A LIVE SHOT AT NIGHT, WE USE THESE LIGHTS. TONIGHT WE'RE GOING TO TURN THEM OFF, BECAUSE SOMETHING ELSE OUT HERE IS PROVIDING PLENTY OF LIGHT. WE WERE TOLD THAT THE LIGHTS HERE AREN'T THAT BRIGHT, CERTAINLY NOT BRIGHT ENOUGH TO READ A NEWSPAPER. WELL, HERE'S A NEWSPAPER. CAN YOU READ IT? I CAN.	The reporter gets right to the point, avoiding a cliché like "That's right, Maureen." Instead he SHOWS us the crisis: the Army base is shining bright security lights directly into the homes of nearby residents. He also demonstrates the conflict between the official story (that the lights are not bright) and the reality (that you can read a newspaper in the bright light). This is slightly longer than two sentences, but the demonstration and movement in the standup hold our attention.
(PKG)	(PKG)	

SUPERS

Figure 4.7 Intro, live shot and package script

Video	Audio	Comments
SW Washington		The reporter ends his standup with a roll cue: "... I can."
Shareen Bundy/SW resident (:18-:21) QUICK!		
Rhonda Hamilton/ neighborhood commissioner (1:31–1:38)		Notice that the anchor intro page also contains the directions for the video package, including the electronic lower-third titles (supers) and times, as well as the total running time (TRT) and outcue.
TRT: 1:49 OUT: "... might as well leave."		
BRIGHT LIGHT FIGHT PACKAGE	(NAT FULL)	The package opens with a video and natural sound establishing the crisis.
(Woman covering window with a blanket, from outside) (Security lights come on) (Door closes)	(KRIS TRACK) WOULD YOU WANT TO COME HOME TO THIS? SHAREEN BUNDY DOES. EVERY DAY.	This story has a diamond structure as the crisis is established through the experience of one person. Opening question engages the viewer. Effective use of sentence fragment.
Super: Shareen Bundy/ SW resident	(SOT) "It's just nervewracking. You are sitting watching TV and you have this big, bright light shining."	Sound bite shows opinion and/or emotion.
(Woman handing up blanket from the inside) (Bedroom window)	(KRIS TRACK) NOW, TRY SLEEPING. FOR OVER A YEAR NOW, BUNDY SAYS, SHE HANGS THIS BLANKET OVER THE FROSTED WINDOWS IN THE LIVING ROOM, AND ANOTHER ONE OVER THE BLINDS IN THE BEDROOM.	Notice the balance of short sections of track and short sound bites. Following the "say dog, see dog" rule, we see the living room and bedroom windows.
Shareen interview	(SOT) "The lights come through, you can't see anything. It's blinding, it's really distracting."	Notice how the narration concentrates on the facts while the SOT focuses on how the situation makes the subject feel.

Figure 4.7 Continued

Video	Audio	Comments
(lights, army base)	(KRIS TRACK) LIKE CLOCKWORK, AS THE SUN GOES DOWN, THESE FLOODLIGHTS ACROSS SECOND STREET SOUTHWEST COME ON. WHO OWNS THEM? THE ARMY. THEY ARE PART OF A CHECKPOINT ON FORT MCNAIR.	Here is a quick explanation of the problem, reinforced by video images. Notice the simple, straightforward language and short declarative sentences in the present tense.
Shareen interview	(SOT) KRIS QUESTION: "Have you talked to anyone about it?" SHAREEN: That's kinda hard to do, they don't listen.	This short q and a establishes the conflict. Neighbors want the lights turned off but the army won't listen.
(army base) (neighborhood) (full screen text of army statement, quotes highlighted)	(KRIS TRACK) MAYBE THEY'LL LISTEN TO US. THE ARMY SAYS IT HAS NO RECORD OF BUNDY COMPLAINING. REGARDLESS, AFTER WE CALLED, THERE WAS ACTION TAKEN. A FORT MCNAIR STATEMENT SAYS OFFICIALS MET WITH DC POLICE, THE WARD 6 STAFF AND THE AREA NEIGHBORHOOD COMMISSIONER TO DISCUSS THE SITUATION. WE WERE NOT INVITED TO THAT MEETING. THE STATEMENT SAYS "THE LIGHTS BREAK NO LAWS AND THE CONSENSUS OF THE MEETING WAS THAT THE LIGHTS ARE NOT INTRUSIVE AND NO COMPLAINTS HAD BEEN MADE." WELL, HERE'S ONE.	Notice the smooth transition out of the bite by repetition of the word "listen." In this case, we are seeing a wide shot of the document and the reporter is paraphrasing its contents. Key quotes are pulled out of the document and highlighted as the reporter reads them. Because he is reading the exact quotes, this track is a little longer than tracks that simply connect video and sound bites.

Figure 4.7 Continued

Video	Audio	Comments
Shareen interview	(SOT) "If I don't put the blankets up, it keeps me up."	Graphic shows the official statement and the sound bite gives the opposing response.
(Bright lights) (Another graphic of a statement, with quotes highlighted)	(KRIS TRACK) AND WARD 6 COUNCILMAN TOMMY WELLS' OFFICE TELLS US THERE WERE OTHER COMPLAINTS DURING A JUNE 1ST COMMUNITY MEETING. HIS OFFICE SAYS THAT AT WARD 6'S REQUEST, FORT MCNAIR MADE SOME CHANGES. AND THE ARMY CLAIMS THE CURRENT POSITIONING OF THE LIGHTS "MINIMIZES LIGHT SHINING INTO RESIDENTIAL AREAS."	Following the diamond structure, we see how the problem is affecting many people and not just one. Again, we see the official document with quotes highlighted as they are read verbatim in the script.
Shareen interview	(SOT) "Even with the blinds down, it comes directly in."	
(Reporter talking to official, interview setup footage)	(KRIS TRACK) WHILE THE ARMY REFUSES TO TALK TO US ON CAMERA ABOUT BUNDY'S SITUATION, HER AREA NEIGHBORHOOD COMMISSIONIER, RHONDA HAMILTON, DID. (SOT)	Again, conflict between official statements and the actual experience of the resident. The reporter keeps pressing for answers, finding at least one public official who is willing to respond on camera.
(Rhonda Hamilton interview)	"It would bother me if the light was bright and shining through my window. I think this can definitely be addressed so they can feel comfortable with the lights and so the base can do the things it needs to do."	He also mentions that he tried to get comments from other officials who would not talk on camera.

Figure 4.7   Continued

Video	Audio	Comments
(Woman and blankets on windows)	(KRIS TRACK) BUT AFTER NINE YEARS HERE, BUNDY SAYS SHE'S HAD ENOUGH OF HER BUILDING'S PROBLEMS. AND SHE'S DONE HANGING BLANKETS OVER HER WINDOWS. SHE'S JUST GOING TO LIVE SOMEWHERE ELSE.	The sound bite gives hope for an eventual resolution of the problem, but the resident profiled in the story has found her own solution: she's going to move away.
Shareen interview	(SOT) "If I want something better, I might as well leave."	Following the diamond structure, the piece begins and ends with the experience of one affected individual.
BRIGHT LIGHT FIGHT TAG REPORTER ON CAMERA LIVE CLOSE	(KRIS LIVE) WE SHOULD TELL YOU NOT EVERYONE LIVING ON THIS BLOCK HAS AN ISSUE WITH THE LIGHTS AND EVENTUALLY THIS PROBLEM WILL GO AWAY ON ITS OWN. THE LIGHTS ARE TEMPORARY WHILE FORT MCNAIR BUILDS A NEW GATE. THE ARMY EXPECTS IT TO OPEN IN MARCH. TONIGHT THE MAYOR'S OFFICE AND THE WARD 6 COUNCIL OFFICE TELL US THEY ARE AWARE OF THE ISSUE AND INTERESTED IN FINDING A COMPROMISE. WE'LL KEEP WATCHING THE STORY AND WE HAVE MORE ON OUR WEB SITE. LIVE IN SOUTHWEST WASHINGTON, KRIS VAN CLEAVE, ABC7 NEWS.	The tag runs over the two-sentence limit because there is late-breaking official reaction to add. Due to the complexity, the reporter did not move during the tag, instead choosing to deliver the information by simply addressing the camera. Although it is good to promote additional coverage on the web site, it would have been better to promote something specific, like additional responses from officials or more background on the complaint. The reporter provides hope for a possible resolution of the story in the future, using the standup close to preview what is likely to happen next.

Figure 4.7 Continued

Live Reporting

Technology allows journalists to report live from the scene of breaking news almost anywhere in the world. Whether you are part of a television broadcast crew or a lone webcaster transmitting video from a backpack, you need to develop the basic skills for live storytelling: clear, concise reporting when you have only *one* chance to get it right. Although it may seem like a reporter is just "winging it," the most memorable live shots involve some level of planning ahead.

Doing a successful live shot is easier than it sounds. If you have a background in performing arts, or in sports, you've already had some experience with the necessary skills. A musician who plays a virtuoso piece of music also has *one* chance to get it right. The performance is based on countless hours of practice, mastering not just the notes, but the interpretation of the music. An athlete who makes the right play at a crucial moment is also performing "live." Based on extensive training, the key player delivers the game-winning performance through individual or team effort. Your power performance in a live report will reflect the journalistic skills you have developed over time.

Write the lead-in first

If someone in the studio will be tossing to you in the field, suggest a lead that will flow seamlessly into your report. Avoid "echo leads" in which the toss tells the entire story, leaving the reporter in the field little to say but, "That's right." Listen to the live toss and react as if it were a conversation.

Establish communication

Ideally, you will have an earpiece to hear the program and a monitor to see when you are on camera. However, that isn't always possible. Arrive at your live location with plenty of time to establish communication with your home base. If you are working alone, you will have to listen for a cue in your earpiece, making sure that you are getting a feed called "mix minus" so that you won't hear an echo. If you are using a monitor, make sure to turn down the sound on the monitor to avoid audio feedback. As a last resort, have someone get on the phone with the control room and cue you with a hand signal.

Live open and close with video package insert

The most basic live shot involves an on-camera standup in which you will introduce and tag your video package. This is sometimes called a "donut" structure, named after the familiar round pastry. Your package is the hole in the middle of the live donut. When the package is over, you will conclude the story with a live on-camera close.

Your opening standup must answer the question: Where am I and why am I here? You must establish:

- your location;
- what is going on;
- a transition to your video, including a roll cue.

Your *roll cue* is a series of words that will tell someone to roll your video package. Sometimes it can be an obvious set-up line, such as, "Let's take a look at the video."

However, you will improve the flow of your story by thinking of your roll cue as the "magic words" or a secret code you have arranged with the control room. The last three words of your live standup should provide a natural transition to the first shot in your video, as in: "When firefighters saw the flames, their first priority was to make sure no one was trapped inside." In this case the roll cue is: "was trapped inside." This line flows into your first video, natsound and images of firefighters searching the burning building.

While we're on the subject of referencing the background, don't feel obligated to turn around and look, as if you are worried that the burned-out house might have moved out of the shot. Focus on your communication with the audience by taking to the camera and make sure the shot is framed and lit so they can see what's behind you. The only reason to turn around is to point out something specific or to interact with the environment. If it is a spectacular picture, walk out of the shot and give the audience an unobstructed view.

Your standup close must provide a resolution to the story. Or, to put it another way, make sure you have communicated the most important point the viewer should take away from the story. Try to add an interesting fact or comment, or preview what is likely to happen next. Follow your style guide for your sign off. Some outlets want you to state your name, your news organization and your location. Others prefer a more conversational toss back to the studio. Stay involved with the conversation until you get the cue that you are no longer on camera. Discuss, but don't rehearse, a possible question and answer exchange with the studio. You want to be prepared, but you also want your answer to be spontaneous and reflect your genuine understanding of the story.

Observe the two-sentence rule

Live opens and closes work best when they are focused. Follow the rule of "two sentences in, two sentences out." Beginners can get into trouble by rambling on about information that we will be able to see for ourselves in the video.

Again, consider the example of our live reporter at the house fire, who will need only two sentences to establish: location, what is happening, and transition to the video with a roll cue: "The burned-out house you can see behind me was once a family's home. And when firefighters saw the flames, their first priority was to make sure no one was trapped inside."

After we have seen the package documenting the work of the firefighters and the heroic action of the neighbor, the reporter will, again, need only two sentences to bring a resolution to the story: "Investigators will be out here first thing in the morning to try and determine what caused the fire. The people who escaped the flames will begin the longer and more difficult process of starting over. Paul Wang, Channel 3 News, reporting live in Pleasant City."

The first sentence of the live close should flow naturally from the final shot or sound bite in the package. With practice, you will find that you can generally get the job done in two sentences, even if you are gesturing or referring to something that is going on in the background.

The live standup without video

If you have just arrived on the scene, but haven't had time to shoot, edit or feed video, you may need to establish your presence with a live standup. Organize your thoughts in terms of crisis, conflict and the anticipated resolution. Relate to what is happening around you and share your impressions with the audience. If necessary, step out of the shot to allow the user to see what is going on. Keep it short and focused. If you don't have all the facts yet, let the viewer know you are working to get more information for later reports.

The live voiceover

If there is not enough time to produce a full package, you may be providing live narration of raw or edited video. In this case, you will open your live shot with two sentences on camera, ending the second sentence with your roll cue. Then, continue narrating to explain what the viewer is seeing. When the video is over, conclude your live report with a two-sentence close. If you are throwing to a SOT, say your roll cue, pause while the sound is rolling, and know the out cue of the bite, which is your cue to begin your two-sentence close.

Using a script or notes

The two-sentence rule makes it unnecessary to read from a script in most live situations. If you are holding a microphone in one hand and a notepad in the other hand, you won't be free to animate your delivery with natural gestures. Avoid waving your notepad at the audience. It's much better to use that free hand for gestures or a prop that has something to do with the story. If you can't write and remember two sentences, you might wish to try another line of work!

Some reporters prepare for live shots by writing down their entire script, becoming familiar with it, and then putting it aside. Others simply note the concept they are trying to convey in each sentence and work from a mental outline. Your delivery will seem less natural if you are reading from a piece of paper or reciting something you have memorized. If you are doing a complicated live voiceover or toss to SOT with multiple roll cues, you may wish to refer to your notes. It's okay to break eye contact once in a while, but try to look down and read from your notes only while the video is rolling and you are not on camera. With practice, you will develop a system that works for you.

Live coverage of breaking news

When you are on the scene of breaking news, you may be involved in open-ended coverage, where you are expected to provide as much live reporting as possible from the scene. Use all of the resources available to deliver a memorable story of crisis and conflict, even when the resolution is not yet known. Refer to what is happening around you and conduct interviews if participants are nearby. This is a true test of your storytelling skills. You will need to observe all of the rules for accuracy, fairness, and attribution while giving your audience the feeling of being there. If you remain calm and focused on your role as a journalist, no matter what is happening on the scene, you will achieve a power performance.

Review: Check-list for Live Segments

- *Crisis, Conflict, Resolution*: Organize your live shot with a beginning, middle and end. Tell me a story.
- *The two sentence rule*: Keep your live shot focused and concise.
- *Open*: Where am I and why? Then set up the tape with your roll cue.
- *Close*: Add value with an interesting comment or fact, preview what happens next. Sign off in the style required by your news organization.
- *Natural delivery*: Have a mental outline of the main points of your script, as well as your roll cues. Don't recite something you have memorized or ramble on. React naturally to the toss and any questions you are asked.
- *Hands free*: Work with a clip-on microphone whenever possible. You will communicate most powerfully when your hands are free to gesture in support of what you are saying.
- *Demonstrating*: Engage the viewer, either with props or some kind of show-and-tell. Interact with the people, objects and events around you. Step out of the shot when necessary to give the audience a better look at what's happening. If you must turn around and point, make sure you are gesturing toward something specific, don't just wave or nod at the background.

Telling vs. selling: teases are different

You may be asked to do a live or recorded "tease" for your story. Tease writing differs from other story formats because it does NOT tell the whole story. A tease should include only the information that will compel someone to watch:

- Include WIIFM. Don't tease: "Why gasoline prices are at an all-time high." Better: "Find out what's causing those high gas prices and the one simple thing you can do to save money at the pump."

- Appeal to a wide audience. Don't write: "If you play video games, stay tuned." This excludes all the viewers who don't play video games. Better: "Why police say a popular video game is teaching kids to break the law."
- Don't give away the ending. Don't tease: "We'll tell you how everyone got out safely. Better: "Find out what one neighbor did that made the difference between life and death."
- Don't sensationalize or withhold crucial information. Don't tease: "Something in your refrigerator could kill your kids." Better: "There's a recall of spoiled meat that was sold in local stores. Find out what to look for to make sure your family's food is safe."
- Avoid stating the obvious. Don't tease: "We'll have the forecast." So what? It's your job to provide a weather forecast every day. Better: "We'll look at the radar to show you when the storm will get here and when it might start raining in your neighborhood."
- Don't tease: "I'll have the story." Again, a reporter should always have a story. Tease what is special about *this* story that will make someone want to stick around through the commercials, or click and watch.

Like a lead, a tease is a promise that you make to the viewer. Be sure you can deliver what you have promised. Don't tease that you'll reveal the reason for the higher gas prices, or when it will start raining, if you have no idea.

Just Do It

While it may seem like there are a lot of rules for effective video storytelling, you can learn only so much from a book. Research a story idea, grab your gear, and get out there. You will make some mistakes as part of the learning curve. Your first package probably won't win any prizes, but that's okay as long as the next one is better. Give your best effort on every story, whether it's a simple VO or a complicated live shot. With practice, your power performance will have an impact on the air and on the web.

Multimedia Exercises

Video

1. Identify story forms within a TV or web newscast. Watch a local or national news program and make a list of the various story forms that are used.
2. Watch a news story package on TV or on the web, then break it down. Make a list of the shots that are used. Time the length of the narration and the sound bites.
3. Shoot a video sequence of a person doing something.
4. Write a 20-second reader. How does it differ from a print story when the copy is intended to be read out loud?
5. Set up a mock news conference in your classroom and demonstrate how to shoot a proper sequence of the event.

6. Take turns doing one-on-one interviews. Get the subject to speak in sound bites, and don't forget to shoot the set-up shots and cutaways.
7. Assign students to shoot an MOS on the topic of their choice, or a question chosen by the class.
8. Shoot, write and edit:
   1. a VO
   2. a VO SOT
   3. a VO/SOT/VO
   4. a package

Role-playing

1. Act out what might happen if a reporter is trying to shoot pictures in an area where the camera is not welcome.
2. Act out the exchange that might happen when a reporter calls a public relations person to request an interview or video opportunity. Then reverse the situation so that the public relations person is pitching an interview or video opportunity to a reporter.

Analyzing live shots

1. Watch a local or national news program that includes live reports. How often do the reporters observe the two sentence rule? Include crisis, conflict, resolution? WIIFM?
2. View TV coverage of a news story, then search for similar video content on the web. What are the similarities and differences?

Works Cited and Further Reading

Frank N. Magid Associates, Inc. "Magid media futures 2009: opportunities in online video," Metacafe, June 2009. Web. 23 Feb. 2010. Retrieved from: http://www.magid.com/metacafe.pdf. Summary of findings on frequency of online viewing and user preferences across multiple demographic groups.

Nielsenwire. "Time spent viewing video online up 49%," The Nielsen Company, 15 June 2009. Web. 11 Nov. 2009. Retrieved from: http://blog.nielsen.com/nielsenwire/online_mobile/time-spent-viewing-video-online-up-49-percent/.

Nielsenwire. "Total online video streams up 41% from last year," The Nielsen Company, 15 Sept. 2009. Web. 11 Nov. 2009. Retrieved from: http://blog.nielsen.com/nielsenwire/online_mobile/total-online-video-streams-up-41-from-last-year/.

Pew Center for Civic Journalism. A *Journalist's Toolbox*. Video.

Pew Research Center for the People and the Press. "Internet gains on television as public's main news source," *The Pew Charitable Trusts*, 4 Jan. 2011. Web. 14 Jan. 2011. Retrieved from: http://people-press.org/reports/pdf/689.pdf.

RTDNA webinar, "Video free for all," Retrieved from: www.rtdna.org, Nov. 4, 2009.

Tyndall report. "More networks putting video reporting online." Retrieved from: http://www.broadcastingcable.com/article/315675-Cover_Story_Network_News_One_Click_Away.php.

COURTESY JOE LITTLE

JOE LITTLE
KGTV-TV San Diego

Job: Reporter, fill-in anchor
Market: San Diego, CA
Hometown: Chula Vista, CA
Education: George Mason University, BA in Speech Communication, 1998; Syracuse University, MA in Broadcast
Journalism, 1999
Career Path:
Internships: Sports intern, WUSA-TV, Washington, DC
GMU-TV, production and hosting intern, Fairfax, VA
Sports intern, WIXT-TV, Syracuse, NY
Reporter/anchor, WHAG-TV, Hagerstown, MD
Producer/reporter/anchor, WWCP/WATM-TV, Johnstown, PA
Writer/reporter, KNSD-TV, San Diego, CA
News Director/anchor, Adelphia Headline News, Carlsbad, CA
Reporter/fill-in anchor, KGTV-TV, San Diego, CA

What is the best career advice you ever got?
All of us former jocks went to Syracuse hoping to be the next Bob Costas or Dan Patrick. One of my professors,
Hub Brown, said anyone could read stats and highlights, but if I truly wanted to separate myself from the pack, (I
should) learn to tell stories first. I immediately focused on news and never turned back. However, I was a Sports
Director for six months and have filled in on the sports desk at KGTV.

Most memorable story.
Easy: 9/11. I was *there*. Not in New York or at the Pentagon. I was four miles from Shanksville, Pennsylvania, when
United Flight 93 went down. My photog and I were one of the first crews on the scene. I walked all the way up
to that hole in the field. I spent the rest of the week out there.

Reporters become accustomed to death and tragedy in our everyday work, but in this case there was no sign
of the devastation. The plane went in at such an extreme angle that it literally buried itself in the ground. The
biggest piece of wreckage was no bigger than a suitcase.

You can go your entire career and never cover a story that will change history. I've heard the old salty dogs (veteran reporters) talk about the JFK assassination or Pearl Harbor, events that change the nation. I was there on the front line, I was part of it. Very early on, we were getting the 9-1-1 calls, passengers saying we're going to storm the cockpit and take the plane back. People forget that was our only victory that day. We won when the passengers fought back and made that sacrifice, and that was one of the things I reported that night.

You started out working with a photographer in a small market, and ended up being a one-man band in a larger market. How did that come about?

At George Mason University they had a very strong television production program. I learned everything I could behind the scenes and learned the on-air stuff at Syracuse. By the time I graduated, I was totally prepared to be a one-man band. In Pennsylvania, I was in charge of a bureau with several counties to cover and we had two sets of gear. I would go in one direction; my photographer would go in the other so we could cover two stories at the same time. We'd meet back at the office and I would write and we would edit.

My wife landed a job in San Diego and I moved there with nothing. The only job I could find was as an associate producer at the NBC affiliate. The news director didn't see me as a reporter, but I did everything, keeping my skills fresh. I left there to go to a very small cable outfit. It was a small, rookie crew and I did a lot of teaching. I shot my own stories, shot for other people and ran the station as a teaching operation for the interns and the young reporters we had on staff. Again, I was keeping my skills up. When KGTV went to the one-man-band system I was one of the first people they hired. It was the perfect opening for me.

My wife and I started a video production business, shooting wedding videos and other visions of other people's happiness. I purchased Final Cut Pro, got a basic lesson for 30 minutes and then taught myself how to use non-linear editing. When KGTV came along, I was able to integrate what I had taught myself into my everyday grind of putting news stories together. They wanted a guy who could do it quickly and creatively, and that was me.

Thousands of people have viewed your standups on YouTube. Does your creative approach work for hard news as well as features?

Not one of those standups is from a feature story; they are all "A" Block (hard news) stories, creatively told. We work under a beat system. I'm the South Bay reporter and I'm also the water reporter, with record-level drought conditions in California. Even in a serious story, it's never okay to just stand in front of the camera and talk. That's terrible television. It's a visual form of communication. If it's not visual, why waste those 10 seconds of television time and the 10 or 15 minutes it took you to set the camera up? Why waste 10 seconds of a viewer's life with just your face? If I'm going to do a standup, I make it informative, active and visual.

When I'm interviewing someone, I would much rather slap a microphone on them and have them continue doing whatever it is they are doing while they talk to me, while I'm rolling. You can tell me the story and entertain the viewers' eyeballs at the same time. As an example, grab a firefighter, have him stand in front of a fire truck and do an interview. Then do the interview again while he's cleaning his fire hoses. What video is better? It drives me up the wall when I see network reporters, with four or five man crews, just standing there talking. As a viewer, that's 5 seconds of my life I want back.

What are the biggest challenges you face in the field?

First, you have to maintain a level of creativity. There's always a way to make a shot or a standup better. Then there is the physical aspect. The simple reality is that you have to wear clothes that look good, and you're lugging a camera, a tripod and a microphone in 90 degree temperatures. You can't stand in the shade while the photographer shoots. I'm sweating my butt off, and then I have to wipe off my face and do a live shot. And finally there's the time pressure. You have to plan your day so far ahead. If the show starts at 5.00 p.m., and your story hits at 5.01, you have to backtrack and figure that you need half an hour to write the script and an hour to edit, so you have to make sure you are done shooting interviews by 3.30. I have to plan ahead, knowing that I have to shoot my interviews, my b-roll, write my story, edit my story, and then get myself ready for the live shot or the studio.

How has multimedia technology affected your job?

I get in at 8 a.m., go to the 9 o'clock meeting, then find out my assignment, whether it's something I've pitched or something that was assigned. Then you go out as soon as possible and start shooting as quickly as possible. When you're working as a one-man crew you're expected to do at least a package, and maybe a smaller package for a later show, and web text for the internet by 3 o'clock. Then I file my scripts and packages for the 5, 6 and 7 o'clock shows and a VO/SOT for the 11. When I have new information, I call our dot-com guys and they "tweet" it for me.

Do you think the "one-man band" approach to story coverage made possible by multimedia tools and backpack journalism has improved journalism or "set it back"?

Honestly, I would say it has set back television journalism a step or two, only because people aren't used to it yet. But our industry has been through this before, when crews went from a producer, audio operator, photographer, editor, and reporter to only a photog and reporter. You would have thought the industry was going to fall into a black hole and we were all going to die. Well, we lived through that disastrous change. And we'll live through this one as well. Give it a few years. The shooting will get better. So will the editing. We have too many dinosaurs – and they will stay dinosaurs unless they get on board – who are fighting this change. One-man bands have set back the industry temporarily, but we're the ones who will be working in the future.

Do you have any tips for journalists from the traditional print side of journalism who want or need to "do it all" for another platform, including shooting their own video and standups?

Go get your own gear and play around with it. Access to equipment has never been easier or cheaper. Get a camera, buy a laptop and learn the basics of editing. Then watch the local news. See what they shoot and how they shoot it. Then go out and mimic it. It's amazing what you can teach yourself. Then, go talk to a few photogs or editors. I've never met a photog who won't give a few minutes to teach me a few things. It will take you a few months before you feel comfortable and not like a buffoon.

What is your advice to people entering the rapidly changing profession of multimedia journalism?

Learn everything. Don't focus on newspaper reporting, or radio performance, or video production, or your anchor voice. News organizations are not going to pay for a photog and a reporter when they can hire one person to do both jobs. Dailies, radio stations, magazines, and TV stations are all downsizing. The more hats you can wear, the more valuable you'll be to an employer.

JESSICA YELLIN

TV Reporter, CNN

Job: National political correspondent
Market: international, based in Washington, DC
Hometown: Los Angeles, CA
Education: Harvard University, AB political science
Career Path:

Freelance writer, Los Angeles, CA
Magazine section editor, *Los Angeles Magazine*
Reporter, *George Magazine*, Los Angeles, CA
Reporter, Central Florida News 13, Orlando, FL
Reporter, WTVT-TV, Tampa, FL
Overnight anchor, correspondent, MSNBC
White House correspondent, *ABC News*
Capitol Hill correspondent, CNN

Why did you become a journalist after studying political science at Harvard?
I thought reporting was not for me. I had zero journalism in my background. I wanted to be in politics and then I decided that I could actually do more good by watching the politicians than by being one. I did enough research to figure out I would have to pay my dues in local markets and work my way up to get to be a Washington TV reporter.

On working as a one-person band in Orlando, FL.
I remember the first day I got to Orlando. I didn't know anyone. They brought out a cameraman and they showed me how to white balance, how to focus, how to set it up on the tripod. And they warned me about blue video. I had no idea what they were talking about. You want me to shoot things that are blue? I was panicked that this blue video thing would happen to me. They also made me do a live shot. It was terrifying, but you survive and you know you can do it again.

It taught me more than I could ever have learned in any course. It is the most hands-on training in every aspect of news you could ever get. In many ways it was also my favorite job in this business. First of all, when it's done, it's really your product. Along the way you feel this enormous sense of challenge and accomplishment when you get something done. It teaches you to appreciate what a camera person does and how difficult it is. You learn how to write to video as you're going through the day. So now in my current role I still think as if I were a photojournalist. You learn how to craft stories differently because you are thinking of video and sound the whole day. It's just this exhilarating experience of really being self-reliant.

How did you make the transition from print journalist to broadcasting?
It's a very different beast because you have to speak in simpler, more declarative sentences. You have to pay attention to the differences in the medium and it doesn't occur to print people all the time. You either get it or you don't. TV is a craft, just like writing a (print) story is a craft. Because it just looks like a bunch of people talking, it's deceptive. You learn the difference on the job and there's no better training. The hardest thing is to watch yourself. After the week is over, grab the tapes, take a look at them and cringe. You can't do it "day of," but with a week's distance or two weeks, you go back and look at what works and what doesn't work and you figure it out for the next time. You have to ask for input and criticism. I would ask the cameramen to give me feedback. The biggest thing you lose while one-man-banding is the second set of eyes.

This is a visual business, especially for women. How did you handle the aspect of the job that required you to look your best on camera?
I was in Orlando, where there is no breeze and 100 percent humidity. You went out and did your thing in full makeup, got your video, and before the standup you got back in the car, turned on the air conditioning, put the vents directly on your face, let the makeup slide back into place, and then ran out and got the standup over with as quickly as possible because if you didn't get it done within five minutes you'd be drenched again. I had my share of people who would look at my tape when I was ready to move on to the next job, and they'd say things like, "Your reporting is great, your storytelling I really like, but your hair is a little fluffy." People only judge based on what they see on the tape and that was an exceptional challenge. It's definitely more difficult for women than for men to do the one-man band thing, also because the camera is heavy. But you feel an enormous sense of independence when you can get it done.

Was it difficult to shoot your own standups?
I had my days when everything was in perfect focus and the sound was great and the standup made sense, but all you saw was from my neck to my waist. Another day, when I tried to correct that, it was so wide you couldn't see me. Trial and error, right? Learn from your mistakes. My biggest frustration was to figure out what the content of the standup should be. During interviews, you are spending a lot of time thinking about the framing and if they've moved, and in my mind I wished I could go back and listen to every interview because I wasn't focused entirely on content. And then it's hard to think of your script during the day. You feel like you want to shoot and get the technical stuff out of the way, and then go back and do the script part, but you can't afford to do that. The standup was always challenging, to stop and say, what will my script be like and where does the standup go? I always did a bridge, so I had to figure out what's the turn in the piece. When I got a camera person, I was so liberated, the job was a dream. I could just think about the piece all day, about my standup. In an interview I'd hear the sound bite and write it down. The biggest plus of one-man banding is that every other job you have after that is so easy.

You worked alone for a year before being promoted to morning anchor and working with a camera person. How does this background help you in your current job covering politics, where many of the stories are not very visual?

People who have never shot video don't have the reflexive, instinctive sense that I need to think about what I'm covering this with. As I'm thinking about my script all day long and listening for sound and info, I'm constantly thinking, how am I going to cover this? When you're in Congress and you have to tell a story that is somewhat dry and conceptual, I talk to the camera person and tell what I'm thinking an hour before we edit. And he might do some tight shots of people's moving feet to show the flurry of activity in the halls. Or if it's really confusing, spin around slowly and get a circular view of a room at the capital, or some other way to show the chaos. I'm in dialog with the cameraman early because I'm thinking that way. Editors say they like editing my pieces because I write to the video.

Do you see a day when all network journalists will be one-man bands?

We already have VJs (video-journalists) and multiplatform producers. I think there will be a lot more asking people to do everything at once. On the other hand, I think people have learned that you can't do that for your entire network format. Too often the network as a whole would end up missing video.

Most memorable stories.

I was one-man-banding at a funeral in Orlando. An entire family had been murdered. One of the suspects was invited. In the middle of the service, the entire church got into a brawl. And I was standing on the balcony shooting it and I was thinking, "Do I flee or do I shoot?" I got the video of the scene, which was so bizarre for so many reasons. I was so proud of myself. I was alone in places that were unfamiliar to me. It always felt like a stretch. I was always pushing myself. When you're one-man-banding, you get a level of intimacy with your subjects that I've never ever had in other settings. There's an intensity that comes from that one-man-band experience.

The other memorable story was when I was in Tallahassee to cover a 2000 Florida Senate race. The morning after the election they woke me up at 6 am and they said, "There's something funny going on at the Secretary of State's office, would you mind going over there?" Within four hours, every hero I'd ever idolized on television was walking through the room. I ended up covering the recount (which ended with George W. Bush being elected president) for 35 days. That was memorable.

How has multimedia technology affected your job?

I follow people on Twitter because it's a good source of reported information. Senators twitter, so you find things out that way. At CNN we use a ton of new technology like the electronic wall on the set. I think that as long as it doesn't take the place of good reporting, it can enhance the experience, because it gets people to pay attention. You can't just use bells and whistles. People will figure it out. They know what feels shallow. I found there's an incredible interest in always using new technology because it gets people engaged. Congress is not the most exciting natural TV story, but there are ways to make a budget process more interesting by using technology.

During the 2008 election you were the first news reporter to appear as a hologram. What went through your mind?

I was excited. First of all, I just think that the hologram was a once-in-a-lifetime experience. When they showed me the room, I was so blown away by the technology that I wanted to be part of it. Part of TV and what we do is fun, there's a sense of playfulness you can have about it. And then there's a place for serious news. It's okay for both to exist. It took a lot of practice and rehearsal. We had a good time, and there was a huge team of people working on it, it felt like a team project. It would make me sad if, after all the dues I've paid, after all the hard work I did, all the humidity I suffered through in Florida, if that was all I was ever known for. I love that it's part of my résumé. It was just fun.

What's your advice to people who want to be multimedia journalists?
It's still an exciting career. You can really make a difference. It's great to start local. It's fabulous to start one-man-banding as soon as you can. Get the experience and move on. Be as flexible and adaptable as possible. There will always be a need for journalism. The people who adapt are the ones who will do well.

5

Presenting the Story on Camera, on Air and Online

Beyond finding, writing, and posting your story across media platforms, as a multimedia storyteller you may find yourself feeling totally unprepared to *present* that story on-camera. If your background is primarily in print or text media, you may not have spent much time developing your presentation skills for broadcast or web audio/video. Those accustomed to web casting or appearing on television already may feel more comfortable with visual storytelling. But multimedia demands that you fully develop these skills. Here's why: the techniques you will learn in this chapter apply not only to TV and computer screens, but also to presenting yourself on small, portable mobile communication devices. The technology may be different, but you increase your credibility with any audience by looking and sounding confident, no matter which media platform is employed.

First, let's admit that for most people, this is an area that can create a lot of anxiety. Telling stories in front of a camera can be intimidating, especially for the beginner. You wonder if the viewers will like you, or more importantly, if they will believe you. You may be insecure about the way you look or the sound of your voice. Or you may be unaware that there are aspects of your performance that can distract the viewer, interfering with his or her understanding of your story. In this chapter you will learn to identify your strengths and target the areas for improvement in the most important presentation skills: time management, voice quality, script preparation, face/body movement and appearance.

Driving the Story

Think back to the first time you rode a bicycle or drove a car. You weren't sure if you could successfully travel from point A to point B without crashing. Eventually, with training and experience, you became an expert navigator, certain to reach your destination and feeling confident enough to bend the rules now and then. Your efficient driving

Power Performance: Multimedia Storytelling for Journalism and Public Relations, First Edition. Tony Silvia and Terry Anzur.

performance is based on preparation. For example, if you aren't sure where you are going, you look up the address and find it on a map or use a Global Positioning System. You know the rules of the road and are prepared to follow them. You have a plan: back out of the driveway, turn right, turn left, stop at the traffic light, turn right again, find a parking space and stop. No one wants to be behind the driver who is lost or too timid to step on the gas. Someone weaving through traffic lanes can be downright scary – or even deadly. This is a useful analogy for on-camera storytellers, because after you have identified and gathered the story, you are responsible for *driving* the story, following the rules of the road for effective delivery. We will now give you these rules for successful onscreen delivery.

Rule #1: Time Management Is Part of Your Power Performance

For every story assignment, you should have some idea of the deadlines you are facing. In a typical day, a reporter might face different deadlines for various multimedia platforms, appearing as the top story on the evening newscast while blogging, networking or posting on the web whenever there is a new development. In the news business, this is called "making slot," and woe to the journalist who fails. Online media, like the traditional wire services, operate on the principle of "a deadline every minute," and disorganized journalists risk being scooped by a competitor. A broadcast reporter who isn't ready for his or her designated slot in a newscast can send the entire program crashing down in a domino effect; the next reporters in line have to be ready earlier than they were expecting, and if everyone is procrastinating, the anchor of the broadcast may have to ad-lib or throw to a commercial to fill the time. The consequences of throwing an entire news program off track can be severe, up to and including termination. Hence the newsroom adage, "Make your slot – or rot." The same is true on the web. Breaking a story like the death of Michael Jackson brought tremendous traffic to the web site TMZ.com. Everyone else came in second.

Managing this time pressure requires planning. Going back to our driving analogy, you start out by mentally calculating how long it will take you to reach your destination. You anticipate traffic tie-ups or roadblocks you might encounter along the way, or where you might have to pull over and check the map. You plan to arrive safely and with plenty of time to freshen up when you get there. As you plan your storytelling, allow for the time you need to gather facts, interviews and pictures, screen the video, select the quotes or sound bites, and write. You may need time to record a voice track before editing your finished product. You may need to confer with your supervisor for script approval. And finally, you need time to present *yourself* as a credible source of information.

The rest of this chapter contains valuable tips on improving your voice, your delivery and your appearance. Be sure you allow yourself enough time to put these techniques into practice. Get in the habit of meeting deadlines without fail and being at your location early, so that you will be prepared to make your slot and drive your story. If you believe you cannot make your deadline, let your colleagues know as soon as possible. It is better to be on time with your best possible effort than to be one second late with total perfection that may never be seen by anyone.

Rule #2: Develop a Multimedia Voice that is Casual, Comfortable and Connected

Voice quality

In the early days of broadcasting, the airwaves were dominated by men with deep, baritone voices. This was a technical necessity due to the limitations of early audio equipment. However, as audio quality improved, it didn't clear the air of discrimination against women, whose voices were perceived as being less credible. Pauline Frederick, a pioneering NBC radio correspondent in the 1950s, recalled being told by one male executive, "Listeners are going to tune out because a woman's voice does not carry authority." Civil rights legislation prompted broadcasters to put more women on the air in the 1960s, but it took much longer to erase the perception that a woman needed to sound like a man to be believable. When Judy Muller was hired to do radio commentary for CBS in the 1980s, she received a back-handed compliment from *60 Minutes* correspondent Mike Wallace, who called her "the woman with balls in her voice."

The emergence of mixed gender and multi-ethnic news teams led to a more relaxed approach to local and cable TV news which has been called "enlarged conversation," but it was dismissed by some critics as "happy talk." Although voice quality remains important for both men and women in multimedia, acceptable voices have come to reflect the diversity of the viewing audience and the changing role of the storyteller:

- *Traditional media voice*: the announcer can be compared to the voice of God, announcing the news from on high; he talks, you listen.
- *The multimedia voice*: the speaker engages the audience, with a specific intention to inform, entertain, or persuade, and always with the goal of inviting the viewer/listener/user to respond in some way.

The traditional "old media" voice, when heard in multimedia, is often presented as a parody of credible speech. A slick, commercial voiceover may be perceived by the audience as a sales pitch, not a news story. Instead, audiences have come to prefer voices that sound *real*, like a friend they would meet for a conversation over a cup of coffee. We all have different physical characteristics, making each human voice a unique instrument. Trying to artificially lower your voice to sound like a stereotype of an announcer is likely to make you sound forced and fake. Voice experts Dave Cupp and Ann S. Utterback have described the desired sound as "casual, comfortable and connected." They write, "What is needed is a new style that breaks out of the traditional format of evening news programs and provides both the immediacy and the casualness that are the hallmarks of the Internet."

Rule #3: Make the Most of the Voice that You Have through Awareness Training

Fixing voice problems

Imagine that you are driving on a remote country road, and you are listening to your favorite song on a radio station. As you drive even farther away from the city, the signal begins to fade, until there is so much static that you decide to change the station or turn the radio off. Even though you like the music, it is too difficult to listen. Improving your multimedia voice means eliminating the static so that your audience can enjoy listening to your entire story and become motivated to respond.

Some problems, like a stutter or a lisp, may require the attention of a professional speech therapist. However, some of broadcasting's most notable stars, such as NBC anchorman Tom Brokaw or ABC interviewer Barbara Walters, were able to connect with vast audiences despite audible flaws in their speech. Most beginners can make significant improvements in voice quality through basic awareness training.

Awareness training #1: Breath capacity and control

You've probably been advised to "breathe from your diaphragm," with little or no idea of where it is or how to do that. This exercise will help:

1. Stand or sit with your back straight and feet firmly planted on the floor. Place your hands on your abdomen. Take two deep breaths, in through the nose and out through the mouth.
2. On the third breath, as you inhale, push out your stomach and think of it as a bag that you want to fill up with air. Continue breathing in and out, filling the bag more with each breath. Your hands will now be over your "poochy" or protruding stomach.
3. Count out loud and slowly release the air in your stomach, pushing in gently with your hands. See how high you can count before you run out of air. If you're a sports fan and you want to have a little fun, have someone time you with a stopwatch as you say the word, "G-o-a-a-l!" like a soccer announcer. You should be able to count out loud to 60 or sustain your breath while making sound for about 30 seconds.
4. Notice how much deeper and richer you sound when your focus is on the "poochy" stomach. That is because you are now speaking – and pushing the air out – from your diaphragm. Awareness of this type of breathing is especially helpful for beginners who have been speaking from their chest, throat or nose.
5. If you have difficulty with this exercise, evaluate your overall fitness level. A regular program of aerobic exercise can help you build breath capacity. And if you smoke, quit.

Rule #4: Relax, Breathe and Speak from Your "Poochy" Stomach

Don't worry about how your "poochy" stomach will look on camera. The viewers should be engaged with your eyes and facial expression. If they're looking at your tummy, it's probably not a very compelling story. When anchoring, your stomach is often hidden behind a desk. When you are tracking audio only, no one can see your "pooch" but they will definitely notice if you sound nasal and whiny, or out of breath. Once you have mastered this breathing technique, you will no longer need to place your hands on your abdomen, and you will be free to use them to add appropriate gestures to your presentation. You are also free to breathe normally as you read the copy, as there is no need to sustain each breath for 30 seconds. Later on, we'll discuss the importance of proper punctuation to guide your breathing.

Before your performance, allow yourself time to take a few deep, cleansing breaths from your "poochy" stomach. Never slide into position at the last minute because you will sound unprepared and your voice will have a higher pitch or a nervous, breathy quality. Be relaxed and ready.

Rule #5: Check Your Posture to Clear Your Airway and Place Your Feet Firmly on the Floor

Awareness training #2: Posture

In order to use your breath efficiently, you must have a clear airway. If you are seated, your back must be straight. Don't cut off the flow of air by hunching forward. Place your feet firmly on the floor. If you have elevated your chair because you have a tall co-anchor, ask for an "apple box" or a small crate to be placed under your feet. You'll notice immediately that your voice is more secure when your feet are not swinging. Find the posture that is most comfortable and allows you to breathe efficiently. Two options shown in Figures 5.1 a and 5.1 b are:

- Seated upright with your back resting against the back of the chair; or
- Seated on the edge of the chair while hinging forward *slightly* from the hips with one foot placed slightly in front of the other. This is called the "starting block" position because it mimics a runner preparing to leap out of the starting block. You want to give the impression of being ready to leap out of the screen, but don't overdo it. Leaning too far forward can interfere with the lighting and create shadows on your face.

Some people sound better when they announce while standing up. Again, make sure that your back is straight, and your chest is lifted, and you are speaking from the "poochy" stomach. If you are on camera, you should place one foot slightly in front of the other to slightly angle your body, so you won't look like you are posing for a police mug shot. Even

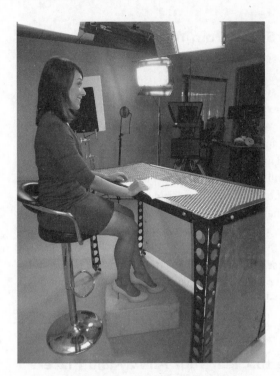

Figure 5.1 (a) Proper posture at desk, using apple box 1, with back resting against the back of the chair

Figure 5.1 (b) Proper posture at desk, using apple box 2, leaning forward slightly in the "starting block" position

Figure 5.2 Proper posture when standing to record a voice track

if you are tracking audio only, don't neglect your posture. You will sound better if you are standing or sitting up straight with your feet planted firmly on the floor and your head and chest lifted. Hold your script up in front of your face or place it on a stand to avoid hunching over to read the copy (Figure 5.2). Don't be shy about moving or adjusting the microphone for correct posture.

Rule #6: Talk as if You Are Speaking to Someone Who is Only Ten Inches from Your Face

Awareness training #3: Volume

Avoid shouting into the microphone. This is the #1 problem that interferes with the "conversational" sound you want to achieve. Imagine that you are face to face with an extremely attractive or interesting person, and you are a mere 10 inches apart. Would you shout? Of course not! When you are telling a story, the microphone is generally less than 10 inches away from your mouth, so adjust your volume accordingly. It is better to be too soft than too loud. You or the audio operator can always boost your volume level. If you are shouting, there isn't much that can be done to prevent distortion.

Common problems and how to solve them

- *Problem*: The camera is farther away than usual.
- *Solution*: Don't shout at the camera. The microphone is still only a few inches away from your mouth.
- *Problem*: There is a lot of background noise, such as music, wind, a crowd or machinery.

- *Solution*: Hold the microphone closer to your mouth and speak in a normal tone of voice. In this situation it is better to use a hand-held microphone than a clip-on. If necessary, use a wind screen, a little sponge that fits over the microphone. Try to have the competing noise turned off.
- *Problem*: You are appearing with someone who has a louder voice.
- *Solution*: This is frequently a concern for women paired with men. Don't feel the need to compete in the volume department. Speak in your normal tone of voice and allow the adjustment to be made in your audio levels.
- *Problem*: You sound "off mike."
- *Solution*: Pay attention to microphone placement. If you appearing with someone, make sure the clip-on mic is on the side closest to your partner. If you are using a hand-held mic, keep it the same distance away from your mouth as you move around. If you are interviewing someone, move the mic back and forth as you take turns speaking.
- *Problem*: You are "popping" your p's.
- *Solution*: When recording audio only, experiment with speaking into the microphone at a slight angle or using a pop filter screen. If you are still popping, reduce the amount of air you are releasing with each "p" sound and relax your lips, making it closer to a "b" sound, and make sure you are not shouting. Practice by using the phrase "big pig," and softening the "p" in pig until it no longer pops.

Rule #7: Allow Time for a Sound Check

Allow time for your sound check. Use headphones if you are recording your own voiceover off camera. Watch an audio-level meter to make sure you are not peaking into the "red" zone. In the field, make sure your camera person is wearing headphones, and if you are working alone, use headphones to check the level before you appear on camera. If you are recording, play it back and use headphones to check the sound quality.

When you are asked for a level check in the studio, don't throw away an opportunity to rehearse for your power performance. Say the first line or two of your script, exactly as you plan to perform it when you get your cue. Counting to ten or telling a joke may result in a very different voice level that won't match your actual performance. Also remember to check the sound level in your earpiece, if you are wearing one in the studio or in the field. If the program feed is too loud or if someone in the control room is shouting in your ear, you will be tempted to shout back.

Rule #8: Speak in a Way that Can Be Understood by Your Intended Audience

Awareness training #4: Accents and dialects

The Standard American dialect, most often associated with broadcast announcers from the Midwestern states, is the most frequently heard and widely accepted form of spoken English for news programs in the United States. But your speech reflects the language you heard and used while growing up. You might use words and phrases that are common in Texas, but wouldn't be understood in Massachusetts. You may also stress words and syllables differently than someone from another region. Your speech may reflect whether you come from an urban environment or a rural area. If English is your second language, you may be speaking it with the accent of your native tongue. Do you need to change your speech patterns to be a successful multimedia storyteller? Well, yes and no.

Despite regional differences, most Americans can understand one another, as well as people from other English-speaking countries like Canada, Britain, South Africa and Australia. But there are great differences in how we perceive various dialects in terms of race, class or level of education. You may hear someone with a Southern US accent and think of your folksy neighbor from down the street. A proper British accent may be associated with a higher level of education and worldly experience. Voice coach Lillian Glass cites a 1931 British study in which listeners were able to correctly guess a person's level of education and socioeconomic status based on their speech patterns. Your reaction to a speaker from Europe, Africa, Asia or Latin America may depend on how people from those areas are perceived in your community.

In countries where the dominant language has different levels of formality and many informal local dialects, officials may require a certain speech pattern for announcers on state-run mass media. CCTV news announcers in China, for example, are required to speak only standard Mandarin. In any culture, it is always wise to learn correct grammar and standard pronunciation in order to be understood and accepted as a credible source by the widest possible audience in your chosen language. Some people have a natural ability to switch back and forth, using the local speech pattern when among friends but switching to the more formal "announcer" speech when reporting a story. Americans who grew up speaking a hybrid like "Spanglish" may need to make an effort to bring both their English and their Spanish to the level expected of professional journalists in either language. Getting rid of an accent or dialect completely is a complex process that does not always end in success. But here's the good news: In the multimedia world, the only "wrong" dialect or accent is one that cannot be understood by your intended listeners.

Depending on your subject matter, an accent or dialect can be an advantage. A country twang in a report on NASCAR racing or an urban flavor to a web cast about rap music may actually enhance your credibility with the target audience. A distinctive speech pattern can become part of your personal brand. For example, moviegoers around the world instantly recognize the Austrian accent of action hero-turned-politician Arnold Schwarzenegger. But specialized programming can limit your options. If listeners associate your down-home dialect with light features, they might find you less credible on a serious story from a war zone.

Rule #9: Warm Up Your Mouth, Lips and Tongue

You should move your mouth and lips to enunciate every word of your script, and every audible letter in each word.

Awareness training #5: Enunciation

Many Americans have lazy lips when it comes to pronouncing the letters "d," "t," and "ing" during informal speech. Before your actual performance, you need to warm up your mouth, lips and tongue for a serious workout. Utterback recommends repeating short tongue-twisters like "put a cup," "hot and cold," or "fat lazy cat." You can also improve your performance by rehearsing your actual script out loud while exaggerating the movement of your mouth. Identify the words that are likely to create a stumbling block.

Be conscious of moving your lips during this exercise: Say the phrase "I'm (name) and here are the stories making news." Open your mouth to properly pronounce the contraction for "I am" as "ime," not "uhm." Instead of saying "nooz," articulate the "ew" sound in the word "news," which involves an extra effort at moving your mouth. Make sure you are not mumbling your name. If you are learning a second language, you may already have realized that you move your lips more distinctly when you are not sure you are being understood. Move your mouth just as much when speaking your first language.

Rule #10: Take Care of Your Voice and Your Hearing

Voice care

Maintain a pleasant, healthy-sounding voice by following these guidelines:

- To keep your throat moist, have water available nearby during your performance and drink plenty of water as part of your daily routine.
- Try not to eat while you are on live or recording, and except for water, avoid eating or drinking anything 15 minutes prior to your performance.
- Make sure to eat something earlier in your shift to keep up your energy level.
- Avoid dairy products just prior to announcing, as well as any food or drink that will create mucus and force you to strain your voice by repeatedly clearing your throat.
- If you must clear your throat, try drinking water instead.
- Avoid situations such as noisy crowds or loud music where you must shout to be heard, putting extra strain on your voice.
- If you use the same cup daily on the set, in the office or in the field, make sure to wash it frequently with hot water and disinfecting soap to avoid brewing a cup of germs that can infect your throat.
- A cold or flu can block your airway, so control germs by frequently washing your hands and wiping off your computer keyboard and desk area with a disinfectant.
- If you have a cold or a sore throat, don't shout to compensate for laryngitis and don't whisper to "save" your voice – shut up and rest until your voice is healthy again.

- See a doctor if you experience chronic hoarseness or a persistent sore throat, which can be signs of a more serious problem.
- Avoid the obvious: smoking, drugs and alcohol.

Protecting your hearing

While we're on the subject of health, you should also take steps to protect your hearing.

You may have been warned about the possible ear damage that can result from cranking up the sound in your ear buds or headphones when listening to music. Broadcasters and web casters often wear an earpiece called an IFB, which stands for internal fold-back. It enables you to hear the other voices in the program, as well as instructions from your crew. Although you should take the time to check the sound level in your ear, occasional loud bursts of sound are unavoidable. Repeated exposure can lead to a persistent ringing in the ears called tinnitus, and eventually, hearing loss.

If you spend extended periods of time anchoring or going live from the field, you should invest in a custom earpiece. Mail-order kits are available, but the best practice is to have a custom impression made at a hearing aid store. "A custom fit will direct the sound into the ear more efficiently and cause less irritation in the ear canal," says hearing expert Dr. Cindy Beyer of HearUSA. You should also clean your earpiece regularly to remove wax and prevent ear infections.

Rule #11: Mark Your Script to Identify Potential Problems Before Your Performance

Prepare your script

The best on-camera storytellers make it look easy. But there's more to power performance than just memorizing your lines or reading from an electronic prompter. The script is the roadmap you will use to drive the story. You need to check for speed bumps before you step on the gas. Good writing is the foundation of a power performance. You must start from a well-written and properly marked script. You also must develop the skill of interpreting your copy, even when you did not write it yourself and you are interpreting words written by others.

Here are some techniques you can try:

1. Cut down long sentences. Short sentences with active verbs will enliven your presentation. Long, newspaper-style sentences are hard to read out loud because they are weighted down with dependent clauses. When a sentence is too long, you are forced to suck in a big breath and race to the next period without interpreting the power and meaning of the words. Stick to the rule of "one thought per sentence." If the sentence has more than 20 words, it's usually best to chop it in half.
2. Decide what you will emphasize, mark your script and make changes to make it your own. Go through each story with the goal of isolating the *one* thing you most

want the audience to retain. What is the new element of a continuing story or the most important fact of a breaking news event? Plan how you will use your delivery to call attention to it. Then go through each sentence to figure out which *one* word or phrase is the most important. Be selective. Punching fewer words will help you avoid a sing-song delivery and sound more conversational.

3. Try a change of pace or pitch. Identify the parts of the story that are background. That's where you can speed up because it's old information. You are literally bringing the listener up to speed. Plan to pause or slow down to call attention to signal what is new, surprising or significant. Selectively raising or lowering your pitch can call attention to a particular word or phrase.

4. Read out loud. You may get a few strange looks in the newsroom as you prepare by reading your story out loud to your computer screen. But isn't it better to find the stumbling blocks before you trip over your tongue at the microphone? Rewrite to eliminate any tongue-twisters, or be prepared to slow down, enunciate and get it right.

5. Empower yourself to change the copy if it makes you stumble, but check with the original author, or your editor, to make sure you have not altered the facts.

6. Check pronunciation. Identify the tricky names in your copy and give yourself time to consult a source like the Associated Press pronunciation guide. For local names, make a phone call or ask someone else who has covered the story if you are not sure. This is especially important if you are new in town and need to learn the local language quirks, like why Houston (How-ston) Street in New York is not pronounced the same way as the city in Texas (Hew-ston), or the difference between Rodeo (Ro-DAY-oh) Drive and Rodeo (ROH-dee-oh) Road in Los Angeles.

By the time you record your script or deliver it live, you should feel a sense of ownership. Listeners can tell the difference between a storyteller who "owns" the story and someone who is "just reading."

Rule #12: Obey Punctuation Traffic Signals for Inflection, Pauses and Breathing

Obey the punctuation signs when you are driving the story. Lazy writers often use three dots as a substitute for actual punctuation. This is like driving around town when every light is a flashing yellow. Think of the punctuation marks as your traffic signals:

- A comma is a slight tap on the brakes.
- A period is a full stop.
- Three dots signal a slight pause … for effect.

Avoid the beginner mistake of ending a declarative sentence on an upward inflection, which sounds like a question mark. You are informing or reassuring the audience, not asking for their permission to tell the facts of your story. What if there is an actual question in your script? Inflect upward at the end of the interrogative sentence and then pause slightly to allow the audience to anticipate the answer that follows.

Punctuation also signals when to take a breath. Writing short sentences and breaking up long sentences will increase your opportunities to take a natural sip of air, just as you do in normal conversation.

Rule #13: Establish Your Emotional Connection to the Story on the Best–Worst Scale

In a multimedia world where any development can be reduced to less than 140-words on twitter.com, messages can range from "World Trade Center attacked" to "I'm eating a sandwich right now." But each of those simple messages touches off a different reaction on the receiving end. The challenge is to adjust your power performance to the anticipated emotional reaction of your audience. Failing to adjust your delivery to match the impact of the story is the #2 problem that interferes with achieving a truly conversational sound.

Try to mentally rate each story on the best–worst scale (Figure 5.3). This technique was developed for actors but is also useful for on-camera storytellers. Think of the best thing that could possibly happen: you win the lottery, for example, and achieve all your dreams of making the world a better place. Now picture the worst that could happen: a holocaust in which the entire planet is wiped out. In between are all the shades of gray that define the human condition. In the middle of the scale is a "neutral" story. In the words of the old TV police drama, *Dragnet*, the neutral story calls for you to deliver "just the facts." Few stories, however, are totally neutral and you will need to adjust your delivery slightly toward either the best or worst end of the scale. Remember, we need conflict to make our stories interesting, and conflict carries emotional baggage for your intended audience.

A story can slide back and forth on the scale as we move from crisis to conflict to resolution. For example, a family faces a crisis after losing everything in a disaster, one of the worst things that can happen to anyone. Then, there is conflict as the disaster victims struggle to get on with their lives. Finally, we learn of the resolution as the community steps forward with donations to help resolve the problems, one of the best possible reminders of the basic decency and resilience of human nature. Your delivery of the story should reflect this progression.

Journalistic storytelling is different from acting. You don't need to "act" sad when relating the tragic details of an event. However, you wouldn't smile while reporting on war deaths. Conversely, when you are reporting something that stirs up your own deep feelings,

I_____	I_____	I
Best	Neutral	Worst
(You win the lottery,	<<<<(Most stories)>>>>	(The end of civilization
world peace is achieved.)		as we know it.)

Figure 5.3   The best–worst scale

look for appropriate opportunities to connect to the audience. Media lore is filled with such memorable moments, like CBS News announcer Walter Cronkite removing his glasses and seeming to hold back a tear at the death of President Kennedy, or saying, "Go, baby, go!" with heartfelt excitement as the 1969 Apollo 11 mission launched the spacecraft that would be the first to land human beings on the moon. Many California residents identified with the local anchorman who ducked under the desk when the studio lights began to sway during an earthquake.

The only wrong reaction is one that is not genuine, such as the incident in the film *Broadcast News* in which the reporter played by William Hurt fakes a tear during a staged shot after an interview. The multimedia audience will quickly spot someone who is acting or faking it. Even when the reaction is genuine, it may be better to keep your composure. It is also the role of the professional journalist to remain calm and reassuring during any situation that he or she is covering and to react only when it is appropriate to do so. Keep it real and let the audience decide for itself how to feel about the story. Avoid comments like, "A tragic story today from Afghanistan …" All war deaths are tragic and the audience doesn't need to be told. Your delivery, however, should reflect your understanding of the situation.

Rule #14: Keep Up the Pace and Slow Down Only for Emphasis

Reading speed

Step on the gas. Be ready to accelerate as you drive the story with confidence. Talking or reading too slowly gives the impression that you are talking down to the audience. Worse, you can put the listeners to sleep with a monotone or sing-song pattern. Don't worry about going too fast. The *Guinness Book of World Records* clocked John Moschitta, the world's fastest talker, at 586 words per minute. For most of us, about 200 words per minute is the maximum talking speed. Research into time-compressed speech, cited in the web *Encyclopedia of Educational Technology* at San Diego State University, has shown that people can easily comprehend 300 words per minute. However, that speed requires compressing the speech electronically so that the speaker does not sound like a cartoon chipmunk. It would be physically impossible for most of us to achieve that pace naturally without tripping over our tongues.

For beginners, if it seems too fast, it's probably the right speed. Terry Anzur Coaching Services uses this exercise to find your perfect pace:

1. Read a paragraph of copy out loud, into a voice recorder at the speed that seems natural for you. Save this recording.
2. Read the same copy again, as fast as you can. Don't worry if you stumble over a word, just keep going. Save this recording.
3. Compare the two recordings. You are likely to find that the first one sounds a little dull, and while the faster version may contain a few stumbles, it is much more lively and easier to follow.

4. Read the same copy again, keeping up your energy level, but easing back slightly from your "fast" read to the point where you are not stumbling over the words. This is your ideal reading speed for multimedia storytelling.

As previously discussed, you have marked your script to anticipate the places where you will pause or slow down to emphasize what is new, or the important information you want the audience to retain. Researchers in the field of artificially compressed speech for accelerated learning have noted that the selective use of silence, or pauses, increases comprehension.

Rule #15: Include a Prompter Check as Part of Your Preparation

There is a saying among television news anchors: "Those who live by the prompter, die by the prompter." Even if your performance will be delivered on the web, the saying holds true; the prompter is only a reminder of what you were going to say.

A prompter, or autocue, is any kind of device at eye-level that will display your script a few lines at a time, in front of or near the camera, as you read it. Some early TV news anchors used hand-lettered cue cards in order to read while maintaining some eye contact with the camera. This evolved into a conveyor-belt system that allowed the image of a paper script to be projected in front of the camera lens. The word TelePrompTer, was the original trade name by the company that first developed the device in the 1950s, but it has come to refer to numerous updated versions, including programs that can be run from a personal computer.

The prompter is only a machine, which can break down. It is operated by human beings, who can lose their place in the script, leaving you stranded in front of your audience. Prepare your script as if, at any moment, your teleprompter could explode and your script could catch on fire. You should "own" your copy to the point of being able to improvise your way through it without the prompter or the script. Do not get in the habit of simply reciting every word that appears before your eyes. The on-camera storyteller is the last chance to catch a mistake in the script before it reaches the audience. Every word should pass through your brain before emerging from your mouth.

Ideally, you will have a crew member who can operate your teleprompter. However, it has become increasingly common for on-camera storytellers to control their own prompter using a foot pedal or hand control. Tying down one hand to the prompter control limits your ability to animate your delivery with appropriate gestures and may make you seem stiff. Operating the prompter may also distract you from concentrating on the finer points of your delivery. Anyone who can read can operate a prompter, so if there is a willing and qualified person nearby and there are no union work rules to prevent it, ask him or her to help. News organizations with limited budgets may consider having a desk assistant or receptionist work part-time as a prompter operator. Some two-anchor teams have managed to work the prompter for each other. Otherwise, you will have to work on becoming comfortable with the prompter controls and make the best of it.

A prompter screen will usually display three to five lines at a time and the screen will scroll upward. Make sure the line you are reading is the first or second line from the top. This will improve your eye line straight ahead to the camera so you don't appear to be looking down your nose at the audience to read the lowest line on the screen. In addition, this will give you a chance for a split-second preview of the next few lines. This may not seem like much time, but in some situations it's all you need to catch a mistake and fix it "on the fly" before you deliver it to your audience.

Include a prompter check as part of your preparation. As with your sound check, rehearse by reading a bit of the actual copy. It's a chance to make sure you are comfortable with the controls, or to ask your prompter operator to adjust the scrolling speed. Scrolling too fast will cause you to stumble as you struggle to keep up, while scrolling too slowly will make you sound uncertain and dull. You also need to make sure that there is the proper amount of space between you and the prompter screen. There are two major problems:

1. *Prompter too close*: This creates a "fish-eye" effect as you move your eyes back and forth to read each line of the copy. It will make you seem shifty and not believable.
2. *Prompter too far away*: This creates a "squint-eye" effect, as you strain to read each line of the copy. This will prevent your from relaxing your eyes and establishing a true connection with your audience.

Look at recordings of your on-camera performances to see if you have fish-eyes or squint-eyes, and adjust the prompter distance accordingly. With time and practice, you will learn your optimum prompter distance in most studio or field situations. Don't be shy about asking the camera operator to move in or back up. If working alone, make the adjustment yourself.

Rule #16: Use Your Script Properly to Enhance Your Performance

Even if you are reading from a teleprompter or autocue, you should also have the paper copy of the script that you marked as part of your preparation for your performance. If you are seated at a desk, coordinate your script with the prompter copy you are reading. If the prompter fails for any reason, you should be able to glance down and immediately pick up the story. Again, this is something that takes practice.

Pay attention to how you are turning the pages. Do not pick up the page with a flourish and turn it over. The paper noise may interfere with your audio, and the sight of the turning page can distract the audience from your story. If you are right-handed, grasp the right edge of the page and pull it off to the side, without turning it over. Slide the next page on top of the first one, until you are finished with a pile of your script pages in reverse order, face up.

If there is no teleprompter, you will have to read from the script. Punctuation becomes more important here, because the natural breaks for breathing are also the places where it will be natural for you to look down and refer to the copy. It is also natural for you to look down and read information that is highly specific or technical, including numbers or lists. Some reporters routinely refer to the script for this type of information, even when there is a teleprompter, to add credibility and provide a natural break in eye contact, which we will discuss in more detail later.

Finally, there are times when you have to read "cold" copy that you have not prepared. The intimacy of multimedia makes it okay to let your audience in on the fact that they – along with you – are getting brand new information for the first time. You might even want to reference the paper as you explain that the story is "just in to our newsroom." It's okay to slow down and read the copy with the unspoken intention of "let's discover this together."

Rule #17: Develop a Consistent Voice that is Part of Your Personal Brand

With experience, you will become comfortable with your voice and delivery, and so will the audience. Beginners often lack consistency. They may sound lively and animated when talking in front of a camera, but when recording a voice track in the studio, may feel the need to adopt the "voice of God." Nerves may heighten your pitch when you are going live, but you sound calm when you are recording in the studio. As your voice becomes part of your personal brand, you should sound like the same person every time and in any situation, reassuring and informing the audience while you present yourself as a credible storyteller in any medium.

Rule #18: Make a Good First Impression on the Viewer through Non-Verbal Communication

People form impressions quickly in the multimedia world. And, as the saying goes, "You never get a second chance to make a first impression." Roger Ailes, the Fox News Channel president who has developed many multimedia stars, states in his book *You Are the Message* that an instinctive relationship is being formed in the first seven seconds of any human interaction. Ailes goes on to say that "the 'magic bullet' of personal communications is the quality of being likable." Power performance means developing the qualities that will make you appear likeable to the audience, even when you are delivering "bad" news.

TV news consultant Kenn Venit says that in focus group research, viewers are likely to spend more time watching a news presenter they perceive to be likeable, and to watch that presenter more often. A storyteller's use of conversational language and inclusive pronouns such as the editorial "we" or speaking directly to the viewer as "you" also enhanced likeability. Venit believes the principles of likeability, frequency and duration translate across media platforms to the concept of "stickiness" on the web. "There's nothing more compelling than a 'talking head' telling me something I need to know," he says. "I don't think the ability to communicate has changed because of the size of the screen. The ideal, in any medium, is to create a vicarious, buffered, emotional experience."

Table 5.1   The Three Vs

Three Vs	Cues	% of first impression
Verbal	The words you are saying	7
Vocal	How you say them	38
Visual	Your body language	55

According to studies of face-to-face communication by UCLA researcher Albert Mehrabian, the audience may take up to four minutes to fully form a first impression, using cues that have come to be known as the Three Vs (Table 5.1).

Notice that under the 7–38–55 rule, your actual words account for only 7 percent of how you are perceived, with the visual impression – by far – the most important factor at 55 percent. The two non-verbal factors account for about 93 percent of your first impression. Additional research also showed that if there is a conflicting message, the audience will tend to believe your body language more than your words. While these studies have their limitations, the message for multimedia storytellers is clear: your audience is likely to judge you by your delivery, appearance and body language before you say a word.

Now that we've addressed your voice and delivery issues, we move on to the basic techniques for improving your body language, gestures, facial expressions, eye contact and appearance. However, it should be clear from the outset that these qualities are intended to enhance your effectiveness as an on-camera communicator, and not as a substitute for the basics of sound writing and solid reporting.

Rule #19: Use Your Body Language Aggressively

In order to hold the attention of your audience, you must claim your space in front of the camera. You must project the image of being open to the audience, and direct the flow of the program to the elements that are most important. A common beginner mistake may stem from your natural instinct to be a polite guest, folding your hands on the desk or table in front of you with shoulders rounded forward in a "tucked in" position (Figure 5.4 a). This may be appropriate in a classroom or in a house of worship, where you are acknowledging the superior position of a teacher, a cleric or a higher power. Experts in corporate behavior have noticed that women are more likely to sit down at a conference table "tucked in," with their materials piled neatly in front of them. Men are more likely to adopt a power position by sprawling out and claiming their space, but were more likely to push back from the table or cross their legs, which can be interpreted as signs of resistance.

In power performance for multimedia storytelling, you are in charge of the screen, whether it's a television, a digital window or a mobile device. You don't need to ask anyone's permission to be there. Claim your space by putting your hands on the desk at least shoulder-width apart. You want to remain visually open to the audience, with your shoulders relaxed down and back, your head and chest lifted and your back straight

Figure 5.4 a   Incorrect "tucked-in" anchor position

Figure 5.4 b   Correct "open" anchor position

(Figure 5.4 b). Never fold your arms across the chest, which shuts the audience out. Don't hide one or both hands under the desk, which is a visual cue that you may not be trustworthy. On the other hand it is possible to be too imposing if you seem frozen in the open position, so once you have claimed your space continue to use natural gestures to vary the angle of your shoulders. When standing, avoid the "police mug shot" pose. Placing one foot in front of the other will angle your shoulders slightly and seem less threatening to the audience.

Throughout your performance, you should turn your body aggressively in the direction of your focus. For example, if you are interviewing a guest, you might begin with a short introduction focusing your body forward to the camera, and then introduce the guest while turning your entire body focus toward the person. Only turning your head may send the message that you are not really interested in what the person has to say. When storytelling requires you to hold up an object, point to something or walk to a different part of the scene, make sure your body language tells the audience where to focus. Your movements should be comfortable and deliberate, giving your viewers the feeling that you are directing the flow of the program, and experiencing the content along with them.

Body focus is especially important in a highly visual presentation such as a weather or traffic report. The storyteller's body language should anticipate the graphics, focusing body direction on the appropriate part of the map and anticipating the movement of graphics across the screen. Your information will seem less believable if it looks like you are reacting with jerky movements to whatever pops up. Think of a person in the water; you want to be the confident Olympian swimming toward a gold medal with strong, deliberate strokes, not flailing about like a drowning person in need of rescue. You should give the impression that you are controlling the graphics, instead of the graphics controlling you.

Because body language is so powerful, be selective. A common mistake for beginning weather presenters is to wave and nod at every temperature on the map. Don't worry; most viewers are capable of reading the temperature for the town where they live. You will be much more effective if you select what is important on the map, such as a record-setting temperature or an approaching front, and then turn your body toward that feature as you point to it. Try to point to only ONE thing in each graphic. Don't stand in front of any important information. Build your graphics so that there is a place for you to stand on one side. Step off camera for a moment and get out of the way if the viewer needs to see the entire screen. Avoid crossing the screen, giving the impression that you are pacing back and forth, unless there is an important reason to do so. Successful weather presenters spend at least 80 percent of their time standing on their mark and looking into the camera, only turning around and pointing to the map for the most significant elements, or stepping out of the way to let the viewer see the big picture.

Rule #20: Use Natural Gestures to Enliven Your On-Camera Delivery

In the multimedia world, your storytelling performance may be seen on a giant HD screen or a tiny mobile device that fits in the palm of your hand. For a movie actor on the big theatrical screen, a raised eyebrow in a close-up can seem like a huge movement. In a wide shot on a small digital window it would hardly be noticed. It is important to adjust your performance to the platform where you will be seen.

As a general rule, you have more freedom to gesture than you think. You need to break through the barrier that technology can create between you and the audience. Terry Anzur Coaching Services uses this exercise to illustrate the point:

1. Frame yourself on camera in a tight shot that shows only your head and neck.
2. Record your performance as you read 30 seconds of copy while flapping your arms up and down like a giant bird.

3. Watch the performance and notice that this extreme movement of your arms is not visible to the audience, but the act of flapping your arms has undoubtedly animated your face.

You should now feel comfortable using normal gestures when you are in front of the camera. If you normally "talk with your hands" in conversation, there's no need to hold back. Keeping your hands low and out of camera range will animate your face. Look for ways to add selective emphasis with your on-camera gestures. For example, you might hold up your right hand when giving one party's position on a controversial issue, then gesture with the left hand while giving the opposing point of view. If reading a list of three or four items, you might count them off on your fingers. Even when you are not on camera, don't forget the power of gestures to animate your voice. Feel free to move your hands naturally when you are recording a voice track.

Gestures become more powerful when you allow your hands to invade the zone in front of or near your face. You may wish to hold up your thumb and index finger if you are making a point about new nanotechnology that is incredibly small. Or gesture with an outstretched index finger when you are stressing the "one thing" that is important in the story. Or, smack your fist into your opposite palm if you're emphasizing the force of a crash.

Rule #21: Visualize the Content of Each Story and Allow Your Facial Expression to Naturally Reflect It

Think of a crowded sports bar or coffee house. A monitor is on in the corner of the room. The news is on, but the sound cannot be heard. Yet, there is something about the storyteller that is so compelling that you want everyone to be quiet so you can hear. Chances are that the storyteller is making effective use of facial expression. Watching yourself with the sound turned off is a good way to evaluate your own use of this powerful communication tool.

Earlier, we discussed rating each story on the best–worst scale to animate your vocal delivery. Now, apply the same technique to your facial expression. Smiling in a story about the newborn baby animal at the zoo will also help you connect with the emotion the audience is feeling. On the other hand, the recovery of a body at a crime scene would call for an entirely different reaction. Again, this is not acting. Try this exercise:

1. Seated in front of a camera, read one hard news story and one light story and record both performances.
2. As you read each story, visualize the scene in your mind.
3. Watch the performances with the sound off. You should be able to tell the difference between the cute animal story and the crime scene.

Let your reactions happen naturally. Avoid the common beginner mistake of bobbing your head for emphasis. You don't want to look like the bobble head toy in the back window of a car. Tilting your head to the side can be misinterpreted as flirting or teasing. Try this exercise: read 30 seconds of copy while balancing a book on your head, allowing only your facial expressions to do the work. If the book falls off, you need to break the head-bobbing habit. The only "wrong" facial expression is one that is forced or suppressed. If you are smiling during a serious story, you will damage your credibility, but if it's a story that genuinely makes you smile, let it shine.

Rule #22: Maintain Eye Contact with the Viewer

Watch any on-camera story teller and put your hands up to the screen to cover up everything but the person's eyes. Are the lights on? Is somebody home? Or is the eye expression more like a disinterested stare? If you are not communicating your interest in the story through your eyes, the audience will have an incentive to click away.

Look for natural places to break eye contact. Remember, the intimacy of multimedia means that your face may be much "closer" to the viewer than it would be in normal conversation. You'd be uncomfortable talking to a person who stared at you. Find natural breaks between stories and within stories to look down and consult the script. According to consultant Kenn Venit, research on newscasters' eye contact has shown that a 90/10 ratio is best. He advises breaking eye contact only about 10 percent of the time you are on camera.

While multimedia storytelling may ultimately be seen by countless people, you are always communicating with one person at a time. Eye contact is a powerful signal that you are interested in them. This is especially important in interactive media, where you are prompting the user not only to listen, but to respond. Even if you are reading a teleprompter, you need to make eye contact with the viewer through the camera. It may help you to visualize your best friend or a loved one, or talk to the person operating the camera. Visualizing your audience as one person is also a good way to calm your fears about appearing before a giant, unseen audience.

Rule #23: Viewers Should Notice the Person, not the Hair, Clothing or Makeup

On-screen appearance

Fortunately, you don't need supermodel looks to succeed as an on-camera storyteller. However, you need to understand the three basic factors that can dramatically affect your on-camera appearance: lighting, shading and cosmetic factors such as makeup and hairstyle. These three factors are interconnected; for example, no amount of makeup can compensate for truly awful lighting or shading, while heavenly lighting and perfect camera settings can't disguise a distracting hairstyle. Trying to fix the problems can be daunting if the camera operator blames the lighting technician, and the lighting expert tells you to change your makeup. Only when all three elements are working well together, do you achieve your best on-camera appearance (Figure 5.5).

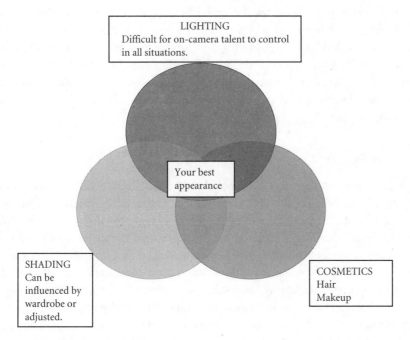

LIGHTING
Difficult for on-camera talent to control in all situations.

Your best appearance

SHADING
Can be influenced by wardrobe or adjusted.

COSMETICS
Hair
Makeup

Figure 5.5   Your best appearance

Lighting

Recording a pleasing image on video requires light. In the early days of television, studio lighting was uncomfortably blinding and hot. In his history of early broadcasts, *Please Stand By*, Michael Ritchie describes the temperature extremes in a Chicago studio in 1943. Announcer Hugh Downs was greeted by technicians in hooded parkas as he prepared to read the news in a dark studio that felt more like a meat freezer. Just before airtime, the female producer removed her parka, revealing shorts and a halter top, and advised Downs to remove his jacket. When the lights came on, Downs felt a "sheer withering force of light," and was soaked with sweat in less than ten minutes.

Technical improvements made it possible to turn down the intensity of the lighting. Today, studios often employ lighting professionals to provide a flattering glow for the talent, especially in High Definition where every detail is visible. Therefore, it is virtually impossible for you to make any changes in the pre-set studio lighting grid. You should be aware of your "mark," the place at the desk or on the studio floor where the lighting is focused. Place an actual mark on the spot if necessary, putting a small piece of tape on the edge of the desk facing your belly button, or taping a small X on the floor.

If you are web casting from a makeshift studio, make sure that your face is well lit. Avoid lighting that makes the background brighter than your face.

In the field, you have more control over the lighting. Bring a simple lighting kit, with light stands, and allow extra time to set up lights at the location. Don't rely on the tiny battery-powered light that may be mounted on top of the camera unless you are in a situation where there is no electrical power, you are on the move or trying for a special effect. Avoid "backlighting," in which the light source is coming from behind you and reducing you to a dark silhouette. During daylight, try to select a camera position that will make natural use of sunlight on your face, often eliminating the need for a light kit. If it is high noon, and the light is directly overhead, use a reflector or a fill-light to eliminate shadows. This added light may cause you to blink, so carry saline solution to moisten your eyes and do your best to get used to it.

Camera shading

Today's camera technology makes it possible to shoot high quality images with little knowledge of the technical specifics. Cameras can automatically adjust for white balance and exposure. A skilled camera operator may prefer to make manual adjustments. Without going into details, the important point for the on-camera storyteller is awareness of how the dominant colors in wardrobe, skin, hair color and background affect the image.

Extremes of black and white as the dominant color in your wardrobe can affect the way the camera captures your features and skin tones. Wearing a bright white shirt or jacket will cause the camera lens to "iris down" to compensate for the brightness, making your features darker and less distinct. This is rarely flattering to people of color, and is also a poor choice for light-skinned presenters who may be trying to camouflage wrinkles and other flaws by artificially darkening their features. On the other hand, wearing all black will cause the camera to "iris up" to compensate for the darker image, creating an over-lit or washed-out effect on your hair and skin tone. It is best to stick to solid, bold colors for your on-camera wardrobe, and avoid solid black, solid white or light pastels, which can appear white under video lighting. Use the extremes only as accent colors; for example, a crisp white or pastel shirt under a navy or gray jacket.

In the field, choose your background wisely. Again, standing in front of a backdrop that is overwhelmingly white or black can affect exposure and cause the camera to overly lighten or darken your features. Be prepared to adjust the camera, compensate with lighting, or move the shot to a different background. Make sure your clothing contrasts with the background so you don't blend in. If your set has a sky-blue background, don't wear the same shade of blue. If you are appearing in a virtual set or in front of graphics that are electronically projected on a solid color screen called a "chroma key," wearing the same color as the screen will cause you to disappear.

Cosmetics: hair and makeup

The 1960 presidential campaign debate between Richard Nixon and John F. Kennedy marked the beginning of the television era in American politics. Those who listened to the debate on radio may have judged Nixon to be the superior speaker, while those who watched on TV perceived Kennedy to be the winner because of his more polished appearance, including makeup – which Nixon declined. Flash forward to 2008, when the US presidential campaign put powerful women such as Hillary Rodham Clinton and Sarah Palin in the spotlight. To win votes, politicians in most cultures seek to present an image of confidence and power. As a multimedia journalist, you are campaigning to win an audience that votes continuously with a click of the remote or the mouse.

Some journalists may be uncomfortable learning about makeup techniques, on-camera hairstyles and wardrobe guidelines. But in a multimedia world, your audience expects to see you. Print, radio and web site reporters may be required to appear in video versions of their stories, or give on-camera interviews, as discussed in Chapter 3. Even if you do your most brilliant work while blogging in your pajamas, you eventually have to get ready for your on-camera close-up. Here are some basic tips to make sure your appearance doesn't distract the audience from the important story you are telling.

The rules for men

√ To maximize your credibility in the studio and in most field situations involving government-related or other hard news, wear standard, international business attire: dark suit or jacket, white shirt and a bold-color "power" tie.

√ Only one item should have a pattern or stripe. If you are wearing a striped tie, make sure you have a solid-color shirt.

√ Ties should not have more than three colors; avoid distracting patterns.

√ Lighter colored jackets, and solid shirts that are not white, are okay for variety.

√ If you think you may have to take your jacket off, avoid a solid white shirt. Remove pens and other gadgets from your breast pocket.

√ Keep in mind that khaki or gray pants with a navy blazer are considered "casual" in the business environment.

√ Avoid tiny patterns such as tweed or herringbone that can create a moray or "rainbow" effect on camera; stick to solids or subtle pinstripes.

√ Make sure your clothing fits you well and get alterations if necessary. Pay special attention to the fit of your collar and shoulder seams.

√ When seated, smooth down the back of your jacket and sit on it if necessary to make sure it does not ride up or look bunchy.

√ Button your jacket and make sure your tie is not peeking through the gap below the buttons.

√ Makeup should even skin tone, cover blemishes and eliminate shine. Keep a powder compact handy for touchups, especially if you perspire in the sun or under studio lights.

√ Keep hair trimmed (every 3–4 weeks) to avoid a shaggy look.

√ Be sure to shave before your appearance so you will not have a beard shadow. Any facial hair, such as a beard or mustache, should be neatly trimmed.

The rules for women

√ To maximize your credibility in the studio and most hard-news situations, stick to a solid-color business suit with a contrasting solid blouse or shell.

√ For knit tops, the same rules apply; solid colors and a V-neckline are most flattering.

√ Choose jackets or tops with long, slimming lines and invest in smooth foundation garments. Avoid anything that looks bunchy or blousy.

√ Avoid prints and patterns; solid, bold colors make you "pop" on camera.

√ Avoid shiny fabrics and leather. Stay away from linen and other fabrics that tend to look wrinkled.

√ Make sure your clothes fit you properly and invest in alterations if necessary.

√ Any jewelry should be non-distracting; avoid anything that is dangling, swinging or chunky.

√ Choose a classic, not trendy, hairstyle that frames your face.

√ Trim hair frequently to keep it neat and out of your eyes.

√ Your haircut should allow the viewer to see your earrings, but do not push your hair behind your ears.

√ In the field, tie your hair back in windy conditions to keep it out of your face.

√ A hijab, if worn, should be in a solid color and smoothly frame the face.

√ Makeup should even your skin tone and define your eyes and lips. Keep powder handy to minimize shine. Avoid "frosted" products and stick to natural colors.

√ Make sure you don't look like a talking wall of hair when turning sideways; the viewers should see your profile.

You should be able to achieve your professional look quickly as part of your preparation time. Get your hair, makeup and wardrobe routine down to 20 minutes or less, and then leave it in the dressing area. Once you are on camera, your main focus should be on the content of your presentation.

Dressing for the story

Obviously, there are exceptions to the wardrobe rules. A multimedia journalist must never look "out of place." You wouldn't wear a business suit to a forest fire, or a t-shirt to a presidential news conference. The emergence of "business casual" as appropriate office attire is changing the standards, but even if you are wearing a golf shirt or a knit top, you must still stick to solid bold colors that look good on camera. The only "wrong" wardrobe for a multimedia storyteller is one that calls attention to itself as inappropriate. As a general rule, it is better to be over-dressed than too informal. You can always remove your jacket and roll up your sleeves, but is difficult to disguise a casual outfit that conveys the impression of disrespect for the story and your audience.

If you are a one-person video crew, you have to be dressed for lugging around your equipment as well as appearing professional when you are on camera. It's always wise to travel with a change of clothing so that you are dressed appropriately for the story and ready to look your best on any assignment.

The double standard

In *Women in TV News Revisited*, Judith Marlane notes that appearance standards can be more demanding of women. She writes: "Viewers are more likely to comment on hairstyle than on story content." She quotes PBS journalist Gwen Ifill as saying, "Part of the deal that you sign with the devil to be on (camera) is that the physical aspects of who you are often override your professional abilities and you just have to find a way to balance that out."

Finding that balance means you should avoid clothing that is perceived as too "sexy" by your intended audience. A study in the *Psychology of Women Quarterly* found that people tend to form a negative impression of women in power when they are dressed provocatively. Researcher Paul Glick concluded that a female manager dressed in a low-cut blouse and tight skirt "elicited less positive emotions, more negative emotions and perceptions of less competence on a subjective rating scale and less intelligence on an objective rating scale."

Various cultures and audiences have different standards for what is "too sexy." A Muslim audience may expect a woman to cover her hair. However, in Los Angeles, it is not unusual to see entertainment reporters in daring attire that seems to fit in with the Hollywood scene.

Where Your Preparation Pays Off

Before your performance, make a last-minute check of your "cockpit," much as a pilot would do a safety check before flying a plane. Check the following:

√ calm and relaxed breathing
√ clear airway
√ audio levels and prompter distance
√ properly marked script
√ open, relaxed body language and gestures
√ non-distracting hair, makeup and wardrobe.

You are now ready to drive the story and connect with the audience. Viewers should immediately form a positive impression of your presentation skills and then concentrate on your story in any media platform.

Works Cited and Further Reading

Ailes, Roger, and Kraushar, Jon. *You Are the Message*. New York: Currency-Doubleday, 1995. Mostly geared toward public speakers, Ailes has adapted the principles in this book to television and other media.

Cupp, Dave, and Utterback, Ann S. "Delivery for the New Media." Utterback Publishing. N.p., July 2009. Web. 14 Aug. 2009. Retrieved from: http://www.utterback

publishing.com. Describes the evolution of the broadcast voice and its adaptation for use in new media.

Glass, Lillian. *Talk to Win: Six Steps to a Successful Vocal Image*. New York: Putnam, 1987. A comprehensive set of exercises to improve your vocal image.

Marlane, Judith. *Women in Television News Revisited*. Austin, TX: University of Texas Press, 1999. A comprehensive series of interviews with prominent women in TV news, including their comments on appearance and voice issues.

Ritchie, Michael. *Please Stand By: A Prehistory of Television.* Woodstock, NY: Overlook, 1994. A comprehensive look back at the early days of television, filled with fascinating pictures and anecdotes.

Shook, Frederick. *Television Field Production and Reporting.* New York: Longman, 1999. Although primarily focused on videography issues, this book includes an excellent chapter on "The Role of Talent Performance in Field Reporting."

Utterback, Ann S. *Broadcast Voice Handbook.* 4th edition. Santa Monica, CA: Bonus Books, 2005. Focusing primarily on the broadcast voice, includes exercises for improving breathing and delivery. Her web site offers regular updates and tips on how to improve your voice for broadcast and multimedia. Retrieved from: http://www.utterbackpublishing.com/voiceupdates.html.

COURTESY CNNMONEY.COM

POPPY HARLOW

CNNMoney.com

Job: Primary host of web site video network and reporter for CNNMoney.com on CNN, CNN International, and Headline News (HLN)

Market: International, based in New York

Hometown Minneapolis, MN

Education Columbia University, BA Political Science, 2005

Career Path:

Internships and part-time work while in college: CBS MarketWatch.com

Assistant producer, CBS Newspath

Anchor-reporter, NY1, covering Staten Island and Northern New Jersey for cable TV

Reporter-producer, Forbes.com video network

Anchor, CNNMoney.com

How did you get started in business news?

I worked at CBS MarketWatch all through college. I started the summer after my freshman year, full-time between the New York, San Francisco and Minneapolis offices. After that they asked me to stay and work part-time during my sophomore year of college in the New York office. Then I worked for them the next summer.

MarketWatch is video on the web, so that's when I started producing video stories for the web. They were really the leaders in video for the web when it comes to business journalism. Also, they had a syndicated weekly (television) show and I helped them produce that as well.

Why did you choose to focus on video for the web, instead of the traditional career path of going to a small market TV station?

It was being there at CBS MarketWatch, because that was video on the web when people weren't doing it as much. I did go to a small market by working for the local edition of New York 1 (NY1) as an anchor and reporter covering Staten Island and a small part of northern New Jersey. I shot and edited all of my own video and I was the assignment editor when I was anchoring. It was totally one-man band.

How did you get your work noticed?

It was luck and persistence. At CBS Newspath they needed someone to go out and cover movie premieres. Of course, I was thrilled. I did these on-the-spot interviews with Sarah Jessica Parker, Matthew McConaughey and all these movie stars. I did it completely on my own time, not being paid, but I was able to build a reel. I didn't want to be an entertainment reporter, but I jumped on the opportunity to practice being on camera and practice doing interviews. With NY1, I sent my tape and no one called me, so I called and got an informational meeting with them. They didn't have any positions right away, and then they needed someone to fill in.

Were you able to advance more quickly because of your web video skills?

It was just the fact that you could do more on the web, you can do longer interviews. In television, normally it's a one and a half minute package or a quick live shot. You can't put up five-minute interviews, but you can do that on the web. Online, you are anchoring at a younger age than you would be on television. You have different opportunities.

Is anchoring on the web different than anchoring for TV?

It's not live. Your videos can be edited. We can cut a ten-minute interview down to five minutes or put the whole thing up. It's different in the fact that it's on demand. If someone turns on the television to "watch" cable news, they can just leave it running in the background while doing errands, taking a shower or getting ready for work. If you're talking about video on the computer, you have to choose to sit down and watch it. You choose to have the screen open to the video rather than minimizing it and listening while you do other things online. You have to make it more enticing for people, I think. There's a remote control for the computer and it's your mouse. In that sense we still face the same challenges as traditional television media.

How do you keep people from clicking out?

You keep asking good questions. You give people a more in-depth look at a story because you have the time to do that.

How important is your appearance?

People are visual. Dress how you want to be taken. You wouldn't go into a business meeting in flip flops, so why would you interview a Fortune 500 CEO wearing something that's not professional?

Are you a web journalist who does television or a television journalist who does the web?

I'm a web journalist who does television, certainly. Whatever medium you are working in, you have to do it all. We have a team of 12 and our producers aren't just writing copy for the anchor and putting elements in graphics and video and sending it to Atlanta. Our producers are going out on their own, traveling across the country, finding stories, shooting the video themselves, coming back, editing it and putting the stories online. It's not ten people putting in to one live hit that's over when it's over. Our producers wouldn't be able to do half of what they do if they couldn't shoot and edit their own video and have a good eye for production.

Did you always want to be a business reporter?

I wasn't a finance or economics major. When you look at CNNMoney.com, they are helpful stories for people, not "inside baseball," derivatives trading and what analysts are saying. It's general news today because the markets and the economy are the top stories.

Most memorable story.

It was a series of stories on Detroit. We went there, interviewed the CEO of General Motors, the head of Ford, and the governor of Michigan. But it was really when we dug deeper and spent time in Detroit, it was an unbelievable story. It's a city right in our own backyard that is dying, in a sense. You look at helping people around the world, but what about Detroit, with 23 percent unemployment and an auto industry that may not be able to stand on its own two feet? You have huge questions about how that city is going to survive. I spent the day with a woman named Fredericka Turner. She took us to her old neighborhood. She talked about the homes that are foreclosed on her block and how she wants to buy one of them and redo it. It's so sad for her to go back to the old neighborhood and see that the school system is rampant with crime to the point that she can't send her own daughter there. It's an amazing city with a lot of stories left to tell.

(Link to the story at: http://money.cnn.com/video/news/2009/08/31/n_detroit_resident_profile.cnnmoney/.)

Most memorable interview.

The Kid Rock interview I did for CNNMoney.com. It's called Kid Rock's Detroit. It's someone you don't expect to be doing so much for his home town. I feel the same way about Brad Anderson, who used to be the CEO of Best Buy, a Minneapolis company from my home town. He's one of the executives who doesn't embody whatsoever the image of corporate greed that Wall Street now holds. He gave away a lot of his stock options to his employees and didn't want anyone to know about it, didn't want to talk about it when I asked about it in the interview.

What's your schedule on a typical day?

6:30am	arrive at work and go to makeup
7:30am	prep for interviews and live hit
9am	CNN international hit (a few times a week – not daily)
9:45am	Disney CEO, Bob Iger, interview
10:30	CNN live hit
11am	Look Ahead taped interview for CNNMoney.com
12:30	CNN live hit
2:10pm	HLN live hit
2:17	CNN live hit
2:30	CNN international live hit
3:45	HLN live hit
4 pm	market wrap hit for CNN Newsource affiliates
4-7pm	Situation Room hits (varies from week to week – not daily)

Prep for interviews coming up tomorrow and work on packages.

How has social media changed your job?

I'm late to the social media game. I didn't have or want a Facebook page until I saw that I should have one to get story ideas and feedback from people. It's been hugely successful. I have a page, http://www.facebook.com/poppyharlow, and I post stories on there. I ask people questions, like when we're doing a story on unemployment benefits running out. We ask people if they have any personal stories to share with us. It's amazing what you can get. Of course, there are the snide remarks, and people joking around. But, all in all, it's useful information.

What's your advice to multimedia journalists?

Be very persistent and think more about what you're going to learn and what you're going to be able to do than about where you are. There's a reason why people come from local (TV) markets, they learn to do everything there. But also look at the growth potential. There are people at CBS or CNN who rise up to be reporters, but you don't see that as much. You see people going places to learn the skills to come back to the network they want to report for. Be persistent about calling. Ask for opportunity. Be willing to work on the weekends, ask if they need someone to go out and shoot. Really mean it. And always be available. At the outset your career should be the most important thing, before you have children, before you're married. I have a better balance now, even though I work 12 hours a day. I love my job.

And the future?

Social media is going to have a bigger impact than we know. It will push journalists further in terms of authenticating information, breaking through the sound, clutter and noise. It's going to be a challenge but it is one that will make us better, I hope.

OWEN J. MICHAEL

KABC-TV

Job: Online news producer for abclocal.go.com/kabc
Market: Los Angeles, CA
Hometown: Chicago, IL
Education: Arizona State University, BA in English Literature, 1998
Career Path:
    Wire editor, *Business Wire*, Los Angeles, CA
    Wire editor, *Market Wire*, Los Angeles, CA
    Copy editor, *Surfer Magazine*, Dana Point, CA
    Online News Producer, KABC-TV

How well did your college education prepare you for the field of multimedia journalism?
I was a journalism major, but at the end of my freshman year I wanted to branch out into magazines and books. I figured that with a degree in English Literature I had more options. I was an unorthodox student. After high school I worked and traveled for a while. I was writing and publishing my own magazine while I was in school, so I never looked into internships.

How did you make the transition from business wire services and *Surfer Magazine* to producing for a TV station web site?
Working for *Surfer Magazine* was a dream job. I'd been reading it since I was 12. I did a lot of copy editing for other magazines published by the Action Sports Group. As far as covering extreme sports, I was in hog heaven. But after a while, I missed the urgency of wire service editing that I had learned at *Business Wire* and *Market Wire*. When the Iraq War started, I wanted to get back to hard news. I made the calculation that if I was going to do online journalism it would be better to do it for a TV station than a newspaper.

How important is the web site at KABC-TV?
I was in the second generation. Before I got there, the web site was just a promotional tool with some wire copy, a few big stories, and a lot of cross-promotion to shows like *Oprah*. They only had two people working on it, and

they had migrated from creative services, not the news department. Starting in 2005, they began to invest more heavily in it, with a new manager and a staff of four covering and updating the news. Now, everything that's on the broadcast is on the web and there's a lot of emphasis on breaking news.

How do you take the content from a broadcast and adapt it for a web page?

It's essential to know how to write and edit copy. You might need to expand a story that was only a VO (voiceover). Television writing is more conversational than it is for print. It doesn't read as well on the page as when the anchor is reading it on the screen. You want to add a few more facts than they have time for in 30 seconds on the show. For an ongoing story, we would link to what we've done in the past several weeks. The Internet is a bottomless pit and we have the space to build the VO up from just a few paragraphs. You try to hire people who have dealt with the state of the art on the Internet, but are also trained in journalism. They need to know AP style, and how to identify the sources for a story. They need to know both "old school" journalism and "new school" social media. Twitter and Facebook are two of the biggest tools we're using now. We have a huge following.

What about putting reporter packages from a TV program on the web?

We start from the anchor introducing the package, then the live shot, package and the toss back to the studio. We'll post the video and we can also post a transcript, but we have to re-work some of the copy to take out visual things like "here on this street" so that it makes more sense in print. We may be able to attach background links or a photo gallery.

But the package itself is the bread and butter of both the station and the site. Just go out there and be a great reporter, but be organized. It's important for reporters to file scripts. It speeds up the process of getting the story online, so it's important to be proficient in using your laptop or mobile device to communicate and clarify the story. The live hit that airs one time on the program lives forever on the web. Your online presence matters.

What's your advice to multimedia journalists?

Be prepared to be an absolute one-man band, from operating the camera to how you look in front of it, and being able to edit and upload your story. You should be able to produce your entire package with no help from anyone else. The one-man band is stronger than ever.

Show that you have an opinion on the ethics of online media. Let's say you have a hot tip that a huge celebrity has just died, but it's only a gossip web site reporting it. Do you tweet it to the world and send out breaking news alerts or do you wait until you have confirmation? Online journalism presents a whole new set of issues and we're still sorting it out.

The most important thing is to be a good writer. You don't have to be a technology wizard. The job is so turn-key now that you don't necessarily have to know html, although it helps.

What is the future of multimedia journalism?

It's hard to see around the corner. We are so close to the point where everyone will be carrying a little information device that can be used for everything. People will be constantly plugged in, having videos fed to their home page. People will be living with your brand, 360 degrees and 24/7. We are just beginning to understand the implications of Twitter for getting the word out about evacuations, traffic closures or breaking news. And there will be a next generation after Twitter; we just don't know what it is yet.

With all this technology, is it still important to be a good storyteller?

I worry that storytelling will get lost in the mix. When you are trying to stock a site, I worry that it could become quantity over quality because you are so focused on getting the bare bones of the news out there. But it's fundamental to know how to tell a story and use a variety of ways to enhance it by offering video, a photograph, a slide show and a bunch of hot links. You have to create a media-rich opportunity, but make sure it doesn't become too distracting. There's no need to add links and pop-ups with every other word. That's very abrasive to the eyeball. We are taking stock of graphic layout and realizing you don't have to put every possible thing on the page. Allow the user to relax and just read the article itself. It's a balance.

6

Practicing Public Relations in a Multimedia World

Think of a famous athlete who has carefully controlled his image throughout his career. Who comes to mind? For nearly all his career, that athlete was Tiger Woods. The golfing icon crafted the public's perception of him as a determined, powerful competitor, but also as someone with strong values and a balanced family life. Of course, that image changed once it was revealed that the best golfer in the world was not perfect and, in fact, had many character flaws. The revelation in 2010 that Woods had been unfaithful in marriage not once, but (at last count) up to sixteen times, caused his "brand" to come unraveled. His story can be seen as the foundation of both good and bad public relations practices in a multimedia world.

The celebrity news web site TMZ broke the story of Woods crashing his SUV late at night, presumably following an argument with his wife related to his infidelity. That was in December, 2009. Tiger Woods' life would never be the same. Until then, he was the consummate public relations machine. "All things Tiger" were disseminated to the media on his terms, in his time, and through his representatives. So tightly controlled was access to Woods that journalists bemoaned the fact that in order to report on him, they had to gain information from the golfer's web site – and pay for a subscription to do so. Even the sports media powerhouse ESPN had to play by Tiger's rules.

What Tiger Woods had been so good at achieving was using technology both to control his message and keep journalists at bay. By regulating how often and how much he wanted to communicate with the public, Woods and his spokespeople ensured that his personal and professional – especially his business interests outside of golf, as in his product endorsements – were protected from the prying eyes of what could at times be a critical news media. For years, it worked, creating a major shift in how sports and entertainment figures, politicians, and the CEOs of large corporations access their audience. And it all began with a simple question.

Power Performance: Multimedia Storytelling for Journalism and Public Relations, First Edition. Tony Silvia and Terry Anzur.
© 2011 Tony Silvia and Terry Anzur. Published 2011 by Blackwell Publishing Ltd.

What is My Message?

In order to write a compelling story, journalists have first to know what that story is about. They need to know its essential elements before attempting to convey it to an audience. For public relations practitioners, the task is the same. PR people, many of whom are former journalists, are, in essence, storytellers. And, like their counterparts in journalism, they are undergoing change – right along with their clients. Tiger Woods isn't the only one who learned from the public exposure of his infidelity; his public relations people learned as well, albeit, some might say, a bit too late. That lesson is centered on some basic principles of PR that take on added urgency in a time when the public has infinite options for gaining information about a public figure or client.

First, know your message and *own* your message. The first is fairly straightforward. Public relations people spend time asking "What story do I want to tell about my company or my client?" Ironically, the most effective public relations storytellers answer this question by looking at the end result of the process – they ask themselves, "How do I want this story to end?" and structure their stories to contain the essential message right from its opening sentence, through its middle and culminating in its ending. Notice that an essential difference between PR practitioners and journalists is the phrase "How do *I want* this story to end?" Where journalistic storytellers follow the facts, effective public relations storytellers lead the story in the direction they want it to go. That means not just knowing your message, but *owning* it.

Owning Your Message

Those who "own" information can tell whatever story they want. Again, Tiger Woods, until 2010, was the perfect example. As CNN put it, "from the time he putted a golf ball at the age of 2 on *The Mike Douglas Show,* Tiger Woods has been a golden child. While athletes in different professions dealt with doping scandals and other controversies, Woods continued to do what he did best: dominate the field of professional golf and rake in endorsements." He – and by extension those he hired to tell his story – created the image of a man who was supremely gifted and fiercely competitive, but also highly principled: a role model for others, young people especially.

That storyline was told over and over, parceled out as a message "owned" by the messenger. There was no one to challenge that story because alternative storylines never made it into the media. How could there be alternative stories published when no one knew anything about Tiger but Tiger? – and he only let the public know what he wanted them to read, see, and hear. Shutting out dissonant messages is hard to do in a multimedia world, but for decades "Team Tiger" had done just that by (1) knowing their message and (2) owning their message.

Soon after Woods' world became unglued in 2009, *New York Post* writer Phil Musnick wrote a column entitled "Tiger's good guy image manufactured from the start." In it, he points to numerous examples of how Woods was anything but perfect, but that those who handled his story, the mega representation firm IMG, both embedded positive messages about their client in all forms of media and strategically kept potentially negative messages from the public's view. "Those stories didn't make it to TV. Natch. Even the softest criticism of Woods & Co., it soon was learned, was prohibited. Violators risked suspension from conducting mere post-round interviews with Woods. From the start, Team Tiger made climate control mandatory."

Who Is the Audience for My Message?

Public relations storytellers most often try to reach a reading, listening, viewing, or clicking audience through positive impressions of the person, organization, or product they represent. That person might be, as in the instance above, a celebrity. She or he could be a political candidate. The company could be a corporation that exists to make a profit, for either its owners or its stockholders. Or it could be a "non-profit" organization that exists to enrich the lives of those in a community, providing anything from medical care or information to artistic performances. A product could be anything from cars to pharmaceuticals. Once you know your client's message and own that message, the next step is to do some very specific research on your intended audience. Box 6.1 summarizes some important information every successful public relations storyteller wants to have at his/her fingertips.

Many factors influence how your audience will receive the story you seek to tell about your client, organization, or product. Young people often view issues differently than those who are older. Women and men often perceive situations differently. Where someone lives, where they work, went to school, whether they practice a certain religion, support a specific political party, or even what they prefer to eat or the brand of car they drive can also determine how your craft your story – and also what medium is likely to be best for telling it.

Box 6.1   Who is my audience?

Demographics	How young/old is my audience? Are they male or female?
Psychographics	Where do they live? Go to school? Religion? Politics?
Self-identity	How do they define themselves?
Predisposition	Do they already like or dislike your client?
Flexibility	Are they likely to change their mind once it's made up?
Values	What do they hold most dear in life?
Aspirations	What are their hopes and dreams?

A person's self-identity is also a determining factor in their receptiveness to a message. If I think of myself as "an independent thinker," I'm not going to think kindly of a story that I perceive as trying to sway me toward a product, a cause, a candidate, or a corporation. Self-identity can also be tied to things like race or ethnicity. Some African Americans, for instance, *might* be more receptive to favorable stories about Tiger Woods' redemption from his flights of infidelity because they see him first as more like them than not. Generalizations, however, can be dangerous. Not all people of a certain race or ethnicity think alike.

Most people are predisposed toward liking certain products, corporations, individuals, or causes based upon their past experiences with them. For decades, Americans fell into the category of either "Ford" or "Chevrolet" families. Children often based their buying decisions on what automobile their father owned – and his father before him. Presumably, they were predisposed in their selection by the previous generation's positive impressions of the product. If you know your audience is predisposed to hear and accept your message, half your job is already done!

It's somewhat tougher, but not impossible, to sway an audience toward your client or cause if they are not predisposed in your favor. As long as the audience can be flexible, your story still has a fighting chance to register favorably with them. As most lawyers know, it's nearly impossible to find a jury that is 100 percent unbiased. All they ask for are jurors who can put aside those biases and be open-minded when deliberating.

Opinions are one thing; values are another. Most of us venture many opinions during our lifetimes and those opinions can change along the way. Opinions, therefore, can be fleeting. Values, for the most part, are permanent. They are the foundation of a human being's belief system and seldom change with time. To use the Tiger Woods example, a person whose values eliminate any possibility of marital infidelity is not going to adhere to a story that tries to evoke sympathy for the offender.

All people – whether they can always verbalize them or not – have hopes and dreams. Many of us daydream about who and what we would like to be, given the choice. Our aspirations might include being a better person or parent, making more money, living in a bigger house, driving a better car, or changing places in life with someone whom we admire. Each can determine how we perceive – and receive – a story about other people, corporations, causes, and products.

Public relations people, like all storytellers, must strive to know their audience before they can best to know how to reach that audience. In 1943, Dr. Abraham Maslow did some groundbreaking work on what motivates human beings toward acting as they do. He devised a hierarchy of human needs that has great application for those in public relations. We all seek survival, safety, love, and self-esteem, according to Maslow. Even seven decades later, that thought is worth keeping in mind when crafting messages for a specific audience.

Control the Message

There are really only two options in public relations storytelling: either you control the message disseminated about your client or the message controls you. How do you control the message? Control, or at least *contain*, the media that spread that message. This is especially important in terms of crisis management, a topic we'll discuss in detail later in this chapter. For now, control of the message means essentially taking charge of every detail, every aspect of a story on your terms before journalists take over and tell the story on theirs. There's a courtroom analogy that applies here. Once a jury hears testimony damaging to a defendant, even if her/his attorney objects and the judge instructs jurors to disregard what they heard, it's too late. The harm has been done. The adage often used among lawyers is "once the bell has been rung, it cannot be unrung." A variation is "once you drag a skunk through the courtroom, you can never get rid of the smell."

The comparison to what trial attorneys do in protecting the interests of their clients is in many ways an apt one. Notice how often those accused of high profile crimes begin appearing on cable news channels, network news broadcasts, and targeted web sites long before they ever step inside a courtroom. It's called the "court of public opinion." Years ago, a wealthy defendant, Claus von Bulow, was on trial for attempting to murder his heiress wife. The motive was money and love for another woman. Von Bulow was anything but a sympathetic character: cold, aloof, erudite, and even boorish. In the trial's final stages, the defendant, against his attorneys' advice, consented to an interview with ABC's Barbara Walters.

The calculated risk was that sitting down next to a respected and likable national news figure might help soften von Bulow's hard edges, making him seem more human and, therefore, both sympathetic and credible. It almost worked. While he was found guilty in the first trial, a second trial was ordered following a successful appeal at the Rhode Island State Supreme Court. Von Bulow was exonerated during that second trial. No one can say for sure, but the way his story was told to Barbara Walters – after much coaching, no doubt – could have played a major role in what was later termed, in a book and movie by the same name, his "reversal of fortune."

Von Bulow and his lawyers had exercised control over the message they wanted to send about their client. Their storyline was clear. Claus von Bulow was a grieving man who missed his wife, had nothing whatever to do with the coma in which she resided, and was truly repentant about his past infidelities. A team of public relations storytellers acting as consultants had successfully controlled the message they wanted to send. It was actually a counter-message, saying in effect, "Our guy isn't at all the way the media wants you to think of him. You might want to dislike him because he's rich, well dressed, and transgressed on his wife, but now that you hear his story, don't you think he's getting railroaded by the system?" This is more than controlling the message. Effective public relations storytellers drive the story.

Drive Your Own Story

Here's another metaphor: in public relations storytelling, you can either be the driver or the passenger when conveying the story you want or need to tell. Being the driver is the goal. You're behind the wheel. You have your GPS set. You know where you're going and you know how to get there. The route is clear and the timeframe is accurate. You can choose to stop en route to your destination or drive straight through. Bottom line: it's your choice. You plot the course, determine the stops, and create the terms.

The opposite is being the passenger. You're not in control of the trip, the destination, the stops, or the terms. You're basically along for the ride and have limited opportunities to impact either the process or the outcome. Others – reporters, editors, producers – set the agenda for what the public will come to know and believe about the client, corporation, or organization you represent. The process and outcome of the storytelling are out of your control; you are forced in this model to be *reactive* to whatever story the media want to tell. Often, that story will work against you and you client. Why? Positive stories normally don't sell as well as negative stories because they lack the conflict that is central to storytelling. Driving your own story means not waiting for the accident to happen; get behind the wheel and steer clear of a crash.

A large part of this process is being *proactive*. Don't wait for the media to come to you. Go to them first. There isn't a single medium, newspaper, broadcast, or web that doesn't live every day to put the headline or banner "EXCLUSIVE" on a story or interview. The more that story is perceived as top of mind for the audience, the more it becomes a priority for news decision-makers. While journalists will reach out to public relations people for access to their clients, reaching out first puts you in the driver's seat. You can establish the ground rules, create the context, establish the storylines you want the audience to hear and see. Both the "Driver" and "Passenger" models constitute strategic approaches to public relations storytelling. They are summarized in Box 6.2.

There are times when letting the media drive the story may work in your clients' favor. How? In instances where the public perceives the news media as being biased, or "beating up" unfairly on a politician, celebrity, or corporation, a "backlash" effect can occur. Basically, that means the audience begins to "side" with the person whom they believe has been singled out for abuse by one or more news media. This can create an "opening" or an "opportunity" – a window for a savvy public relations storyteller to slip through with her/his counter-message. It's another way of suggesting if you don't "drive" the story at the outset, there may be opportunities later – but it's better to be in control from the start!

Unfiltered Access to Your Audience

Everything you've read so far about how to interact with traditional journalists suggests that you may never have to interact with them at all. Remember that the premise of this book is multimedia storytelling and it's useful also to recall that technology makes it nearly

---

Box 6.2   Driver vs. Passenger Model of PR Strategy

Driver (Proactive)   Controls message, establishes storylines, defines agenda
Passenger (Reactive)   No control of message, storylines, or agenda.

possible to tell your story without cooperation – or interference – from mainstream media. Effective storytellers in public relations have the writing, networking, visual, and technological skills needed to create and distribute stories without relying on traditional media. In other words, it's possible to bypass journalists and take your story directly to the specific audience you want to reach. By doing so, skilled PR storytellers avoid having their stories "filtered" by reporters or editors.

Here's how it used to work when those with a story to tell had to rely on the mainstream news media for transmitting that story to the public. It began with what was once called a "press release." The term "press" referred to the fact that PR people primarily dealt with newspaper reporters. Later, that term was changed to "news" release, acknowledging radio and TV as major players in story distribution. Finally, the even more inclusive term "media" release gained favor to accommodate so-called "new media" – the Internet, social media, and mobile communications. Still, the "release" survives as an important part of how PR people tell their stories to the public. Where once it was mailed (can you believe it?), then faxed, it is now more often than not e-mailed or tweeted. The format for an effective public relations release remains the same, however; it still needs to be a compelling story, following the basic elements of effective storytelling outlined in Chapter 2. A good public relations release looks something like this:

For Immediate Release

Contact: Joe Crane   555-3467   jcrane@creativepr.com

Better Batter Makes Batter Better

Inventor creates flapjack craze

Picture yourself this Easter Sunday morning whipping up a batch of pancakes for your friends or family. What's the biggest challenge you face? Maybe it's mixing the batter, pouring it perfectly in the pan and hoping … just hoping … that it comes out perfect! That's how the inventor of "Better Batter" found a better way. Looking at the ingredients spread around his kitchen counter one day, he said to himself, "Why can't this be in a can, just like whipped cream?" Out of that came the idea for pancake batter in an aerosol can. And now it's revolutionizing how weekend breakfasts are made all over America. From his New Jersey kitchen to the shelves of major drug stores, "Better Batter" is just, well, better batter.

Notice how there is a "pitch" right from the start of this story. "Picture yourself" invites the reader in to the narrative and promises to solve a problem – what we call a "benefit" to the audience. In this instance, the immediate audience is the news editor, news producer or news director reading the release; the ultimate audience is that person reading, viewing, or online following. The story also appeals to timeliness, looking ahead to a looming holiday weekend. It also suggests that the product is more than the sum of its parts. Pancake batter isn't the biggest deal in any one's world; the story of one man's innovation *is*. Notice also how closely the release follows simple news writing style, incorporating crisis, conflict and resolution, although in this case the "crisis" or problem to be solved is simply, "What can I serve for breakfast that's tasty, quick and easy?"

It pays to do a little homework on the news outlets where you are pitching your story. The #1 complaint heard from content editors is that PR people request coverage without first researching the types of stories that are routinely covered by the station, publication or web site. Look for bylines and target reporters who have done similar or related stories, and adjust your pitch accordingly. When pitching the pancake batter story to a business reporter, for example, you might emphasize the inventor's entrepreneurial success in a tough economic climate for new businesses, instead of the holiday cooking angle.

Timing is also important. A good story that would be covered on a normal news day will get lost in the shuffle during a major news event such as an election, a disaster or a championship game. You may have to find a "tie-in," a way to connect your story to whatever is dominating the news. Be aware that most news outlets, and especially television stations, are short-staffed on weekends, when many "feel-good" events occur. There simply aren't enough camera crews to cover them all. Be prepared to point out in your news release why your story stands out as must-have coverage on a busy news day.

The purpose is to "sell" the product, but research suggests the most effective way to do so is not to buy advertising time, but to gain news media attention. Would the release, as drafted, accomplish that goal? If it does, it wouldn't be because of the product, but due to *the story*. Just as in news writing for any medium – and that can't be overstressed – capturing any audience's imagination through a good, compelling story spells success. That's as true for a media release as it is for a front page story, a web post, or a TV news package. Tell a good story and people – even experienced news people – can put aside their knowledge that what you are really doing is selling them on a product, candidate, or corporation. In this instance, the actual product described above made it to air on *CBS Sunday Morning* in 2010 (though the release drafted above was not the one actually used, one similar could have conceivably led to that event).

Of course, the print release, however distributed, is only one form for communicating your story through mainstream news media. A good public relations *packet* or *media kit* might contain still photos of the product, audio or video interviews with the inventor, perhaps a sample aerosol can of the product, maybe even a finished television or web story, written by you or one of your associates, called a VNR (Video News Release). The VNR sometimes is part of the overall media kit, delivered by mail or e-mail, via a company's web site. Often it is distributed by satellite to stations with which the public relations firm or individual has contacts and, therefore, an existing relationship. In large television markets, VNRs seldom make it to a newscast unedited or unfiltered; often, if at all, sound bites and video are lifted for a VO/SOT or made part of a reporter's package. In smaller markets, however, where resources are often fewer and the need for material greater, VNRs may make it into a newscast with little or no editing.

As we said in Chapter 1, this is the tried and true route that public relations writers were forced to follow before the advent of the Internet and its accompanying social media components. Given Facebook, YouTube (with its many channel options), Twitter, and an infinite number of "apps" on cellular telephones, direct, non-filtered access from you, the PR storyteller, to your intended audience is not only entirely possible, but highly desirable. The more you can fine tune and target your client's message to individuals or a group who are already receptive to that message, the better that client looks. When all is said and done, the goal of this form of storytelling: creating, maintaining, or cleansing the image of an individual or organization's *image*. More discussion on using social media for direct access to your audience follows later in this chapter.

Viral Media

If you're looking for evidence that an audience's perceptions, opinions, and decisions can be influenced by the various media surrounding them, look no further than Douglas Rushkoff's (1995) book, *Media Virus: Hidden Agendas in Popular Culture*. While not intended as a textbook for practicing public relations, Rushkoff's theory suggests that, when prominently placed within credible media, a story takes on a life of its own.

Not only are those who see the original story influenced, but, if it's strongly and strategically placed in highly viewed media, its influence will spread through other media – much like a rumor gets passed throughout a workplace or akin to the way a virus spreads through an entire population. Media history is filled with such stories. They are perennial and powerful. Some deal with celebrities, other with politicians. Still others spread the word about products or the corporations that make them. Create a "buzz" about your client – individually or institutionally – and let others do the work for you.

So, how do viral stories begin? There's no one answer, but there are some real-life examples to support a series of strategies. Anyone who has ever watched NBC's *Today Show* has seen the large crowd assembled on Rockefeller Plaza outside "Studio 1-A," where the show originates in New York. Have you ever noticed what happens when the show's anchors step outside to greet the crowd, do the weather, or conduct an interview? Think about that crowd. Are they all so-called "average viewers," vacationing in New York from around the country? Not by a long shot.

Sure, many have signs proclaiming where they're from, a birthday, or greeting to those back home. But have you noticed the other signs? Look closely. They're often for products or services. That's right – they're "selling" a message and they're doing it in a "viral" manner. The repetition of the product or company in such a prominent venue helps spread the viral message to "check this out." Web sites are an important part of the message contained on these signs. Holding up a sign in front of a crowd may be old-fashioned, but it works.

And who are those people holding up the signs? Most often, they're hired to do so. Sometimes they're public relations people themselves. The short-term goal is to get on-camera displaying the client's name, brand, and contact info. The longer-term goal is to peak interest, create "buzz," and be in a spot where your message is replicated many times across other media. Think, for example how, when the stories run on the web, the client's logo gains more visibility. The chance always exists that still photos from the segment could end up on the web or elsewhere. Multimedia has made viral messaging more prevalent – and powerful – than ever.

The best part is that this kind of high-level exposure to a massive audience is virtually free. That's why radio stations, legal firms, beauty products, even startup entrepreneurs, use the streets of Manhattan and proximity to a television network camera as a means of spreading their messages. No wonder that this form of public relations is often referred to "gorilla PR." It takes some gumption to go out and, in essence, be insistent about getting your message up front and out front. The key is to be *subtle*; simply placing your client's message prominently behind those they respect creates an unconscious connection between that message and the messenger: almost like an endorsement.

It's called "gorilla" messaging for a reason. It sneaks up on you. You may not think about it till later. "What was that radio station playing country music?" you might ask. Off to the web you go to find it. "How about that free beauty treatment; what was the company's name and how do I get it?" The seed has been planted. In a way, a story has been told, not one with a complete narrative, but maybe something that's more powerful: *viral imaging* revealed through the power of suggestion.

Either way – through the adoption of your client's message in a news story or through viral imaging – when public relations storytellers see their work in print, on television, or the web with a minimum of editing, they call it a "win." There are many more ways to "win" in today's multimedia environment. As a public relations student who went on to work for a large pharmaceutical company once put it: "The goal is to advocate for your client, however and whatever that takes. Seeing your message on one of the morning shows or on the front page of the *New York Times* is the same. They're both 'wins' and we go out and celebrate at the end of the day."

Interview Placements

The more traditional way to assure your client's message will be heard is to get her/him booked for an interview, either resulting in a newspaper article, a radio/television interview, a web story, or, increasingly all three. Access is a key to reporters and editors in both traditional and new media. New media may be less formal, but you still have to build a relationship with the contact person. For some media outlets, the contact is with the editor who assigns the story or the reporter who will write it. The higher up the media ladder you go, the more likely you will be dealing with someone called a *booker*. This is especially true for the broadcast television networks. Each has a booking department, filled with people whose job it is to find "experts" or "eyewitnesses" for stories that will be covered in that day's newscasts.

Sometimes bookers come from a journalism background; equally often they come from a public relations background. Either way, they are, like you, storytellers. They may not write a complete narrative, but they contribute a significant number of elements to how that narrative is shaped and told – including the essential questions that reporters and/or anchors ask. It's important to build a relationship with people in booker positions. Why? When a story calls for a live interview, the booker would be more likely to call, or recommend that a news producer call, the person she/he knows best. That could also mean the public relations person who has a track record of delivering good spokespeople for past stories. *Build credibility for your clients by building credibility for yourself.*

You might also offer the services of your client to comment on specific kinds of stories. Let's suppose, for example, that CNN is planning a news story about some new digital technology that will apply to all forms of identification each of us commonly carry: drivers' licenses, passports, credit cards, etc. Let's all suppose that you are a public relations story-teller for a large corporation like Polaroid that is working to become the dominant manu-facturer of ID cards using this technology. Instead of waiting for CNN to find you, you should be proactive and reach out to them.

This example comes from an actual case in 1996 when one of the authors was working on a story for CNN involving issues related to digital fingerprint identification technology. Any one of a number of firms developing similar technology could have been spotlighted in that story. Polaroid became the face of the story in large part because of their willingness to fly not one, but two, of the corporation's top CEOs to Atlanta for the interview. They flew overnight, arrived at 8 in the morning, and were interviewed for a half hour before flying back to Newtown, MA, Polaroid's home base. By being *proactive*, Polaroid's public relations person accomplished a number of things, among them (1) he assured that Polaroid would get exclusive exposure in a story that would make them look good; (2) he did so by executing a *preemptive strike*, meaning that once Polaroid told their story, they defined the terms of that story. No competitor of Polaroid's appeared in that story, which exposed the firm favorably all over the world. Now, that's good PR!

Interview Preparation

The key to having a good interview is *preparation*. Do some research on the person who will interview you or your client. Not all interviewers are equally skilled; nor are they all friendly. By that we mean, don't assume that the person on the other side of the microphone is on your side; he or she is paid to get the story or a particular point of view. Beware of so-called *ambush interviews*. Watch past interviews this person has conducted. Are there "traps" he or she is known for setting – places where the interview subject gets put in a corner and ends up looking bad? Develop a strategy for sidestepping those. Is there a pattern in the order or kinds of questions the person asks? If so, develop a corresponding strategy to take full advantage of that pattern. One of the most famous television interviewers of our time, Barbara Walters, is known for asking extremely personal questions, many of which address sensitive issues from a subject's past or present. If such issues are lurking in your client's past, or if she/he has some current "skeletons in the closet," it's your responsibility to know about them – and develop a strategy to address them.

Don't be afraid to rehearse the interview in advance. Select questions that are likely to be asked during the actual interview. Listen to the answers you or your client give. Do they sound logical? Credible? Authoritative? Memorable? How can they be improved to help strengthen the image you seek to convey? Rehearse, but don't over-do it. Over-rehearsing can be counterproductive. If speech begins to sound rehearsed or memorized, it's perceived as insincere.

There's no template to guarantee an interview will go well, but there are ways to maximize your chances to come out looking good or to enhance your client's image. Here is a tip sheet to help guide you through the process of interview preparation. While we will spend a good deal of time in this chapter discussing how to bypass journalists and gain direct access to your audience, even in today's multimedia environment, traditional media still occupy a place of some power. Equalizing the distribution of that power relies upon being savvy about how all media work – traditional, social, and, increasingly, mobile media.

Media Interview Tip Sheet

☑	Know your stuff	The more you know, the more confident you'll sound.
☑	Answer the question	Sounding evasive makes the audience distrust you.
☑	Be conversational	Talk with the person interviewing you, not at her/him.
☑	Dress the part	Don't overdress, but a CEO should look like one.
☑	Anticipate	What questions might be asked and how will you answer them?
☑	Deflect criticism	Avoid criticizing competitors; be positive about *your* message.
☑	Be the expert	But only on what you know; don't speculate about what you don't.
☑	Never argue	Politely disagree and move on.
☑	Build talking points	Embed your most important points in every answer.
☑	Repeat talking points	Given the chance, say them again … and again.
☑	Summarize	Everyone won't hear every point. Sum it up at the end.
☑	Listen	Great opportunities come not when we're not talking, but hearing.

Kinds of Stories

Looking back on Chapter 2, you will see the kinds of timeless, universal stories that are compelling in every medium. These apply to public relations stories, but there are also elements that are particular to this form of storytelling. Remember, your goal as a public relations writer is to either (1) build a positive image for your client or (2) restore an image in need of repair. The best way to do the first is to create a measure of *currency* with your audience. That means making your message top of mind for the constituency you most want to reach. Stories about people, companies, or products need to focus on the good will they express toward others. Sometimes that means philanthropy – in other words, it means focusing on those stories in which the client looks good by doing good.

Have the employees of the corporation you represent volunteered their own time to help make others' lives better? If so, that's a story – and a good one. Sometimes the opportunity to tell such a story is tied into a seasonal event. One way in which many corporations receive a positive image boost is through stories related to holiday giving. It may be a "giving tree," in which a corporation's employees contribute gifts to people in need. Many media outlets, both local and national, have their own giving initiatives around Christmas and Chanukah and other religious or cultural holidays. Corporations may be asked to donate their products and sponsorship to the cause. It's also a public relations opportunity to create storylines showing your client to be generous, caring, and socially aware.

An example is the *Today Show* toy drive run annually on NBC each November and December. Donations by toymakers, publishing houses, and child product manufacturers measure into the hundreds of thousands of dollars. Spokespersons for the corporations that donate to this and other causes, both nationally and locally, get free air time to tell their story. That story normally includes humility for being included in the effort and self-recognition of the need and desire to give back to the community that has supported them all year long.

Image Builders

Stories that create a strong, positive image of a client – be it an individual or corporation – are stories that have the potential to make that client visible to segments of the audience to whom they may have been previously invisible, or at least not "top of mind." How best to accomplish that goal is illustrated by the media release below.

For Immediate Release

Contact: Joe Crane   555-3467   jcrane@creativepr.com

Haircuts for Haiti

Major hair salon chain gives profits to earthquake victims

Need a haircut or style? You can just get a cut or you can give a hand to those in need. Stellar Cuts, the newest national chain of hair stylists, with 120 locations across the US will give all of its profits from haircuts, styles, and shampoos this Saturday to help victims of the recent earthquake in Haiti. "We are so fortunate to live in America and have all that we have," said Stellar Cuts corporate vice-president Justin Sharpe. "All of us at Stellar Cuts want to help others less fortunate gain safe shelter, have clean drinking water, and adequate food." Estimates are that this weekend's efforts could raise up to $200,000 for Haiti relief efforts. Stellar Cuts will open early at 7 a.m. on Saturday and stay open late until 10 p.m. in order to raise more money for the cause.

Because everyone likes a story of sacrifice or self-sacrifice (remember those timeless storytelling formulas in Chapter 2), chances are that news media would pick up on the "Hair for Haiti" story, in part because it is written in a simple, straightforward manner, much like a news story. But also keep in mind the *timing* of the event linked to this story. It takes place on a weekend when all newsrooms are low on staff. A story like this one, taking place when it does, is ready made, especially for television and the web. Even if a reporter is not able to be dispatched, a photographer, on his or her own, can shoot the needed stills or video. In many ways, this story, due to its theme and timing, is a homerun for the client corporation.

Image Makeovers

The story above presupposes that the company named Stellar Cuts simply needed an image boost – that is, had a need to become more visible in the marketplace compared to its larger competitors. Instead, what if Stellar Cuts had recently been the object of negative news coverage? For the sake of argument, let's say it was reported that the company had hired undocumented workers and paid them lower than average wages. Would that make a difference?

It would, to the extent that now the *goal* of your story becomes not to make the audience aware of the company – they're already more than aware if they've seen the negative coverage – but to *change their minds* about Stellar Cuts, its management, and its operations. Could the same media release used above also work in this scenario? It could, but one that more fully extols the company's virtues might work better. Given the negative image of exploiting undocumented workers, a stronger emphasis might be placed upon how the company is renewing its commitment to social consciousness. Helping the Haiti victims is one example of that renewed commitment.

By doing so, the haircutting firm shows that (1) it recognizes it could have made a mistake (without ever admitting that it did); and (2) it takes an active role in fostering better corporate behavior for the future. In this instance, different quotes from the corporate VP would be included in the story, something perhaps along the lines of "This is just one way in which we at Stellar Cuts want to show that we do care about people – all people – and that we're committed to treating others with respect, compassion, and dignity."

One reason that effective public relations storytelling is so successful has to do with the forgiving nature of people – Americans, especially. Once a strong negative message is replaced by a strong positive one, the latter becomes, to use a term we've stressed throughout our discussion, "top of mind." It's what people retain and remember. Consider how few people remember that Johnson and Johnson corporation was once featured in news coverage about cyanide-laced Tylenol tablets. Even those who do remember have long since replaced any negativity associated with that memory. It's testimony to how well and how quickly the company reacted, pulling the product off the shelves and showing its executives cared more about people than profits.

Crisis Management

Building an image is hard work. It takes compelling stories and time for the audience to assimilate all the positive messages they contain. Repairing an image is even harder, but hardest of all is trying to manage a client's crisis. It could be a crisis of public confidence, as in a company that has been accused of wrongdoing in the marketplace. It could be a personal crisis that negatively affects an individual's public image, as with the Tiger Woods' sex scandal that began this chapter.

Putting positive stories into the public sphere becomes intensely important when an individual or corporation is under constant siege from negative news reports. When in "crisis," stories must be written quickly, but also strategically. Knee-jerk reaction to a client's dilemma can be costly in the long run, but so can reacting too slowly. Every day a negative claim goes unanswered in the media is one day more that the perception and reputation of a client sink lower in the public's opinion.

Of course, there are also crises that result from severe storms or other natural disasters, such as floods, earthquakes, or mudslides. They also call for swift response from spokespeople for government agencies. That response, however, is to supply the public with the facts, the information they need to remain safe and recover from actual damage. Response to a PR crisis, by contrast, may depend upon disseminating factual information, but it's less information the public needs and more information your client wants them to have. It is meant to help the client, not the public, by countering harmful claims already present through other media.

An effective response to a public relations crisis depends upon many factors, the majority of which can be summarized as shown in Box 6.3.

Box 6.3   Planning a Response

√	Get out front	Define the terms of the crisis before the media define it for you.
√	Act quickly	Begin to draft stories that show the positive side of the person or situation.
√	Don't hide	Invisibility or silence is often taken by the public as admitting guilt.
√	Target	Define the audience who you most need to see/hear your message.
√	Build trust	Enlist others perceived by the audience as credible to vouch for your client.
√	Use the past	Contact reporters who have previously been positive toward your client.
√	Rehearse	Review likely questions (and appropriate answers) to reporter questions.
√	Test first	Do a trial run of your strategy before enacting it in public.
√	Adapt next	Use the feedback to fine tune your message.
√	Connect	Utilize social media sites to spread your message.

Many experienced public relations professionals will tell you that the single most important thing you can do as a storyteller in a crisis situation is *be honest*. While this may be essential advice for day-to-day dealings with other media professionals (as well as the public), it is never more important than when in the middle of a news media firestorm. Reporters have long memories. Fabricating or outright lying about a client's culpability is very different from accentuating positive elements of the story you want the public to retain.

Many historians have suggested that former President Richard Nixon might never have been impeached had he (and his staff) been honest about the circumstances surrounding the Watergate break-in and burglary. Sometimes the best strategy is to acknowledge responsibility, apologize, and move on. Doing so can make reporters appear to be "piling on" the client and that can cause what we saw during the administration of another US president, Bill Clinton, a backlash against the news media following revelations of the Monica Lewinsky scandal.

More recently, critics of how Tiger Woods handled his own marital indiscretions point to his lack of response early on. Once he did respond, nearly three months after the revelations, it was through what some public relations experts called an "orchestrated" event. Woods, surrounded by family members and supporters, delivered what appeared to be a forced apology. Only two pre-selected reporters were allowed in the room and no questions were permitted. "I found nothing sincere or true," said Eli Portnoy, an Orlando-based brand strategist. "I think … it caused him more harm. I didn't sense true remorse. I think this might backfire to some extent … There's nothing there to make him any more likeable than he has been."

Less than two months later, a penitent, remorseful Tiger Woods held his first real news conference on April 5, 2010. He took questions from all the assembled news media and talked about how he had "taken a hard look" at himself and was now "a better man." He expressed appreciation for his fans, whom he said he had not appreciated nearly enough in previous years. He referred to reporters by their first names. He invoked his deceased father's memory and his living mother's support. In other words, he went a long way toward correcting some previous gaffes.

Saving his personal relationship may be beyond the scope of a news conference, but rescuing his fast depreciating professional brand – and the financial prosperity that comes from product endorsements – was certainly within the purview of that setting where, finally, he faced the media. In many ways, he had learned to become better at telling the story *he* wanted to tell, replacing the stories others were telling about him. Whether he was a better man wasn't the point; he had become a better *communicator*. When in crisis, that's the key that opens every other door.

Social Media, Front and Center

Research suggests a student majoring in journalism or public relations today is well advised to put social media on her/his "most needed skills" list. This is especially true for public relations storytellers. A 2010 media survey jointly conducted by the trade publications *PR*

Week/PR Newswire shows more journalists using Facebook and Twitter and, in general, relying on social media for their stories. Among the findings:

- 24 percent or journalists say they consider sites like Facebook and Twitter an important way to connect with experts. That's up from 13 percent in 2009.
- 46 percent of journalists say they sometimes or always use blogs for research.
- 33 percent report using social networks in their research, compared to 24 percent in 2009.
- Overall, 43 percent of journalists have been pitched through social networks, compared to 31 percent in 2009.

This constitutes, according to the experts, a quantum change in how public relations storytellers do their jobs. "Across the board you can see a change in journalists' behavior," said Sarah Skerik, VP of distribution services at *PR Newswire*. "Journalists are doing more with less. They seem to be acting more aggressively about finding their stories, digging a bit deeper for story angles."

Others quoted in response to the survey agree. "Coverage oftentimes comes from building a relationship with a journalist, and it's becoming more frequent in the industry to establish those relationships through social media," says Amy Prenner, founder of the LA-based Prenner Group. According to Erica Iacono, executive editor of *PR Week*, journalists are coping with "heavier workloads, shorter deadlines, and increased competition." All "are causing journalists to seek out new sources of information to help them get their jobs done, including social networks."

So, pitching your story ideas to those in traditional news media, ironically, involves using "new" media including mobile communication. Most media people today receive and post their Facebook and Twitter messages while on the go – via their iPhones, iPads, BlackBerries, or smartphones. This gives public relations people unprecedented access to an important audience of media gatekeepers.

Creating demand using social media

When the iPad was first introduced early in 2010, relatively few paid advertisements or commercials were seen as part of the product's roll-out. Instead, dozens of print, web, and television stories captured the public's imagination for this newest high-tech gadget. Some of the attention was sparked by debate. Stories focused on its similarities to other personal data devices, the Kindle reader, for instance. Would it be as good? Better? What made it different from many other devices already in the marketplace?

Maybe these story ideas came from reporters' and editors' own brainstorming. It's more likely, however, that they came from Apple's social media strategy. Months in advance, an avalanche of FB postings, Twitter tweets, and online discussions sparked fascination with the product while piquing expectations for its release. News media paid attention to all that social media "chatter" and helped advance Apple's goals through mainstream stories on morning news programs, nightly news broadcasts, not to mention posting Apple's video demos on their web sites.

Within hours of the product's release, Facebook pages for iPad cropped up. It was difficult to determine which were "fan" driven and which were official. The largest of the pages had close to 9,000 members in the initial week iPad hit stores. It's more difficult to count tweets, but one media group captured 50,000 on release day. Of those tweeting, 87 percent indicated an intention to buy the product. This doesn't go unnoticed by the news media; they increasingly use social media to gauge audience interest in a potential story before committing to it. Their own interest intensifies with the perception that their readers, viewers, and online users care about the story.

Apple's web site touted its many applications (called apps), including ones that made the iPad the place to interact with brands like Netflix, Major League Baseball, and the *Wall Street Journal*. "Read the *Wall Street Journal* on iPad and soak up news from around the globe, everywhere you go," read the product features page. "In-depth analysis, real-time quotes, and video – all your favorite sections of the Journal are here – and they're even better on iPad. The large display shows you an entire page of award-winning news. You can even customize this app to get only the news you want, when you want it."

This one device – whether or not the three million sold on the first day are a predictor of its eventual success – is instructional in terms of how effectively social media can be used to create demand for a product or service. Let's look at what worked from a multimedia storytelling perspective.

- They captured attention through a variety of means: direct and social media contacts.
- They targeted those who cover the "tech" beat for mainstream media.
- They used social media to provide resources, many interactive, all visual.
- They used mainstream media to raise the audience's excitement level, create urgency, and suggest scarcity.

The last point – raising excitement, creating urgency, and suggesting scarcity – is the bread and butter of any public relations storyteller. In the first instance, the job is to create a storyline suggesting that the release of this product is one of the most important developments since Gutenberg invented movable print. That's excitement! Next comes the suggestion that there's a need to buy one *now!* It's a variation of the old adage in early television commercials "be the first on your block to own …" That's urgency. Finally, there's a limited supply, so don't be left out. That's scarcity.

You can better conceptualize how to "pitch" a story on a new product like the iPad to mainstream news media if you look at how it is a "fit" with the kinds of stories they already cover. Think in trends. Among the most covered stories every year are those that involve the most popular "toy" of the holiday season. Its popularity means anxious parents will arrive before dawn to line up at stores hawking that toy. There's the excitement of the chase, but also the urgency to get the item before it's gone, and you're a victim of scarcity.

This story is replicated over and over in all media, but especially in television news. It's the stuff of live shots, with a morning show reporter waiting with those in line outside the store, helping to build desire for the product. Maybe not at the conscious level, but it's likely that the reporter was influenced to some extent by an effective PR storyteller. Remember, stories don't just happen. Stories are built. In contemporary public relations storytelling, the job is using the many tools you have – personal relationships, a well-written release, an articulate spokesperson, and all the social media you can gather. The job is leading others to tell the story you want them to tell.

Leading the Way in Storytelling

Social media is one way, but it's not the only way to get your story into the public's consciousness. Sometimes the most effective approach calls for a blend of "old" and "new" media. Use social media to measure the "pulse" of a particular target audience or group and create a connection with that audience. But don't forget that there are many other ways to use the Internet for storytelling. Some of them involve creating content that might have once appeared on traditional media like television. Increasingly, public relations storytelling involves reaching out to consumers on web sites designated for messaging about clients and their products. Some of those sites are the corporate web sites of the client; others aggregate the content of many clients.

As an example, a company named About Face Media creates short films that tell a story about a variety of clients. The firm describes itself on its web site (aboutfacemedia.com) as "a content marketing company that makes short form video documentaries for brands, and then optimizes that content for use within social media." The documentary form is, of course, traditional or what we might call "old" media. Its use on the Internet constitutes a transfer to "new" media.

The specific concept behind the company involves putting together a team of celebrated and award-winning documentary film makers – people who have the storytelling skills to make films featured at festivals like Sundance, Slamdance, South by Southwest, Tribeca and Toronto. Once the films are made, they are turned over to a client's "social media team to use web tools like Twitter, Facebook, blogs and YouTube to get the videos seen by the widest possible audience."

The clients range from corporate giants like Staples, Sears, and K Mart to universities like Marquette and state tourism councils. They created the Florida Tourism documentaries found on the visitstpeteclearwater.com web site. Short documentary style films contribute information and images to the stories of events (the Grand Prix auto races), cities (Dunedin, a small town with strong Scottish heritage), and art galleries (St. Petersburg's Dali Museum). The slogan of About Face Media is appropriate, given its approach to practicing public relations: "Let's tell your story."

For those accustomed to working in the more traditional film-making world, it's an extension of the storytelling skills they already possess. Christopher Rish is a film maker whose skills have transferred well to making videos that brand a product or corporation by using social media. "I think that the reason documentary-style work is so well suited to PR and to corporate message-making, particularly in the social media world, is that people don't believe the over-hyped, over-produced, sound-tracked, voiced-over media messages anymore," says Rish. "People have become more media savvy and many corporate messages are just too slick to pass muster with a halfway media-literate consumer."

Instead, he maintains that "the documentary style allows for people to make up their own minds about a character, event or brand symbol. It's more like saying, 'here we are, this is what we're about, I hope you like us', and leaving the choice up to the consumer about who and what to believe. Choice is very important now." So is the afore-mentioned direct access to an audience – something multimedia storytelling has made not only possible, but desirable.

"As manufacturers and brands now communicate directly with their consumers over the Internet, they are getting into the message-making business themselves, bypassing the traditional media and communicating directly to their audience through the content on their web sites, YouTube videos and Facebook pages," Rish says. "These videos often need to feel 'actual' or unscripted for their viewers to pass them along. They either need to feel honest and true or be amazingly entertaining. Just OK isn't good enough in the post-TV world."

The YouTube PR Campaign

YouTube is another storytelling medium we've come to think of as part of social media. Telling stories with video is not new. Television has done that since its inception more than six decades ago. What's new is posting the user-generated content on line. As a medium, YouTube's popularity has strong implications for all storytelling genres, journalism especially. But it also creates tremendous advantages for those whose stories are told in the public relations sphere. Far from the traditional press or video release, which reaches only a fraction of a total audience, YouTube allows public relations people to tell their stories to a vast, global audience.

Early in 2010, while in the middle of a massive recall of its vehicles for safety reasons, the world's largest automaker, Toyota, faced a public relations challenge: restoring the consumer's faith in what had been the industry's gold standard for reliability, longevity and, most of all, safety. Toyota executives used a combination of traditional media (television) to lead the audience toward their multimedia story (YouTube).

First, they released a series of "funny" television commercials for the 2011 Sienna minivan. Instead of other television ads used by the company – ones that featured testimonials from loyal Toyota owners proclaiming that they wouldn't hesitate to buy another Toyota and Toyota workers thanking buyers for their faith in the brand – these spots had a compelling storyline. They featured the adventures of *The Sienna Family*, a mom and dad with two kids. The mother, especially, loves the family's Sienna so much that she often seeks refuge inside while it's parked in the driveway. There, she sits back, watches a DVD, looking as if she's in the middle of a spa treatment. The television commercials just give a small glimpse into the family's lives. The voiceover then tells the audience: "see how it unfolds on YouTube."

On YouTube, the entire stories closely resemble episodes of a TV sitcom. In fact, an entire YouTube channel (youtube.com/Sienna) was dedicated just to the Sienna Family. Its essential message – Toyota can still be trusted – is embedded in a humorous storyline that stresses family, value, and *family values*. What could be better for a company that was in dire trouble, mired in a consumer confidence crisis, only a month earlier?

What are the lessons? First, by using a social media site known primarily for user-generated content, the giant car manufacturer looked less like a mega corporation and more like it was in touch with average Americans. Like them, Toyota showed it had a lighter side in the midst of the serious news cycle surrounding it. The corporation modeled what many Americans do when they're under stress: they go to a site where people and animals do silly things and become "famous" in the process; remember the rapping wedding party, puppy cam, and numerous other viral videos that captured the attention of the nation. Toyota fit right in.

Second, whether it's a news story or a public relations campaign, people love a good story. If that story contains humor and prompts our laughter while making us feel "warm" and positive toward the brand behind the story, so much the better. That, after all, is the goal behind every PR campaign. Evidence that Toyota hit a homerun with the Sienna Family came in the first quarter car sales report in April, 2010: the Japanese car maker actually sold more cars than during the same period the previous year, despite the controversy over the safety recalls.

Use it All

It's not enough to learn how to write media releases, create media kits, and send out video news releases. As a public relations practitioner in today's multimedia world, you have to use everything available to you, especially tools that didn't exist when Ivy Lee, commonly referred to as the "father of modern public relations" created the very first PR campaign in 1906. It was on behalf of a coal company trying to fight its negative public image during a workers' strike. Some of the principles Lee espoused can be adapted to the multimedia age; the medium may change, but the message remains true to what Lee espoused in his "Declarations of Principles" over a century ago. Among those principles are:

- This is not a secret press bureau. All our work is done in the open. We aim to supply news.
- Our matter is accurate. Further details on any subject treated will be supplied promptly, and any editor will be assisted most carefully in verifying directly any statement of fact.
- In brief, our plan is frankly, and openly, on behalf of business concerns and public institutions, to supply the press and public of the United States prompt and accurate information concerning subjects which it is of value and interest to the public to know about.

In other words, whatever story you tell, *be honest*. A good story is only a good story if it's true. *Be transparent*. Don't give the impression you're hiding something. *Know what's interesting*. If you try to pass off self-serving information as news, neither the news media nor the public will believe you. The proof in Ivy Lee's case was that he completely revamped the image of John D. Rockefeller as a ruthless tycoon who cared less about the public or the country. How? Lee made him the subject of a storyline that involved the robber baron as someone who changed his business practices from ruthlessness to caring for his workers, their wages and working conditions; there were even stories touting Rockefeller's extolling the value of building new plants in communities where they were most needed. Lee told his client's story well. And the audience, at that time a newspaper audience, listened and responded.

Imagine what he could have done if he had the multimedia options available to today's public relations storytellers. You can be sure of one thing: he would have used every one of them to find the audience wherever they are, whether that's in traditional or new media. One can imagine a Rockefeller Facebook page, tweets updating the client's actions on behalf of his employees and customers, a YouTube channel dedicated to his business philosophy – all granting the tycoon direct access to his public.

Lee was so successful because he paid attention to every minute detail within the stories he wanted others to read and believe. That means concentrating on what you want the public to know or do as a result of reading your story. As we said at the start of this chapter, "know your message." Once you do, decide which media are best for conveying it. Finally, make your message easy to find.

Directing the Audience

With the advent of social media, the audience is constantly being extorted to "find us on Facebook" or "follow us on Twitter." The public relations web site "Firebelly" (http://blog.firebellydigital.com) points out that "we talk a lot about making things easy to *share* online, but it's also crucial to make them easy to *find*." The Toyota Sienna television spot referring the audience to YouTube is cited for not clearly directing the audience to the company's message.

Says the writer, Chad Richards: "They tell you 'see how it unfolds on YouTube,' but when I did a YouTube search for *Toyota sienna minivan commercial* (and variations of that) I was presented with a lot of Sienna minivan commercials – none of them were what I was looking for, however. I eventually found an entire channel dedicated to them at youtube.com/Sienna. That URL should have been included in the first place." Richards suggests it happens more often than you might think. "I still see a lot of companies simply saying 'Find us on Facebook' or 'Follow us on Twitter' without providing a URL," he writes. "Make it easy for them to do so by providing the URL!"

Beware of Backfire

It's not political correctness, but media savvy to remember that everything you write in a story isn't going to be perceived as you intended. Even the best storytelling can backfire. Some elements of a story or strategy can actually create a *disconnect* with the audience you've targeted. Not all audiences are the same. When we make assumptions about people, it's usually based upon the belief that they share certain ideas and values with the mainstream population. But that may not always be true.

There are all kinds of ways to alienate an entire audience. For example, if the "mother" in the Toyota storyline above is portrayed in a stereotypical manner as "dumb" rather than "empowered," that presents a gender divide with at least half the audience (if not more, based upon the US population where women outnumber men). The "Sienna Family" is also seemingly white and middle class. Does that present a false representation of today's America? What about a broader range of consumers: African-Americans, Latinos, and every other racial or ethnic segment of car buyers? That doesn't even begin to address the issue that they appear to be an intact or "nuclear" family. What about all those in your audience who are not?

Creating separate storylines that serve specific segments of your audience doesn't divide the audience; it expands the message. When others see themselves reflected in the media they consume, half the work of storytelling is done for you. To the extent that others can identify with the message, they will embrace the action you propose – whether that involves voting for a candidate or buying a car.

The point is that assumptions can be dangerous when practicing public relations storytelling – as they are when telling a story in any genre on any media platform. They are especially so in an area of media where the entire goal is to get the audience to like your client. It's the polar opposite of what you want to achieve: positive impressions of those people, corporations, organizations, or causes which you represent.

Finally, in the age of global media, never forget that practicing public relations doesn't simply mean relating to the American public. That's especially true if a client does business outside the US. Even if that isn't the case, because of the Internet, almost everything we write, photograph, or design ends up being disseminated globally. That creates new challenges and new demands for storytellers whose work crosses global boundaries. Without intending to do so, it's easy to create messages that may be inappropriate for readers and viewers in other countries. As outlined in our next chapter, the multimedia storyteller must be sensitive to cultural, social and political differences and committed to the ethical standards that are shared by journalists and public relations practitioners everywhere.

A Multimedia Exercise

In March 2007, Sea World San Antonio used a social media release to build attention for its "Atlantis" ride. The ride itself wasn't yet in use at the park, but Sea World's PR firm released a series of videos on YouTube as a strategy to create excitement around its launch. Atlantis was described as a combination roller coaster and water ride. The campaign was successful. In its second day, the release had 1,339 stream hits and a total of 490 page hits from 117 media outlets. Using the concepts and the skills taught in this chapter, how would you create an effective media campaign for the "Atlantis," one that would both attract the news media and serve as way of interacting directly with your audience? What storytelling elements would you include and why?

To see how an actual public relations company told the "Atlantis" story, go to: http://overtonecomm.blogspot.com/2007/03/case-study-seaworld-uses-video-to.html.

Works Cited and Further Reading

Breakenridge, Deirdre. *PR 2.0: New Media, New Tools, New Audiences*. New York: FT Press, 2008.

Fearn-Banks, Kathleen. *Crisis Communications: A Casebook Approach*. 3rd edition. London: Routledge, 2007.

Fitch, Brad and McCurry, Mike. *Media Relations Handbook: For Agencies, Associations, Nonprofits and Congress*. Washington, DC: TheCapitol.net, 2004.

Hiebert, Ray Eldon. *Courtier to the Crowd: The Story of Ivy Lee and the Development of Public Relations*. Ames, Iowa: Iowa State University Press, 1966.

Mushnick, Phil. "Tiger's good guy image manufactured from start," *New York Post*. December 1, 2009. Retrieved from: http://www.nypost.com/p/sports/more_sports/tiger_good_guy_image_manufactured_SYCnhDVhWlOf CLBTqSPl2I.

Pedecini, Sandra. "Tiger Woods' apology falls short, public-relations experts say," *Orlando Sentinel*, February 19, 2010. Retrieved from: http://articles.orlandosentinel.com/2010-02-19/news/os-tiger-woods-image-20100219_1_woods-apology-tiger-woods-endorser.

Richards, Chad. "Toyota's 'Sienna family YouTube campaign," February 17, 2010. Retrieved from: http://blog.firebellydigital.com/2010/02/toyota-sienna-family-youtube.html.

Sachoff, Mike. "More journalists using Facebook and Twitter," *Web Pro News*. April 5, 2010. Retrieved from: http://www.webpronews.com/topnews/2010/04/02/more-journalists-using-facebook-and-twitter.

Wauters, Robin. "More iPad sentiment analysis: 87% of tweets indicate intent to purchase," April 6, 2009. Retrieved from: http://techcrunch.com/2010/04/06/ipad-sentiment-analysis/.

COURTESY JAMES LEE

JAMES LEE
Lee Strategy Group

Job: President, Lee Strategy Group
Market: International, based in Southern California
Hometown: Encino, CA
Education: University of Southern California, BA in business, BA in journalism
Career Path:

  Copywriter, Paramount Pictures
  Deputy Campaign Manager, Pete Wilson for US Senate
  Press Secretary, Senator Pete Wilson
  Deputy Press Secretary, Pete Wilson for Governor
  Press Secretary, California Governor's Office
  California Press Secretary, Bush-Quayle presidential campaign
  Communications Director, California Environmental Protection Agency
  Manager, Burson-Marsteller
  Director, Burson-Marsteller
  President, Lee Strategy Group, Santa Monica, CA

You earned two undergraduate degrees in business and journalism. How did you end up in public relations?

By accident. My emphasis in business was marketing and my emphasis in journalism was in broadcast management. I didn't want to be a journalist. When I got my first job at Paramount, I wanted to work in entertainment and move my way up. Then the writers strike hit, and I was disillusioned. Someone suggested I go work in politics. I didn't know anything about it, but I had an interview and was hired on the spot. Sometimes you start out with one plan and you end up in something else.

Did you have any experience in college that prepared you for the public relations field?

I was editor of the *Daily Trojan* (campus newspaper) for a year. It was like running a small community newspaper with 30,000 in circulation. I had an internship every semester, including KABC-TV in the promotions department,

CBS radio national sales, KIIS-FM radio promotions and a real estate trade publication. Internships give you a leg up on the competition. Most important, you develop contacts that carry through into your career.

Was it an advantage to have experience in both print and broadcasting?

As a business and journalism major I could look at the world through two different sets of eyes, seeing the financial bottom line and the creative content side. When you start looking at content from a business perspective, you begin to understand intuitively that journalism fulfills the role of the fourth estate, but it also has to make money. So you have a better understanding of what's going to work.

In addition to looking at the bottom line, was it important to develop your storytelling skills?

You have to be a storyteller. What sells to any consumer of content is capturing the imagination. In an increasingly fractured media universe with attention spans becoming shorter and people's available time becoming smaller, you have to break through the clutter. Technology allows you to better organize a search for the content you're looking for, but you have to make it interesting or no one cares. The old saw that "content is king" is still true. Technology can help deliver the content, but it can't create content. Someone has to write or shoot a story.

What skills helped you adjust to public relations in the political arena?

It's a different set of skills. Early on, politics was about promoting issues and good policies, telling a story. Political media has de-evolved into a series of "spins" and "gotchas." How many times do you have to whack (your opponent) in order to win? The thoughtful, reasoned political analysis about political issues has de-evolved into how much dirt can you dig up, or can you catch the other guy saying the wrong thing?

How is social media changing the roles of the journalist and the public relations practitioner?

In the social media environment, news companies are asking reporters to create additional content. Before, in a typical news cycle on a newspaper, you might write one story a day. That evolved into a morning and evening edition, a wire service or syndication. Then you had to write a personal blog, a Twitter feed and other social media. Now, a single reporter is a mini-publishing house. The value of social media in aggregating an audience is to become a mini-brand, a personality. Journalists now are not just reporting news, they are creating content for their own personal channels of delivery.

PR practitioners have responded by creating our own channels for the client to talk directly to the consumer instead of through the media. When Dell computers has its own Twitter feed or YouTube channel, that becomes a powerful medium for people to access information directly. But the content still has to be creative, useful and arresting, otherwise no one cares. PR people also use the alternative media sources to engage journalists. You used to send out a pitch letter or e-mail. Now you pitch a journalist on his Twitter feed. It's a platform journalists can use to find sources. We haven't changed the process of what we do, which is talk to reporters. What has changed is how we talk to them.

Is this a change for the better?

Old line journalists will tell you the world is falling apart, while a lot of PR people are caught in the fervor of using social media. I take a third view, that it's not good or evil. You have to look at technology as it develops. The one truism about technology is that it creates new platforms for content. When you think about it, we went from the printing press, to radio and television, then we introduced electronic communications on the web, and then multimedia elements on the web. Every time there is a platform adjustment in technology, content providers in media, journalism and public relations rush in to figure out how to adapt and exploit it.

If you are an aspiring PR student, you have to be a technophile. You have to understand how technology operates, what it can do in terms of how it delivers, aggregates and displays content, and then you can exploit it to maximum advantage. That is the most significant change in the last 15 years in our business.

The future of media, journalism and PR is still the classic battle. There are people who will create critical content that examines products, goods, services, politicians and issues. And then there are people who will attempt to influence that creation. But the difference you will see is that the line between those two will become increasingly blurred, as PR people morph into pseudo-journalists because they are capable of producing content, and journalists looking for monetary opportunities will form alliances with PR people to reach a broader audience.

Should PR practitioners be entrepreneurs, or sign on with an established company?
You have to do it on your own and learn from your mistakes. You have to go through the painful process of starting a blog, only having five followers and feeling a little bit of despair in order to understand aggregating an audience. That makes you more valuable to a company that you work for.

What's the best advice you ever received?
My first boss at Burson Marsteller told me that the first thing you should do when you meet your clients is shut up and listen. Very smart people have a tendency to want to talk right away and demonstrate to everybody how smart they really are. The smartest thing they can do is shut up, listen to everybody else and really understand the dynamics of what is being said. That makes you a better person in terms of being able to respond to the clients' needs.

What's your advice to people entering this field?
When I was coming out of business and journalism school, I wish someone had told me about the importance of making the human connections. The networking … is really the recipe for success in the modern business world. It's not about how smart you are. It is your ability to shake someone's hand, look them in the eye and inspire confidence. At the end of the day, as we get into a world that is increasingly separated by communication channels that distance us from one another, the ability to make the human connection in person or through media is more and more important. Whatever communication vehicle you choose, you have to exert the same energy and conscious thought that you would when you are meeting somebody in person. If a person's first impression of you is your Facebook page, it's just as important as sitting in an interview in your best suit.

ANN KELLAN

Intermedia Marketing & Production, Atlanta

Job: Video producer, media consultant and voice-over talent
Market: Based in Atlanta, with corporate and non-profit clients reaching a worldwide audience
Hometown: Vienna, VA
Education: University of Virginia, BA in Communications; Duke University, Nicholas School for the Environment, Fellowship
Career Path:
  Morning news anchor and reporter, WHAM-AM radio, Rochester, NY
  Reporter, WHAM-TV, Rochester, NY
  Anchor and reporter, WPRI-TV, Providence, RI
  Medical Reporter and News Anchor, WJZ-TV, Baltimore, MD
  Freelance reporter, media consultant, video producer, voice-over talent, Atlanta
  International Science and Technology Correspondent, CNN, Atlanta
  Host, *Science and Technology Week*, CNN, Atlanta
  Segment Producer, Iraq War military desk, CNN
  Interim Bureau Chief, CNN, Boston
  President, Intermedia Marketing & Production, Atlanta

How did your college education and student media experience prepare you for a career in journalism and public relations?

My college education taught me how to think analytically. It didn't teach me how to operate a camera or write a news story. My education gave me tools to tackle most subjects. If I had it to do over again I would have taken a wider variety of courses in business, politics, history, law, and science. Actually I was intimidated by science, so it's ironic that I ended up being a science correspondent for CNN.

Getting your foot in the door to cover news took some creative maneuvering. I worked my butt off in college media for four years. I was the first woman to be president of the University's radio station, WTJU-FM, and directed a half-hour student-run news program at the local cable TV station in Charlottesville. After graduation, I moved to Rochester, New York, and took an advertising job to get job leads from the radio and TV sales staff about broadcast jobs. It worked. I learned about a job opening at a small radio station and got a news reporter job working the night shift in a three-person newsroom. From there I accepted a morning news anchor job at WHAM radio, and from there to WOKR-TV which is now WHAM-TV. A few years later I moved to Providence as an anchor and general news reporter and started pursuing medical reporting. No one else was covering that beat. Actually, medical reporting was a new concept in TV. I pitched medical stories to the assignment editors and they let me cover them. The experience paid off. When I left Providence for WJZ-TV in Baltimore, I started as a general assignment reporter. The station's medical reporter was a doctor, and when she left, my boss gave me a chance to cover the medical beat. I was the Healthwatch reporter at WJZ for the next five years.

At CNN, I covered the science and technology beat and hosted *Science and Technology Week*, which included covering one story a week for the show. I covered everything from Comet Hale-Bopp to the annual hackers conventions in Las Vegas. When my CNN contract ended, I resumed my freelance career, always looking for ways to re-purpose my skills. I found opportunities in public relations and media consulting. Companies are always looking for ways to get their stories to the public. I help them find relevant and newsworthy messages and conduct simple media training sessions to help experts better present their messages on the air.

How would you describe your typical work day?

I get up early, let the dogs out, check the latest news, my e-mail, and then I might start working on a script for a science story. I might work with a new client on an environmental campaign. It's a mix of science writing, video producing and corporate communications work. I am constantly learning new ways to tell a story in a changing media landscape.

How has multimedia changed your job?

Perhaps the biggest challenge is the ever-changing technology. Video equipment is less expensive and more portable and more varied than ever. It has become a useful tool like a pencil and pen. Pretty soon, everyone will use video as a form of expression.

I'm learning that a video shot for the web is different than one shot for wide screen TV. Images on a small web screen have to be bolder and simpler to captivate the audience. It's all about getting the story out and keeping an audience's attention. The challenge is finding the best combination of tools to tell the best story possible.

As far as the technology, the formats are more varied today than when I first started so there's the added challenge today to know the type of camera you're using, the format, the audio, how the video will be stored and archived, how it will be logged, transmitted, and ultimately viewed by the client and the audience.

How do you develop your relationship with a client?

By listening. I try to achieve a client's objectives using the tools appropriate to the task. If you want to tell teenagers about a new product, don't target a mass audience. It's a cardinal sin to deliver the right message to the wrong audience.

A number of my clients today can use web sites to distribute video, audio, and text to news outlets. They can download a wide variety of video and audio clips to suit their needs. With news budgets so tight, most journalists welcome opportunities to access video and audio from corporate and non-profit clients. Often, it's footage they couldn't otherwise obtain.

How important is it to be a good storyteller?

Storytelling is important but more important is finding a good story to tell. That's a big problem in journalism today – having the time, the budget and permissions needed to delve into the story behind the story whether it's controversial, libelous, or could tick off an advertiser. Any news reporter can fill up two or three minutes with entertaining pictures and talk and say absolutely nothing. It happens all the time. The storytelling is just fine, but there's no story.

What career accomplishment are you most proud of?

There is nothing like feedback from your audience. When I was a medical reporter in Baltimore people would stop me on the street and thank me for alerting them about having their blood pressure checked. After reporting on a new colon cancer screening, I received a thank-you letter from a viewer saying that screening saved their life. A huge number of kids got excited about science and technology after seeing our CNN reports on the FIRST Robotic competitions. These are the kinds of things that make you feel good. I'm proud of all the stories I've done that have touched anyone, even just a little.

How do you see the future of multimedia journalism and public relations?

The future for public relations is bright. Companies will continue to find ways to use all forms of media to reach a target audience with messages via TV, radio, cell phone, or Internet devices. It's about designing an appealing and provocative message.

Journalism, on the other hand, has a tougher road. With less emphasis on discovering the truth and more emphasis on making a profit, its future is questionable. Journalism is a noble profession that relies on public interest and people's insistence to know what's going on, whether it's in their home town or on the other side of the globe. So what happens when what's relevant can't make a profit? It's often the flashy Hollywood star, the sensational car crash or murder that draws a crowd, not the tax hike or the impending water shortage or school board vote, which are perceived as boring. It's an important profession hanging on by a thread. We can only hope there will always be people interested in journalism and the means available for them to make a living.

7

Ethical Journalism in Multicultural Media

Multimedia journalists confronted difficult ethical choices while reporting on the human suffering caused by the 2010 earthquake in Haiti. Some reporters with medical training found it hard to watch from the sidelines. CNN's Dr. Sanjay Gupta operated on injured children and tweeted that his video crew had become a "crack med team." NBC's Dr. Nancy Snyderman splinted broken bones, saying, "I am first and foremost a physician." ABC's Dr. Richard Besser also treated patients with immediate needs but said that reporting on the public health consequences of the disaster was his primary responsibility. "I don't want the story to be about me," he told *The Washington Post*. "It's about the situation here."

The potential conflict of interest sparked a debate among news executives and academics. Paul Friedman of CBS denied any conflict of interest, saying the dual role of doctor-reporters is "something we can do without prostituting ourselves or misleading the audience." However, Stephen J.A. Ward, a journalism ethics expert at the University of Wisconsin, voiced concern about the prospect of networks competing to showcase the medical feats of their correspondents, saying it left him with "an uncomfortable, queasy feeling."

Ultimately, it is left to the audience to decide if reporters who get personally involved with a story have abandoned the traditional ethics of the journalism profession, or whether the first-hand experience provides a more compelling story. Is it better for a journalist to help one injured person, or pass by the victim in order to file a story that eventually motivates a platoon of doctors and nurses to join the relief effort? To answer such questions as a multimedia journalist, you will have to develop your own ethical framework.

Power Performance: Multimedia Storytelling for Journalism and Public Relations, First Edition. Tony Silvia and Terry Anzur.
© 2011 Tony Silvia and Terry Anzur. Published 2011 by Blackwell Publishing Ltd.

The Basic Principles of Journalism Ethics

The Society of Professional Journalists has proposed four basic principles for ethical reporting:

- *Seek truth and report it.* Be honest, fair and courageous in gathering, reporting and interpreting information. Journalists should:
  - Tell the story of the diversity and magnitude of the human experience boldly, even when it is unpopular to do so.
  - Examine their own cultural values and avoid imposing those values on others.
  - Avoid stereotyping by race, gender, age, religion, ethnicity, geography, sexual orientation, disability, physical appearance or social status.
  - Support the open exchange of views, even views they find repugnant.
  - Give voice to the voiceless; official and unofficial sources of information can be equally valid.
- *Minimize harm.* Treat sources, subjects and colleagues as human beings deserving of respect. Journalists should:
  - Recognize that gathering and reporting information may cause harm or discomfort. Pursuit of the news is not a license for arrogance.
  - Show good taste. Avoid pandering to lurid curiosity.
- *Act independently.* Be free of obligation to any interest other than the public's right to know. Journalists should:
  - Avoid conflicts of interest, real or perceived.
  - Remain free of associations and activities that may compromise integrity or damage credibility.
  - Refuse gifts, favors, fees, free travel and special treatment, and shun secondary employment, political involvement, public office and service in community organizations if they compromise journalistic integrity.
- *Be accountable to readers, listeners, viewers and each other.* Journalists should:
  - Correct mistakes.
  - Clarify and explain news coverage and invite dialogue with the public over journalistic conduct.
  - Encourage the public to voice grievances against the news media.

You can download a printable copy of the full code of ethics at: http://www.spj.org/ethicscode.asp.

Ethics in a Global Context

While news organizations all over the world strive to practice ethical journalism, there are many places where these ideals are far from the reality for working journalists. They operate under restrictions on where journalists can go, or what they may be allowed to report. Governments may attempt to control the content of news reports by requiring journalists to have a permit. In countries without a tradition of free expression as a fundamental right, government officials may see little distinction between a reporter and a dissident or a spy. Ignoring these political and cultural restrictions can be perilous. Consider the case of freelance journalist Roxana Saberi, an American of Iranian and Japanese descent. In 2009, she was detained in Iran for reporting without a permit and for buying a bottle of wine, which is forbidden under Islamic law. Although she was working for NPR and the BBC, she was accused of spying for the United States and sentenced to eight years in one of Iran's most notorious prisons. After 100 days behind bars and a hunger strike, Saberi was freed only after President Obama appealed to Iranian authorities to release her as a gesture of "Islamic mercy." Saberi, who insists she was nothing more than a working journalist, returned to the United States. She could be re-arrested if she attempts to practice journalism in Iran during a five-year probation period.

Coverage of Iran's 2009 Green Revolution also demonstrated how the phenomenon of user-generated content has further blurred the line separating the professional journalist from the concerned citizen with a video camera and an uplink. An internet video of a dying young woman, wounded by a sniper's bullet, became an international symbol of the Iranian protest movement. One of the top prizes in journalism, the George F. Polk Award, was bestowed on the unidentified "brave bystander with a cell phone camera" who recorded the unforgettable image and shared it with a global audience. "You don't need the imprimatur of a huge news organization to be taken seriously as a journalist," columnist Jeff Bercovici concluded. "Journalism is not a profession, or even a trade, really. It's an act. And anyone who performs that act is, at that moment, a journalist."

Most news organizations have their own codes of ethics. When something doesn't feel right to you, the wisest course of action is to seek advice from an editor or a more experienced reporter. Reporters for the Reuters news service are encouraged to always have a "second pair of eyes" to review their story. However, multimedia journalists often must act on their own, with only seconds to decide if it is ethical to publish a given fact, image or point of view. Your ethical choices will determine how your personal brand of journalism is perceived by the audience. Before you hit the "send" button, make sure you have chosen wisely and are prepared to accept the consequences.

Media and Politics: A Changing Landscape

During the Cold War, scholars began to analyze the role of the press in different countries as a reflection of the social and political structure. One study advanced four major theories of the press:

1. *Authoritarian:* based on the idea that truth is the product of a few wise men. In this system, the government decides what the people should know.

2. *Libertarian:* based on the idea that the search for truth is one of man's natural rights. The press is a partner in mankind's pursuit of the truth, unrestricted by government.
3. *Social Responsibility:* based on modern-day concepts such as equal time for opposing political candidates. This theory developed as the Libertarian press became concentrated in the hands of powerful media elites, often motivated by profit.
4. *Soviet Communist:* an expanded version of the Authoritarian theory. The press is controlled by the government, which claims to seek the truth on behalf of the people, not for profit.

Times have changed, as the "press" has evolved to include broadcast and Internet mass media. Governments have also developed beyond the two-sided conflict that defined the decades after World War II. The old saying that "freedom of the press belongs to those who own the press" has taken on a new meaning in a world where anyone with a computer and an uplink can be a publisher. However, multimedia journalists must be aware of social and political boundaries. In a more recent study of the mass media in Arab nations, William Rugh theorized that "the most powerful factor influencing the structure and functioning of the media ... is the actual political reality that prevails in each country at a given time." He defined three types of mass media:

1. *Mobilization:* The government controls the content of the news and uses the media to build support for its programs. Opposing views are not permitted.
2. *Loyalist:* Media outlets may be in private hands, but laws prohibit criticism of government policies and religion. Journalists practice self-censorship.
3. *Diverse:* Media ownership is diverse and journalists operate under few restrictions or laws that are rarely enforced. Citizens are exposed to a variety of political and cultural views.

The transformative nature of new media will undoubtedly lead to new classifications in the future. Scholars already have noted the "Al-Jazeera effect" as the wide availability of satellite news and online programming presents an alternative to state-controlled media. Journalists in highly restrictive environments may feel powerless to attempt the type of reporting they can watch on CNN or the BBC. At the same time, multimedia journalists operating under international press freedom guidelines may not realize when they have broken the law in the country where they are working. Case in point: Laura Ling and Euna Lee, two reporters for Current TV, were taken into custody in 2009 while covering a story on human trafficking at the border of China and North Korea. The journalists claimed they unintentionally set foot on North Korean soil for only a few moments, then rushed back. The North Korean government charged the two women with illegal entry and hostile acts. They were found guilty in a secret trial and sentenced to 12 years of hard labor. Imprisoned in one of the most isolated countries in the world, the reporters were allowed little contact with the outside during five months in captivity. Only a personal intervention by former US president Bill Clinton persuaded North Korean leader Kim Jong Il to pardon and release the two journalists.

Dangers Facing Journalists

In some parts of the world, journalists are literally dying to tell a story. *San Diego Union-Tribune* columnist Ruben Navarrette observed, "It's open season on Mexican journalists who cover the drug trade and are being murdered while trying to report their stories." He noted that one newspaper announced it would stop covering drug violence rather than risk the lives of its reporters.

According to the group Reporters Without Borders (known by its French acronym RSF), more than 800 journalists have been killed in the past 15 years while doing their job and over 90 percent of the killers have not been punished. RSF estimates that about 100 cyber journalists are imprisoned for what they published online. The RSF handbook for journalists states that while nearly all the world's rulers claim to support press freedom, they regularly fail to do so. "Repression of journalists is no longer just a government affair," the handbook says. "Terrorist organizations, gangs, drug-traffickers and extremist religious and political groups are all keen to get rid of the inconvenient witnesses they consider journalists to be." The RSF handbook, available online, offers advice on how to stay safe, as well as resources for training, insurance and protective equipment.

International Principles of Press Freedom

Fortunately, in much of the world, the principles of media freedom are well-established. The foundation is Article 19 of the United Nations Charter. It states:

> Everyone has the right to freedom of opinion and expression; this right includes freedom to hold opinions without interference and to seek, receive and impart information and ideas through any media and regardless of frontiers.

Waving a copy of the UN charter probably won't help much in a violent or repressive situation, but it is comforting to know that, as a journalist, you are part of a worldwide community of truth-seekers who share a common set of ethical values. As journalism ethicist Deni Elliott has written:

> Ethics serves as a bridge across cultures. Every culture has ethical content, explanations and processes. Every person, regardless of culture or race, is susceptible to the harms that we all want to avoid ... However, cultures differ substantially from one another in how they rank goods and evils; they differ in the most fundamental beliefs of the role of human beings in the larger physical world ... And cultural groups differ widely in their power, politics and ability to control the expression of their values.

The bottom line for multimedia journalists is to know the laws in the country where you are working and always observe the global principles of ethical journalism. Ethics are important because they enhance the way the public perceives journalists as a group and your personal brand of journalism. As more citizen-journalists post their stories for a worldwide audience on YouTube, the web site has launched a Reporters' Center, with videos of noteworthy journalists offering advice on everything from how to conduct interviews to personal safety in a conflict zone.

Avoiding Conflict of Interest

- Do not accept bribes or any form of payment from a source for a story.
- Do not accept gifts from sources.

Declining small gifts can be difficult in some cultures. Know the policy of your news organization or develop standards of your own. If a source wants to buy you a meal, try to pay for your share. If the same hospitality is being offered to everyone covering a story, such as refreshments at a news conference, it is generally not a problem. However, a substantial gift, like a lavish weekend at a resort with the expectation of favorable coverage, should be declined or disclosed in your story. Journalists who fail to disclose their freebies could find themselves under government scrutiny, like the "mommy-bloggers" who prompted the US Federal Trade Commission to issue 81 pages of guidelines for product reviews in 2009.

Commercial conflicts of interest commonly arise when covering business. Reporters can be required to disclose their personal investment holdings and avoid reporting on companies where they may have a conflict. If you're a tech reporter, and a company wants to give you the latest hot tech gadget so you can write about it, you're on shaky ground. You could refuse the gift and have your news organization purchase the item. Or you could disclose in your story that you evaluated the item for your research and returned it. The unethical choice would be to write about something that was given to you with the expectation of favorable coverage, and then failing to disclose this arrangement to your audience.

On some beats, such as entertainment, access to celebrities can depend on a close working relationship with public relations practitioners. In one instance, a film company threatened to bar certain critics from free advance screenings and publicity interviews because of negative reviews. An obvious solution would be for reporters to wait until the movie is released in theaters, then purchase a ticket and remain free of any pre-conditions for their coverage. The film company later relented, deciding it had more to gain by allowing all qualified journalists to preview and publicize its films. Audiences can often tell which critics have a reputation for honesty, and which reviews are bought and paid for by film companies. The value of your integrity? Priceless.

News vs. Advertising

Traditional news organizations have a firewall between the news department and the advertising department. People who want to promote their products in the media should buy commercial time or ad space; journalists should be able to make news judgments without considering how a story might affect the news outlet's bottom line. Once again, new business models are blurring the line. If your health report is sponsored by a local hospital, you will have some tough choices to make if hospital officials are accused of financial misconduct or endangering patients. Do you ignore the story to please the sponsor? Do you report the story and risk losing the financial support for your segment? Ethical guidelines would argue in favor of being responsible to the public's right to know by reporting the story and disclosing your relationship with the hospital as part of your report. However, powerful sponsors may try to stop a damaging story.

Co-author Terry Anzur uncovered a story for KCBS-TV in the 1990s on workers at a local automobile factory who were crossing the street to a liquor store during their break time and consuming large quantities of alcohol before returning to work on the assembly line. A law enforcement officer analyzed the video and determined that the workers were too impaired to legally drive a car, much less build one. Despite the fact that this behavior was "caught on tape," the story never aired; car dealers put pressure on the station by threatening to withdraw their advertising. Several years later, KCBS made a different decision on a similar story. Investigative reporter Joel Grover exposed local car dealers who were using deceptive practices to inflate the price consumers paid for an automobile. Among other things, the report showed how dealers were breaking the law by requiring Spanish-speaking customers to sign documents printed in English. A trade publication reported that KCBS-TV General Manager and CBS Stations Group head John Severino told the complaining dealers that they could certainly pull their advertising in response to the story, "but that we would report that as a news story, and to explain why they were pulling their ads, we would have to rerun the story." The story not only aired on KCBS; it made national news on the CBS network and went on to win awards for investigative journalism. Clearly, ethical behavior has both its risks and rewards.

Engaging in Political Activities

Traditional media organizations value objectivity and require their journalists to avoid even the appearance of a conflict. Consider these provisions of the Reuters code of ethics:

> Displays of political affiliation or support for partisan causes have no place in our newsrooms. No member of editorial, whether a journalist or support worker, may wear campaign buttons, badges or items of clothing bearing political slogans on the job, nor bring posters, pamphlets and other political material to the workplace to distribute or display.
>
> Outside work, Reuters respects the right (and in some countries the obligation) of staff to vote in elections and referendums and does not seek to interfere with that right. The company also recognises that staff enjoy certain fundamental freedoms as a result of their nationality or where they live. Reuters, however, expects journalistic staff in all branches of editorial to be keenly sensitive to the risk that their activities outside work may open their impartiality to questioning or create a perception of bias.

While this may be as easy as confining your political expression to your secret ballot on Election Day, it's not always that simple. The multimedia environment is challenging the traditional assumption that journalists must not advocate for partisan causes or candidates. Certain media sources appeal specifically to niche audiences that want the news delivered with a point of view. Faith-based journalists, such as Frenita Buddy who is profiled in this chapter, serve an audience that expects news coverage to reflect their religious beliefs. Social networking has complicated efforts to avoid the appearance of bias, as statements on a reporter's personal web page may conflict with the requirements of his or her news organization.

Transparency and Disclosure

Many ethical dilemmas can be resolved through transparency. Simply put, you will disclose any potential conflicts to your audience as part of your coverage. It's okay to be biased, as long as you disclose it. When your content goes beyond the facts to include the journalist's opinion, it should be labeled "opinion" or "analysis." Multimedia news organizations often make use of the "about us" section on their web page to disclose their political leanings or business affiliations.

It's also a good practice to post your code of ethics on your web site, as Reuters does, so that your audience will understand how you are attempting to fulfill your journalistic responsibility to seek the truth. Allow the audience to "peek behind the curtain" to learn how your stories are put together. For example, if you agreed to certain ground rules as a condition of getting a big interview, share that information in your story.

Slander and Libel

The Media Law Resource Center defines slander and libel as "legal claims for false statements of fact about a person that are printed, broadcast, spoken or otherwise communicated to others." Often grouped under the heading of "defamation," libel generally refers to statements or visual depictions in written or other permanent form, while slander refers to verbal statements and gestures. Under the constitutional guarantee of freedom of speech in the United States, it is rare for a journalist to be sued for slander or libel. If the story involves a public figure in the US, such as a politician or a celebrity, he or she must prove that the false information was published with malice and reckless disregard for the truth. It's not possible to cover an entire media law course in a few paragraphs, but the simplest way to avoid defamation problems in the US is to be certain that everything you publish is true.

Defamation laws differ in countries around the world. The global reach of multimedia journalism raises the possibility that you could be sued in another country, such as the United Kingdom, where libel is much easier to prove. In some countries, the law makes it possible for public officials to sue for damages, even if the story is true. This becomes a form of intimidation because journalists may practice self-censorship, rather than risk an expensive legal battle that could put their news organization out of business. Be aware of the laws in the countries where your work is published and seek the advice of a qualified legal expert if you have any questions.

Social Networking

The demands of multimedia require news organizations to have a presence on social networking sites. You may be encouraged to blog on the company's web site or use Twitter to promote a big story. But conflicts arise because many journalists maintain their own pages, not only to communicate with friends, but also to build an audience for their personal brand of reporting, especially if they are freelancers working for many outlets on multiple platforms.

It may be impossible to build a firewall between your personal and professional web identity. A TV news anchor in Monroe, Louisiana, declared on his personal Facebook page that he was the only person on the news staff under the age of 40 who could identify the "Enola Gay" as the aircraft that dropped the atomic bomb on Hiroshima during World War II. The anchor added, "Not sure whether to be proud or not." His boss, however, decided that the comment reflected badly on the TV station's news operation. The anchor was fired.

Most news organizations have developed policies on personal and professional internet activity. Consider these guidelines from the *Washington Post*:

> In general, we expect that the journalism our reporters produce will be published through *The Washington Post*, in print or digitally, not on personal blogs, Facebook or MySpace pages, or via Twitter or other new media. We are happy to have reporters post links to their stories or other *Post* material.
>
> On the use of new media outside of work: We assume that our journalists won't embarrass *The Post* or impair their journalistic independence through anything they may publish on Twitter, Facebook, blogs or any other new media. We don't and can't practically monitor everything our reporters might do in their own time, so we rely primarily on their good judgment and common sense.

The policy at the *Los Angeles Times* states that staffers are always linked to the paper when they engage in online activities. "Assume that your professional life and your personal life merge online regardless of your care in separating them. Don't write or post anything that would embarrass the LAT or compromise your ability to do your job," the policy states. "Assume that everything you write or receive on a social media site is public and knowable to everyone with access to a computer."

The bottom line is that you could be accountable for any social networking that reflects badly on your news organization, like complaining to your friends about a boss or a co-worker. Be sensitive to cultural differences; what may seem like a harmless beach party picture may be offensive in some cultures if it shows too much skin or alcohol consumption. You may also damage your career with any posts that cast doubt on your professionalism. If you are covering both sides of a political campaign, for example, don't announce to the blogosphere that you personally favor one side over the other. Be prepared to explain why you are listed as a "friend," "fan" or "follower" of a politician or cause, even if you are only monitoring their feed for possible news stories. The Radio Television Digital News Organization (RTDNA) offers ethical guidelines for social media and blogging on its web site at: http://www.rtdna.org.

Ethics in Public Relations

Take another look at the basic principles of ethical journalism at the beginning of this chapter. Telling the truth, accountability and minimizing harm are core values in both journalism and public relations. However, the public relations practitioner is not independent. Instead, he or she presents a client's message from a specific point of view. Transparency and disclosure are the keys. You may produce a multimedia news release that looks like a news story. However, it should be clearly labeled as advertising or promotional content. You want news organizations to use your material, but encourage them to identify the source. When reaching your customers directly through multimedia, users might find your story even more credible if it's the "official" advice from the company that makes or sells the product. But your good reputation must be earned.

The field of public relations in the US has its own standards for ethical decision-making, some of which share common elements with other media. The Public Relations Society of America centers its mission on the premise that "protecting integrity and the public trust are fundamental to the profession's role and reputation." PRSA has a code of ethics which can be found on its web site (www.prsa.org). The following "principles" are identified by PRSA as originating from the organization's core values:

- Protect and advance the free flow of accurate and truthful information.
- Foster informed decision making through open communication.
- Protect confidential and private information.
- Promote healthy and fair competition among professionals.
- Avoid conflicts of interest.
- Work to strengthen the public's trust in the profession.
- Be honest and accurate in all communications.
- Reveal sponsors for represented causes and interests.
- Act in the best interest of clients or employers.
- Disclose financial interests in a client's organization.
- Safeguard the confidences and privacy rights of clients and employees.
- Follow ethical hiring practices to respect free and open competition.
- Avoid conflicts between personal and professional interests.
- Decline representation of clients requiring actions contrary to the Code.
- Accurately define what public relations activities can accomplish.
- Report all ethical violations to the appropriate authority.

Ethical guidelines for public relations are often tested in a crisis. As columnist David Lazarus wrote in the *Los Angeles Times*, serving the public interest can be good for business. The often-cited example is Johnson & Johnson's response to a 1982 scare involving the pain-relief medicine Tylenol. Seven people died after someone poisoned several bottles with cyanide pills. The manufacturer quickly recalled 31 million bottles nationwide, redesigned the packaging to be tamper-resistant and launched a public awareness campaign to restore consumer confidence in the product. On the other hand, companies can pay a price for holding back crucial information. When safety issues were raised about some of Toyota's vehicles in 2010, company officials appeared in the media to assure the public the situation was under control, while internal communications told a different story. "Toyota's actions … – the initial denials, the obfuscation, the *gradual* acknowledgment of safety issues – suggest that its priority first and foremost has been to cover its crankcase, not safeguard its customers," Lazarus wrote in a story headlined, "What's so hard about doing the right thing?" The best advice, according to chief executive Ben Allen of the risk-consulting firm Kroll Inc., is to "Be clear, be honest and say what you don't know."

Civic Journalism: Beyond the Press Release

Consultant Bob Andresen advises journalists: "Report, don't repeat." Think of a press release as only the starting point of a story. A journalist should be prepared to put official statements in context. What led up to the statement? What are the opposing views? Who will be affected by the statement or policy? Will the announcement have any unintended side effects?

Journalists are often accused of presenting only the extreme points of view in the name of delivering "both sides" of a story. For example, if the government has announced a controversial new policy that will raise taxes, a television story might provide "balance" by showing the anti-tax protestors in the streets. Civic journalism seeks out stories in the middle: the people most likely to be affected by the news. A hardworking citizen may be more than willing to pay a fair share of taxes, but have concerns about how the money will be spent. Joe or Jane Citizen, however, is unlikely to call a news conference. You must seek them out. Public relations practitioners should anticipate such requests. If you are preparing a news release, help journalists find real people who can explain how the announcement will make a difference in their lives.

Civic journalism can also reveal new and better ways to serve your audience. Tampa Bay Online editor Rick Scheuerman changed his perspective on sports coverage when he spent less time asking coaches about their strategy and spent more time in the stands, asking the fans what the game meant to them. Similarly, voters asked to submit questions for a political debate might have different interests from journalists, who are more focused on the "horse race" aspect of the election and the memorable sound bites. At the height of the sex scandal during Bill Clinton's presidency, a Cincinnati newspaper invited readers to send in the questions they would like to ask the president. Not one question involved Clinton's relationship with Monica Lewinsky. Citizens wanted to know about the environment, jobs and the country's economic relationship with China. By listening to your audience, you will uncover the stories that will keep users engaged with your content.

Investigative Reporting

Investigative reporting is another way to go beyond a press release. It is a basic function of the news media as a watchdog over the workings of government and the public's right to know. While it is a very specialized field, the basic elements are:

- following the "paper trail" of official documents;
- developing sources;
- revealing information that was previously hidden or unreported;
- demanding accountability from those responsible.

Access to documents

Most open societies have established procedures for citizens to access official documents. In the age of the Internet, a wealth of public information is available online. However, some records may only be examined in person. Other records may be obtained through a formal request. In the United States, the Freedom of Information Act (FOIA) allows for full or partial disclosure of previously unreleased information and documents controlled by the government. The procedure can be time-consuming and expensive if substantial copying fees are charged. Some information may be withheld or "redacted" due to privacy or national security concerns, and you may have to appeal.

To track down the documents you need for a story, you should first visit the web site of the agency you are writing about. You may find that the information is already available online. If not, the agency should post its guidelines for FOIA requests. The American Society of Newspaper Editors sponsors an annual "Sunshine Week" to encourage all government agencies to open their records to journalists and the public. Know the laws in your area and be persistent if you believe there are documents that will shed light on an important story. But don't stop with the documents. Tell the stories of the people affected by what you have uncovered.

Computer-assisted reporting uses data from official sources to create a picture of how an issue is affecting a community. For example, information from a public safety database of the registered addresses of convicted sex offenders could be used to develop an interactive map, showing which neighborhoods have the highest concentrations of known predators and whether they are close to schools, churches, parks and other areas where potential victims gather. Again, you will want to talk to citizens and law enforcement to complete the story of how this information from a database affects the community.

Sources and attribution

Try to keep all information "on the record." As long as you have identified yourself as a reporter working on a story for broadcast or publication, you have the implied consent of the subject to conduct an interview. Once you have obtained the interview, it is "on the record" and may be quoted. You are under no obligation to put the information "off the record" if the person changes his or her mind later on. In rare cases, when there is no other way to obtain the information, you may agree in advance to talk "off the record." This means that you will not quote the source by name and will not publish or broadcast the information unless you can attribute it to another source that can be quoted. You may also go back to the original source and ask for permission to quote specific parts of the conversation.

Your news organization should have a policy on officials who are willing to talk "on the record, but not for attribution." For example, an official who would lose his job for criticizing a rescue effort may be willing to tell you why a necessary piece of life-saving equipment was cut from the budget, if you are willing to withhold his name and quote him only as "a source within the department." Again, you should make every effort to confirm the information from official documents or a named source.

Withholding the identity of a source presents a special challenge for the video storyteller. You may need to do an interview in which the subject's face is concealed, either through extreme backlighting or a digital effect. You may also wish to disguise the source's voice by electronically altering it to sound lower or higher. Again, these techniques should be used only as a last resort when you have tried every possible means to obtain the crucial information from a source that can be quoted by name or interviewed on camera.

Some countries have "shield" laws which allow reporters to protect confidential sources, but in some situations reporters can face a court order to reveal their sources, especially when national security or public safety is involved. Reporters who do not reveal their sources may face fines, jail time or other punishment. When someone wants to talk "off the record" or "not for attribution," ask yourself if this information is worth the possible consequences to you and your news organization. There may be a way to obtain the same information from a quotable source or an official document. If you must use a confidential source, get the approval of a manager and be prepared to accept the consequences of keeping your promise of confidentiality, even if it means going to jail.

Use of hidden cameras and microphones

ABC's *Primetime Live* told a powerful and important story in 1992 by using hidden cameras to show that a supermarket was selling spoiled meat. Five years later, a jury ruled that the TV news magazine was also in the wrong by using reporters who lied about their identity in order to obtain the video. The Food Lion chain was awarded more than five million dollars in damages.

According to guidelines from the Radio Television Digital News Association (RTDNA), hidden cameras should be used only when all other alternatives for obtaining the information have been exhausted. The information must be of vital public importance and outweigh any harm caused by a possible invasion of privacy. In the Food Lion case, reporters used fake résumés to obtain jobs in the store, putting them in a position to record video of tainted meat being repackaged for sale. The jury took issue with the fact that the reporters lied to get the story. "I don't have anything against undercover investigations," said juror Carla Jackson. "But if you're going to do them, do them legal." Know the laws in your area. In some US states it is legal to record pictures with a hidden camera, but not sound, unless the person has given his or her consent.

When Disaster Strikes

Your news organization should have a disaster plan that will enable your station or web site to serve your community under emergency conditions. If you are a freelancer, plan ahead. How will you file stories if the power goes out? Do you have emergency supplies of food, water, cash and fuel? How will you communicate if the phones are not working? Do you have a network of sources that can provide reliable information? The time to answer these questions is *before* disaster strikes.

There are three major sources of information in a disaster:

*   survivors living in the affected area;
*   emergency personnel;
*   representatives of government and social service agencies.

You may not have much official information in the early stages of a disaster. But don't delay simply because you don't have solid facts to report. Let the audience know that you are aware of the developing situation and are working hard to get more detailed information as quickly as possible. Have attribution for everything that you report. Quote police, rescue workers, medical personnel, eyewitnesses, or people living in the affected area. If you have a report that is not attributed and confirmed, broadcast or publish it only if the information could save lives. State clearly that it is unofficial, unconfirmed information and keep working to confirm it. Let the audience know if you check on a rumor and find out from a trusted source that it is NOT true. Never scare the public or present unverified information as solid fact.

If authorities are unavailable or unwilling to answer your questions, report it and keep trying to get answers. Verify information from more than one source and be alert for situations where the stories differ. When Hurricane Katrina struck New Orleans in 2005, people were stranded and fighting for their lives. Responders lacked resources to complete rescue and relief efforts. At the same time, President George W. Bush commended the nation's top emergency official for doing "a heck of a job." These conflicting narratives deepened the tragedy of the monster storm, revealing snarled government red tape, as well as race and class distinctions that were reflected in the response. Although officials defended their actions in the months that followed, they could not repair the political damage. US News and World Report later assessed the impact of the disaster on the president's second term, noting that "his failure to act while thousands of desperate people, unable to find food or water, were appealing for help on national television erased his image as an effective decision maker."

The human side of the story

Within the overwhelming scope of a disaster are many individual stories of tragedy and survival. Profiling victims and survivors, interviewing rescuers and following relief workers into the field will put a human face on the need for help. Let's examine the emergency response to the 2004 tsunami in the Maldives. The Red Cross, in partnership with the Red Crescent, the United Nations and the Maldivian government provided the following services in the days following the disaster:

- 200 large community tanks for safe water storage.
- Basic necessities like soap, towels, toothbrushes and other toiletries for more than eight thousand displaced families.
- School supplies to help children resume normal play and express their feelings.
- Training for social workers and teachers, providing psychological first aid to more than 22,000 people on 26 islands.
- Vaccinations against measles and rubella for 145,000 children, young men and women.

Looking beyond the numbers, consider how each of these programs could have been the starting point for a compelling individual story. Interview a teacher who is trying to help her students cope with the loss of loved ones and resume their education. Photograph the smile on the face of a child receiving a new toothbrush. Talk to a young mother about her concerns for the health of her children, or the older brother who is carrying a bucket of clean water to his family's temporary shelter. Show the survivors' living conditions and follow someone through a typical day in their struggle to meet basic needs. Official facts and figures can be included in your narration over the pictures of the recovery effort. Ideally, the journalist is the bridge between those offering help and those who need it.

Interviewing victims

Some people find it therapeutic to talk about their feelings, while others will refuse to speak with a reporter. Journalists should follow some basic rules when covering disaster victims who may be grieving, disoriented, frightened or in shock:

√ Identify yourself as a reporter working on a story and let the person know you would like to print their name and include their comments in your story. Be sensitive to any concerns.

√ When interviewing survivors who have lost friends or family members, focus on the lives of their loved ones. Express sympathy for their loss. Encourage them to talk about their memories of the person before asking the more difficult questions about how he or she died. Allow a friend or relative to be nearby during the interview to offer encouragement and support.

√ Ask to see a family photograph of the loved one, and be sure to return it if you need to take it back to the newsroom to include it in your story.

√ Avoid the question, "How do you feel?" Obviously, someone who has suffered a devastating loss feels terrible. A better way to ask the question: "What goes through your mind when you think about what you have lost and how you will go on from here?"

√ Listen more than you talk.

√ If the person you are interviewing breaks down, show some compassion. Offer a tissue or a drink of water and turn off the camera or recording device to allow him or her to regain composure.

√ Double check the facts with official sources. People who have suffered trauma understandably may be confused about the exact details.

√ Conclude the interview by asking if there is anything the person wishes to add.

√ Make eye contact and sincerely thank them for sharing their story.

√ Respect the wishes of those who don't want to talk to you. Leave a business card and encourage the person to contact you when he or she is ready.

Take care of your audience and yourself

After you have served your community during the disaster, people may turn to your news organization for help during the recovery. Set up a phone line or web site to connect people with relief efforts. The public may also call or e-mail with suggestions for follow-up stories. Social networking can be helpful because it allows the audience to enrich your coverage with their own experiences.

Without even realizing it, journalists can suffer from the effects of covering disaster and conflict. Recognize the symptoms of burnout or stress disorder among the people in your news organization, including isolation, emotional drain, loss of compassion, insomnia, excessive drinking or drug use, and other health problems. You should consult a health professional to discuss these symptoms.

Reporting in Conflict Zones

Portable multimedia tools make it possible for even freelance journalists to go where the action is. When inexperienced reporters venture into conflict zones they may underestimate the danger. Freelancers often lack the support of a major news organization to help them get out of trouble. *The New York Times* reported on the plight of Amanda Lindhout, a Canadian who used her savings from a waitress job to finance her dream of freelance reporting from Somalia. She lacked the resources of established news outlets that were hiring armed guards to protect their journalists. While visiting a refugee camp, she and an Australian colleague were taken hostage by Somali kidnappers and held under abusive conditions for 15 months. Families and friends raised a reported $600,000 for their release.

"The main driving force is instant fame or instant recognition of some sort," says Rodney Pinder of the International News Safety Institute, a Brussels-based group that offers training for war-zone reporters. "It's a way of breaking into the business at a very competitive high-end level." A safer way to approach a war zone is to become embedded with a military unit. While this vantage point provides compelling stories, the journalist is obviously limited to only one point of view. There may also be restrictions on what may be reported in order to protect military intelligence and personnel.

Of course, the story doesn't end when the armed conflict is over. For reporters from the state-run Rupavahini TV channel in Sri Lanka, covering their country's 30-year civil war became a way of life. As one battle-hardened reporter explained, finding crisis and conflict is not difficult when both sides are shooting at each other. When the war ended in 2009, war correspondents faced a different challenge: building equally compelling stories around the challenges facing their country and its people in the post-war period.

Respect Community Standards

War and disaster coverage is filled with disturbing images. Multimedia journalists must respect community standards when choosing to publish pictures of human suffering. The family of a US Marine who was killed in Afghanistan asked the Associated Press not to publish graphic photos taken of Lance Corporal Joshua Bernard as he was dying from combat wounds. AP withheld the pictures until after the young man's funeral, but then distributed them, saying the images showed "the real consequences of war." Defense Secretary Robert Gates criticized the AP's "lack of compassion and common sense," saying, "The issue here is not law, policy or constitutional right – but judgment and common decency." Following the criticism, some news organizations admitted they were unaware they had published the image because it was posted on their web sites automatically from the AP feed. Some editors rationalized showing the photos on a web page, with a warning for those who might want to click away, but not publishing the images on the front page of the printed newspaper where consumers could not avoid it.

Use good judgment when deciding what gruesome details to report and what to leave unsaid or unseen. For example, a reporter at an explosion doesn't need to describe the human body parts scattered over the scene. Similar guidelines apply to images of the dead and dying. Avoid extreme close-ups of faces. Think about how you would want the victims to be shown if they were your own family members.

Journalism Across Cultures

The Maldives Media Training Project, conducted by Terry Anzur Coaching Services in 2008, revealed some fascinating contrasts between American journalists and their counterparts in a different culture. The Maldives' Ministry of Legal Reform, Information and Arts hired a group of American consultants to help prepare journalists at the state-run

TV and radio stations for the country's first multi-party presidential election. For the Americans, accustomed to working under the First Amendment freedoms of speech and press in the US Constitution, it was culture shock. Opposition candidates had never appeared on Television Maldives. A special crew provided flattering videos of the ruling president that were televised as announcers read press releases exactly as written by the president's office. Advertisers received the same fawning coverage in "business" stories. New recruits to the job of "newscaster" were teenagers with little more than a high school education. One TVM executive described the evening newscast as "propaganda read by children."

Under a new constitution that guarantees freedom of expression, Maldivian journalists embraced the challenge of fair and independent election coverage. The state TV and radio stations reached an agreement to give free political airtime to opposition candidates. TVM organized its first-ever presidential election debate and launched a weekly interview program modeled after *Meet the Press*. News reports began to include opposing views and the voices of ordinary citizens. Privately owned stations provided alternative coverage. Voters elected a former journalist, who was once jailed for his dissident views, as their new president. Shortly after the election, the Maldives College of Higher Education enrolled its first class of journalism students.

Alongside this rapid political change, cultural boundaries proved more difficult to cross. A seemingly harmless feature story on Valentine's Day caused an unexpected controversy. Despite warnings from Islamic authorities that Muslims should not celebrate a holiday named after a Christian saint, stores in the capital city were doing a brisk business in flowers and candy. Building a story around the cultural conflict, TVM reporters interviewed an Islamic scholar, as well as shopkeepers and customers. But when a reporter concluded in a standup that the celebrations raised the possibility of a more "secular" society, cultural alarm bells went off. Maldives, a chain of idyllic islands in the Indian Ocean, is a 100 percent Muslim country which requires adherence to Islam as a condition of citizenship. It's not unusual for a religious topic – the annual award given to those who memorize the entire Koran, for example – to lead the newscast. Multimedia content, from music videos to news stories, must take into account the religion's ban on such things as kissing in public or same-sex relationships. These restrictions can be puzzling to Americans, whose First Amendment rights include freedom of religion, as well as freedom of the press.

This example illustrates that, while technology is connecting the world through multimedia, cultural differences remain. Standard news content in one country may be highly provocative in a different cultural context. But you don't have to go halfway around the world to appreciate this diversity. Working as a multimedia journalist allows you to discover a whole new world of people and cultures in your own community. Perhaps you've never ventured into the poor neighborhood on the other side of town, or experienced a cultural event in an ethnic community that is different from your own background. Try to put aside any stereotypes or assumptions you may have and help your audience understand the similarities and differences. Through your power performance in multimedia, you will establish your reputation as an ethical journalist with a global audience.

Multimedia Exercises

1. Choose a country and do some research on its media laws. Look at examples of that country's multimedia on the Internet. How do journalists operate in that country's political and cultural climate? Check the country's ranking on web sites that evaluate press freedom. Now imagine that you have been assigned to report a story from the country you have researched. How would you get the story without putting yourself and your sources at risk?

2. Role-play the following:
   (a) a journalist being offered a free laptop computer or a free trip in exchange for a favorable story;
   (b) a journalist interviewing someone who has just lost a loved one to violence or disaster;
   (c) a journalist and a public relations person negotiating the conditions for a high-profile interview.

3. Develop a disaster plan for your campus or community news organization. Invite a local first-responder to your class, such as a police officer or firefighter, to discuss their concerns about news coverage of emergency situations.

4. Examine your own social networking pages for any content that might compromise your integrity as a journalist. Better yet, pair up with a fellow student and critique each other's social networking pages for potential conflicts of interest.

5. Analyze a news release about a government statement, policy or program. (Hint: many agencies post their news releases on their web sites.) How would you go beyond the official statement through civic journalism? Computer-assisted reporting? Investigative reporting?

Works Cited and Further Reading

Amanpour, Christiane. "Analysis: what journalist's release means for Iran, US relations," *CNN.com/world*. Cable News Network, Turner Broadcasting System, 11 May 2009. Accessed 9 Mar. 2010. Retrieved from: http://www.cnn.com/2009/WORLD/meast/05/11/iran.analysis.amanpour.saberi/index.html#cnnSTCText. Review of Roxana Saberi case by CNN's chief International Correspondent.

American Society of Newspaper Editors. *Sunshine Week: Your Right to Know*. 24 Mar. 2010. Accessed 21 Apr. 2010. Retrieved from: http://www.sunshineweek.org/. Freedom of Information web site with special section for students and educators.

Austen, Ian. "For novice journalists, rising risks in conflict zones," *The New York Times*. 29 Nov. Accessed 2009. Retrieved from: 21 Apr. 2010. http://www.nytimes.com/ 2009/11/30/business/media/30somalia.html?_r= 1&ref=media.

Bercovici, Jeff. "The new journalism," *The New York Observer*, 23 Feb. 2010: Accessed 6 Mar. 2010. Retrieved from: http://www.observer.com/2010/media/new-journalism. Journalism prize awarded to cell phone video shot by an anonymous Iranian citizen, and its implications for the profession.

Black, Jay, Steele, Bob and Barney, Ralph. "Guidelines for use of hidden cameras," in *Doing Ethics in Journalism*. The Society of Professional Journalists. Radio Television Digital News Association. Accessed 20 Apr. 2010. Retrieved from: http://www.rtdna.org/pages/media_items/guidelines-for-hidden-cameras156.php.

Broadcasting & Cable Magazine. "Nobody walks in Los Angeles," 21 May 2000.www.broadcastingcable.com,

April 20, 2010. Account of KCBS response to car dealers' threat to withdraw advertising over Joel Grover report on deceptive practices.

Dart Center for Journalism and Trauma. "A global resource for journalists who cover violence." Retrieved from: www.dartcenter.org.

Dart Center for Journalism and Trauma: News University free online course with strategies for interviewing disaster victims and coping with stress, Poynter Institute for Media Studies and Dart Center, University of Washington, United States. Access the free training at: http://www.newsu.org/courses/course_detail.aspx?id=dart_trauma05.

Dunlap, David. "Behind the scenes: to publish or not?" *The New York Times*. 4 Sept. 2009. Accessed 21 Apr. 2010. Retrieved from: http://lens.blogs.nytimes.com/2009/09/04/behind-13/?scp=1&sq=Joshua%20bernard%20+%20photo&st=cse.

Elliott, Deni. *Ethics in the First Person*. Lanham, MD: Rowman & Littlefield, 2007. An overview of ethics as a bridge across cultures.

Farhi, Paul. "In Haiti, reporters who double as doctors face a new balancing act," *Washington Post* 20 Jan. 2010: n. pag. Accessed 5 Mar. 2010. Retrieved from: http://www.washingtonpost.com/wpdyn/content/article/2010/01/19/AR2010011904293.html. Reporters, scholars and executives of American TV networks debate the role of doctors who are also journalists covering a disaster.

Gunter, Johnny. "Former KTVE anchor Scott wins appeal," *The News Star*. Gannett, 3 Mar. 2010. Accessed 4 Mar. 2010. Retrieved from: http://www.thenewsstar.com/article/20100303/NEWS01/3030318. News story on TV anchor's appeal of his firing for posting a negative comment about his co-workers on a personal Facebook page.

International News Safety Institute. Accessed 21 Apr. 2010. Retrieved from: http://www.newssafety.org/. Training and guidelines for journalists in conflict zones.

Lazarus, David. "What's so hard about doing the right thing?" *Los Angeles Times* 11 Feb. 2010: B1 + 4. Article on contrasting public relations responses in crisis situations

Ling, Lisa. "Journalists Laura Ling and Euna Lee pardoned and released from North Korea," *Oprah*. Harpo Productions, 4 Aug. 2009. Accessed 15 Apr. 2010. Retrieved from: http://www.oprah.com/world/Journalists-Laura-Ling-and-Euna-Lee-Released-from-North-Korea. Journalist Lisa Ling reports on her sister Laura's detention in North Korea, along with Current TV colleague Euna Lee.

Media Law Resource Center. MLRC, Inc., 2010. Accessed 11 Aug. 2010. Retrieved from: http://www.medialaw.org. Resource for multimedia law issues in the United States.

Meier, Barry. "Jury says ABC owes damages of $5.5 million," *The New York Times*. 23 Jan. 1997. Accessed 20 Apr. 2010. Retrieved from: http://www.nytimes.com/1997/01/23/us/jury-says-abc-owes-damages-of-5.5-million.html.

Navarrette, Ruben. "When reporting is dead-on in Mexico," *San Gabriel Valley News* 27 Jan. 2010: A15. Article on killings of Mexican journalists writing about drug wars.

Pew Center for Civic Journalism. "Doing civic journalism," *Civic Journalism Is … True Stories from America's Newsrooms*. Accessed 20 Apr. 2010. Retrieved from: http://www.pewcenter.org/doingcj/pubs/cjis/index.html.

Reporters Without Borders. *Handbook for Journalists*. Reporters Without Borders USA, Jan. 2010. Accessed 15 Apr. 2010. Includes press freedom documents, ethical guidelines, how to stay safe in a war zone or disaster area.

RTDNA Ethics Committee. "Social media and blogging guidelines," *Radio Television Digital News Organization*. RTDNA, 2010. Accessed 6 Mar. 2010. Retrieved from: http://www.rtdna.org/pages/media_items/social-media-and-blogging-guidelines1915.php?g=37?id=1915.

Rugh, William A. "Do national political systems still influence Arab media?" *Arab Media & Society*. Summer 2007. The American University in Cairo, Kamal Adham Center for Journalism Training and Research. Accessed 25 May 2009. Retrieved from: http://www.arabmediasociety.com/topics/index.php?t_article=143.

Siebert, Fred S., Peterson, Theodore, and Schramm, Wilbur. *Four Theories of the Press:* Champaign, IL: University of Illinois Press, 1963. *Google Books*. Accessed 14 Apr. 2010. Retrieved from: http://books.google.com. Classic Cold-War era study, comparing and contrasting the role of the press in society under different forms of government.

Society of Professional Journalists. "Code of Ethics," Eugene S. Pulliam National Journalism Center, 1996–2010. Accessed 5 Mar. 2010. Retrieved from: http://www.spj.org/ethicscode.asp.

Thomson Reuters, *Handbook of Journalism*. Apr. 2008. Accessed 15 Apr. 2010. Retrieved from: http://handbook. reuters.com/index.php/Main_Page. Complete stylebook for international multimedia news service, including ethical guidelines for corrections, sources, use of social media.

Walsh, Kenneth T. "Hurricane Katrina left a mark on George W. Bush's presidency," *US News and World Report*. US News and World Report LP, 11 Dec. 2008. Accessed 14 Apr. 2010. Retrieved from: http://www.usnews.com/articles/news/politics/2008/ 12/11/hurricane-katrina-left-a-mark-on-george-w-bushs-presidency.html. Assessment of wider political implications, following a disaster in which the official story of the response differed from the experience of the victims.

YouTube. "YouTube Reporters' Center: helping you report the news," Accessed 15 Apr. 2010. Retrieved from: http://www.youtube.com/reporterscenter. Videos of prominent journalists offering multimedia reporting advice.

COURTESY DIANA DERBY

COREY FLINTOFF

National Public Radio

www.npr.org

Job: Foreign Desk correspondent
Market: National, based in Washington, DC
Hometown: Fairbanks, Alaska
Education: University of California, Berkeley, BA, English Literature; University of Chicago, MA, English Literature
Career Path:
   Researcher and editor, *Encyclopedia Britannica*
   Freelance reporter, *Chicago Reader* weekly newspaper.
   Reporter and News Director, KYUK-AM/TV, Bethel, Alaska
   Reporter, KSKA-FM, Anchorage, Alaska
   TV documentary producer and radio news reporter, KYUK AM/TV
   Reporter and executive producer, Alaska Public Radio Network, Anchorage
   Newscaster, *All Things Considered*, National Public Radio, Washington, DC.
   Foreign Desk correspondent, National Public Radio, Washington, DC

Did you always want to be a war correspondent?
Absolutely not. I thought I would be an Alaska-based radio person for my entire career.

   In the early days I didn't anticipate coming to Washington. I was very involved in the basic Alaska issues: energy, oil and gas, Native Alaskan sovereignty and business, what they could do with their land.

You worked at a bilingual radio station where you learned to announce the station ID in the Yup'ik Eskimo language. What was it like covering the Native Alaskan community?

It was a period of colossal change. (A law) had passed to compensate the Native Alaskans for the land they gave up and for the exploitation of oil and gas in Prudhoe Bay.

In order to settle all the land claims along the Alaska pipeline, the state first had to settle the claims in general. They did it by setting up corporations for all the native regions. Some of them failed spectacularly. They were unprepared for the world of business. But others succeeded very well. It was a wonderful story, full of drama and very colorful personalities. It had everything: crime, fraud and skullduggery, but also heroic action to protect the rights of the native shareholders.

You worked in print, radio and television long before the idea of multimedia came along. How has that affected your career?

When you work in any small place, you don't require a lot of qualifications to get the job, but once you get the job, you can do pretty much anything that you can teach yourself to do. It pays off for me now, because I do both radio and the web. It's a huge priority for NPR and it's a tremendous opportunity, but it also raises a lot of questions about what our core product really is.

How do you approach a major story in terms of different media platforms?

When I'm in Washington, I do almost exclusively web material, but when I'm overseas I do radio first and then before the piece goes on the air I do a web version with photographs that are shown simultaneously.

How do you deal with the risk involved in reporting from a war zone like Iraq?

We make our own choices. NPR makes it clear that it's up to us to decide whether something is safe. We don't have guards or security details because we prefer to be low profile, but we have security consultants who advise us on the current conditions and what we should be doing to protect ourselves.

Do the security issues make it harder to get the story?

From 2005 to 2008 it was very difficult to get around. Being embedded with a military unit was almost the only way for a foreigner to go out on the street in Baghdad. You're looking at the world from inside a Humvee and everything looks like a bomb, everyone looks like an enemy. It helped me understand the perspective of the American soldiers and Marines. Then, when you went out to interview Iraqis you were in the company of American military people, which shut down any communication you might have. Beginning in 2008 the security was good enough that we were able to go out by ourselves. Now we can travel very freely.

How do you deal with the misery that you see in a disaster situation, such as the aftermath of the earthquake in Haiti?

We were surrounded by people in the camps who simply wanted to talk about their plight (Figure 7.1). They were not expecting anything from us. We talked to a lot of people and walked on. Ethically, you don't want to give someone the impression that there's a quid pro quo. I gave my interpreter some money and told him to look for discreet opportunities to help people, but always after the interview.

It was one of those stories that periodically, when you got away from it, you would have to cry. I met people who had to do horrendous things. But they were still standing and their spirits were unbroken. It

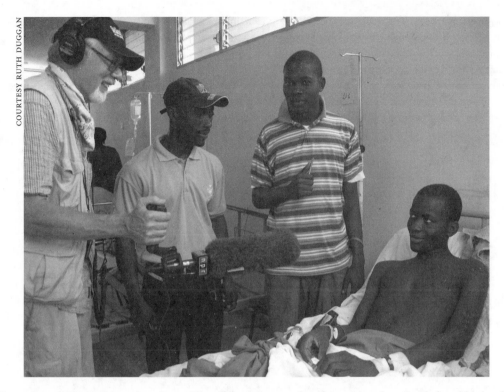

Figure 7.1 NPR Correspondent Corey Flintoff interviews earthquake survivor Jean St. Phal and his brother Marc at the Hôpital de la Paix, Port-au-Prince, Haiti in January, 2010, with Haitian interpreter Joassaint Descollines (second from right).

was incredibly inspiring. Don't be afraid to cry. You're going to have human feelings and you might as well let them out.

Do you use social networks as part of your reporting?
NPR was developing sources and lists on Twitter and Facebook to connect me with sources in Haiti. It proved to be very useful.

What accomplishment are you most proud of?
In the news business, it's "what have you done for me lately?" So for me, it's almost always my latest reporting trip. I'm tremendously proud of the work from Haiti and even after 33 years in the business I'm still learning.

How do you see the future of multimedia journalism?
My big question is who's going to pay for the kind of journalism we've always had the privilege of doing. Journalism will always be there. There will always be a need for great radio reporting, but there might not be radio as we

know it. It might be Internet radio or podcasts. I'm hoping that radio and video will survive and thrive, not just what people can shoot with their cell phones, but real news photography and radio recording.

What's your advice to aspiring journalists?

If you understand basic journalistic skills, you can learn the technology du jour. You can learn videography and how to use Internet tools. Everything technical that I've learned in my career has gone obsolete. The basic principles of how to do the job haven't changed. In some ways, it's gotten better, easier and more fun.

COURTESY THE HOPE CHANNEL

FRENITA BUDDY

Hope Channel

Job: Producer of weekly, live interview program, *World of Hope* and a health program called *Life's Beat*

Market: The network of the Seventh-day Adventist Church reaches a worldwide audience via satellite, TV and the web

Hometown: Akron, OH

Education: Oakwood University, Hunstville, AL, BA in Communication, minor in Political Science, 1999; Northwestern University, Medill School of Journalism, MSJ in Journalism, 2000

Career Path:

Morning show producer, WAFF-TV, Huntsville, AL

English and Bible teacher, Tokyo, Japan

Producer, Hope Channel

How did your college education prepare you to be a journalist?

As an undergraduate, I worked at the college radio station, for three years and by the time I left I hosted my own drive-time show. I also worked on the college newspaper for one year. My internships included working in the communication office of the local congressman and as a public relations intern for a firm in Atlanta. At Medill, we had new media classes for the Internet, along with basic reporting, writing and editing classes.

How would you compare a secular newsroom to a church-based environment?

At the local news station it was always about ratings. My mission is different now, to find the best way to share God's love and not to see if I can beat my competitors with the best story at six o'clock. However, I do miss the breaking news element and the organized chaos of the newsroom.

After the January 2010 earthquake in Haiti, you covered many of the same stories as the secular network news programs.

Definitely. News is part of my background. That's how I think. We had a reporter there who provided "on the ground" reporting. We discussed what doctors are encountering and the medical needs Haiti is facing. We also talked to two people of Haitian heritage who lost family members and are waiting to hear news about others. And then we did a spiritual devotional towards the end.

How has multimedia changed your job?

I don't think of television anymore as just using the remote to turn on the TV. A lot of our viewers are watching Hope Channel online. The Internet allows me provide additional resources to viewers to help take the story a little bit further.

I think faith-based programming will continue to expand in multimedia. There are countries where you cannot openly share your faith, but people are able to share in other ways such as podcasting and video streaming.

What is the best advice you have ever received?

A weekend anchor and executive producer at WAFF told me to always do my best, and that she was proud of me. We don't hear that enough from senior journalists, our mentors. Her encouragement meant a lot because I really knew that someone believed in me. Granted, I made mistakes but I learned from them and always tried to do my best. My advice to others is that it is okay to panic when something new develops. Give yourself a moment to have a normal reaction. Panic or grief is okay … for a moment. Then, get it together and form a strategy to handle the situation. If you don't react naturally once in a while, your emotions will come out when you least expect it.

When did you know you wanted to be journalist?

I decided to go into journalism when I was in high school. My father and I would listen to National Public Radio in the morning on the way to school. I was really into jazz music, and my father said we could listen to jazz, but we had to hear the news headlines first. The more I listened and learned what was happening around me, the more interested I became in sharing the stories of other people. I credit my father for helping me to become a journalist. Not only would we listen to the news, we would discuss it. I really think that inspired me. As I became older, I saw so many people who didn't have an outlet for sharing their story and I hoped that I could be the one to do that. Everyone has a story. Some might be more remarkable than others, but everyone has something to say.

How do you approach a story?

I try to see the situation from the subject's viewpoint. I try to get into their proverbial shoes, and help them share the story in the best way possible. Too often, there are packages with a whole lot of reporter narration, but sometimes the story is told beautifully by the person in their own words. I'd advise someone new in the business to really LISTEN as they interview.

Is a faith-based program able to tell stories that don't get told in the secular media?

I think so. We interviewed a woman who wrote an article for our church magazine about putting her mother in an assisted living facility for people with Alzheimer's and dementia. The secular media would probably talk about how one cares for an aging parent, the mental and emotional stress, and medical advances in research. In a faith-based program, I can let the woman share how the experience has strengthened her faith. The mother, in her altered state of mind, said some unkind things to her daughter, but the daughter has been able to forgive and continue to care for her mother with love. There's nothing wrong with either approach, but working at Hope Channel I am able to tell stories from a perspective that highlights my faith and trust in God.

You also appear on camera to deliver Hope Channel news updates. How did you make the transition from behind the camera, and what challenges did you face?

There's a whole different set of things to worry about, including the way you look, speak, and how you enunciate your words. I also find that it has brought me closer to my crew, which is primarily male. I am often amused when the guys are more concerned that my hair looks good and that there's no lipstick on my teeth! Always take the time to develop a rapport with your crew. Not only can they help you in a pinch, they also have good ideas, a suggested question or an angle for an interview that you might not have considered.

What's your advice to others who may be looking for a way to combine journalism with something they are passionate about?

Don't be afraid to take a chance. Do everything you can. Volunteer. I was able to dabble in radio and that parlayed into voiceover work. I dabbled in public relations and that has helped me in my current job. In graduate school, I worked in print and wrote stories for newspaper and the internet. You never know how a passion or a hobby can provide a unique perspective to your job. Today, it's a great blessing to do something I'm passionate about, and be able to exercise my faith at the same time.

8

Putting Your Skills to Work

Career advice for journalists in the US used to be simple: Get an entry-level job in a small town and work your way up through bigger cities until, at last, you reach the national or international level. Multimedia has opened new career paths in journalism and public relations. The goal of your power performance is to develop the essential skills and qualifications to follow the path that is right for you.

Preparing to Enter the Job Market

Want a job in multimedia journalism or public relations? Get in line. An annual survey by the University of Georgia counted more than 216,000 students in US graduate and undergraduate journalism and mass communication programs in 2008. During that same year, more than 55,000 students graduated and entered the job market. You face the challenge of standing out in a crowd. At the same time, the crowd is competing for a limited number of opportunities. The US Bureau of Labor statistics is forecasting these trends through 2016:

- *Writers and Editors*: Average job growth of 10 percent with many new positions being created through online publications. Demand will increase for writers in specialized areas such as science or law. Many will be self-employed; others will leave the profession "because they cannot earn enough money."
- *Public Relations Specialists*: Above-average job growth of 18 percent, with intense competition for entry-level positions as the number of new college graduates exceeds the number of openings.
- *News Analysts, Reporters and Correspondents*: Little growth in jobs, with keen competition for scarce openings at major mass media outlets. Journalism graduates more likely

Power Performance: Multimedia Storytelling for Journalism and Public Relations, First Edition. Tony Silvia and Terry Anzur.

© 2011 Tony Silvia and Terry Anzur. Published 2011 by Blackwell Publishing Ltd.

to work as freelancers, report for specialized publications, work in small, local markets, or find jobs in other fields. Consolidation and technology will limit overall job growth, but openings will be filled by people with multimedia skills.

Many traditional journalism jobs have already disappeared from advertiser-supported broadcast and print media, while online content business models are still developing. Some media organizations are generating content with freelancers instead of full-time staff members. As a result, making a living in multimedia journalism and public relations can be an impossible dream for all but the most talented, persistent and well-prepared applicants. Fortunately, multimedia skills are transferable to many fields in which communication is important. You should begin building your résumé now.

Working in Student and Community News Media

A college diploma is a major achievement, but by itself it is not enough to land you a job in multimedia journalism. Some notable journalists in the US, such as the late ABC News anchor Peter Jennings, never graduated from college or even high school. Employers value practical experience and want to know that you have worked on your campus or in your community to build the skills needed for a paying job.

The Internet has created many opportunities for unpaid "citizen journalists" to publish their work. YouTube and CNN iReport, as detailed by Lila King in this chapter, allow citizen journalists to reach vast audiences. You may have the opportunity to "do" citizen journalism while you're still in school. Philadelphia's Temple University, for instance, has its MURL (Multimedia Urban Reporting Lab). Situated in the Center City area, it's described as "the cornerstone of the Journalism Department's mission to better tell stories in the under-covered and under-served neighborhoods of Philadelphia." Students post their work online (http://philadelphianeighborhoods.com) where potential employers can access it.

The same is true of the University of South Florida St. Petersburg's "Neighborhood News Bureau." Located in the heart of Midtown, the city of St. Petersburg's historically African-American neighborhood, NNB is a working newsroom, where students, both undergraduate and graduate, interact with the community around them, work "beats" and produce multimedia stories. Founded on the best traditions of community journalism, NNB provides a forum for students to practice their citizen journalist skills and a forum for the audience to read or view their stories. (http://www.nnbonline.org).

The Importance of Internships

An internship, also known as a practicum, allows you to learn first-hand how the news business works while you are still completing your education. Most interns are unpaid, but many news organizations are sensitive to criticism that they are exploiting free labor, and require interns to be enrolled in a journalism program for college credit. The best internships allow you to contribute to the news product and publish stories under your own byline. You can later use these clips to build your job-hunting portfolio. You may get more hands-on experience in a smaller news organization, rather than a large network that may assign interns only to menial tasks. As you read the profiles of Casey Cora, Poppy Harlow and Kris Van Cleave, notice how they took advantage of any opportunity to be part of the newsgathering process during their student internships. Their work was noticed by hiring managers when there was a paid position to be filled.

The Multimedia Portfolio

The point of all this preparation is to create a body of work. Take a look at the sample résumé from Mazen Hafez, a recent graduate of California State University at Northridge (Figure 8.1). Notice that his background includes jobs and internships in radio, print, broadcast and online media, as well as leadership positions in campus organizations. Similarly, you will draw on your experience to put together your job-hunting portfolio, which should be accessible online and include the following elements:

- A professional résumé
- Your contact information
- Representative examples of your best work:
  - video stories you have produced and/or presented
  - page images or links to your published print stories
  - photographs or slide shows you have created
  - examples of web graphics you have designed
  - interactive media packages
  - links to your blogs and other online content, such as social media.
- A cover letter that is customized to the requirements of each job application. The cover letter may take the form of an e-mail or postal-mail letter that invites the employer to view your portfolio online or on a DVD.

The Home Page

The home page for your portfolio (Figure 8.2) should reflect good web design and make it easy for the potential employer to access each essential element. Online journalism expert Paul Wang advises students to "keep it clean and simple." He cites studies showing that users will spend an average of only about 30 seconds with your home page, or as research-ers Nielsen and Loranger put it, "The Home Page: So Much to Say, So Little Time."

Wang advises students to be well organized: "Decide if you have enough video stories or print stories to create a separate button for that, or if you are better off creating a section called multimedia."

Your home page should give an immediate impression of who you are, but save the details for the interior pages where the user may be willing to spend more time. Avoid long

Mazen Hafez

1357 Any Street, Fresno, CA 93703   (661) 555-5352   MazenHafez1@email.com

Experience

KGPE-TV, (Fresno) Producer
- Produced Morning Newscast (5am–7am) and morning cut-ins
- Wrote all scripts and teases in a clear, conversational, and concise method to make each story feel new and current
- Worked overnight assignment desk to update stories, gather facts, ingest video and coordinate live shots
- Ordered all graphics for ots, maps, and full screens to create a more visually appealing newscast
- Posted articles onto station website and social media pages
- Set-up and booked guests on a weekly basis to promote community events and special reports
- Contributed enterprise story ideas for sweeps and daily newscasts

KNBC (Los Angeles) Editorial Assistant   June 2009–January 2010
- Edited video to use for our daily newscasts
- Assisted assignment desk with finding news stories and updating story plan
- Conducted bi-hourly beat checks and fact checking scripts
- Contributed to morning meetings with managing editor, producers and reporters for the evening newscast by offering story ideas and organizing storyboard
- Printed scripts and placed them in rundown order for anchors to read

NBC Dateline (Los Angeles) Intern   January 2009–April 2009
- Coordinated Pre-Interviews and Pre-shoots
- Pitched story ideas and worked on location shoots; assisted/produced "A Step Too Far" episode
- Logged tape, researched data; fact checked several stories

Valley Views Reporter (Los Angeles) Writer, Producer,   Sept. 2008–May 2009
- Worked as a reporter, writer, camera operator, teleprompter, anchor, and editor for a weekly 30-minute college news cast
- Wrote scripts off wire-copy, produced rundowns, audio technician, field reporting
- Wrote teases, and turned in bi-weekly news packages

KCSN (Los Angeles 88.5 FM) Radio News Writer   Jan. 2008–July 2008
- Wrote local stories daily based off wire copy for a 30-minute "Morning Drive" news cast
- Various field reporting assignments in Los Angeles ranging from hard news to features
- Conducted and edited telephone interviews

RTNDA President, CSUN Chapter   May 2008–May 2009
- Chaired weekly meetings
- Moderated and conducted several panel discussions about journalism issues
- Organized fundraisers and community events
- Vice President from September 2007 to May 2008

Director of Elections of CSUN Associated Students   June 2007–May 2009
- Chaired and coordinated weekly Elections Committee meetings
- Made reports to A.S. Council regarding the elections process
- Administered the election in accordance with the Election Code
- Developed marketing strategy and managed a budget to increase student participation

Education

California State University – Northridge   2005–2009
(Journalism Major/History Minor) GPA: 3.3

Figure 8.1   Mazen Hafez résumé

Figure 8.2   Home page of multimedia photojournalist, Ashley M. Jones

blocks of text on your home page and make sure the user can see all the important content without having to scroll down. Wang encourages students to focus on the *one* aspect of their background that should leap off the home page. For example, if you have a strong video demo reel, design the page to encourage the user to click there. Users won't wait forever while your content loads. Choose a video playback format that will display quickly, such as Flash Movie. Don't make it hard to find and click on important details like your résumé, contact information and links.

Keep in mind that there is no such thing as "one size fits all" in job applications. Depending on the medium involved, certain job postings may have specific requirements. A TV station may want a stand-alone copy of your video stories and on-camera work on DVD, while a newspaper might be interested in paper copies of your clips attached to your printed résumé and cover letter. However, in the online world, everyone will be able to link to your "master" portfolio as the summary of your best work across various media platforms. A potential employer may discover your work through an online search, but then ask you for more examples.

One final note before discussing how you submit your work: be aware of *key words* in a job description and try to match the words you use in your résumé as closely as possible to the qualifications they contain. Failing to meet minimum qualifications, such as prior experience, may automatically disqualify you from being considered. The other is that, increasingly, that decision isn't made by a person, but a computer program. Many companies/organizations now use such programs to scan résumés submitted electronically for key words. If enough key words aren't present in the résumé, it gets kicked out by the program and is never seen by a human!

Submitting Print and Online Work Samples

Because of the growing importance of multimedia skills, your portfolio should include print, online and video versions of content you have created. Don't just put up links, showcase the work as you would on any web page with a headline, blurb, "read more," etc. Make the point that you know how to motivate people to "click through".

"Click throughs," as they're called in web storytelling, are incredibly important. The idea is to entice the reader with a small portion of your total story, then get them to read the rest by clicking on the "read more" link accompanying your story. Simply scanning stories or grabbing screen shots from the web site where they were published is not going to show a potential employer that you know how to "sell" that story in a cluttered media environment.

Keep in mind that showcasing your print work within the portfolio means demonstrating that someone else thought enough of it to *publish* it. Strive to include only published work; class assignments, as good as they might be or as high a grade as they might have received, were usually seen by only one person – the professor. Published or posted work shows validation by a broader audience.

Finally, don't showcase ALL of your written work. Part of what employers seek in a new hire is a measure of judgment. That means they want to see that you can select from among a body of work what is the *best* work. Only showcase those stories that you truly believe represent your skills at their best. If you think everything you do is great, chances are you're not being selective. Ask the opinion of a professor or a seasoned journalist if you find it difficult to choose.

The Video Demo "Reel"

Whether your video storytelling is intended to reach the audience on air, online or both, your demonstration or demo "reel" is your calling card. Although the term dates back to the days of film canisters and VHS tapes, today's aspiring video journalists no longer have to struggle with duplicating and shipping expensive cassettes. The only place you'll see an actual "reel" is in a museum. Your work samples can be played back on a DVD, or posted on a web site. However, you should carefully read the job posting for specific instructions on how to submit your work. Some may prefer a DVD, others will click on your web link. Failing to follow the instructions could prevent you from being considered for the job.

In order to present yourself in the most professional manner on a DVD or web site, it is best to follow the following format:

- Opening slate
- Video montage
- Complete story packages
- Closing slate

Of course, you could also display a menu of shorter videos on your home page, inviting the viewer to click on the individual elements of your video résumé. Let's explore each element of your demo reel in more detail.

The opening slate

Most DVD-burning programs allow you to customize the menu screen. Or you may be posting your résumé and a link to your reel on a web page. Either way, you should make sure to include:

- Your name.
- Your phone number and e-mail contact information.
- A photo or representative freeze frame.

Why is this information needed? In the chaotic hiring process, your reel may get separated from your résumé and cover letter. You want to make it as easy as possible for prospective employers to contact you if they like what they see, without searching for another piece of paper or an e-mail attachment.

This is a good time to evaluate your personal contact information for the message it is sending and make some changes if necessary. An e-mail address like "babygirrrlxoxox" or "wassupdude" is fine for your social life, but it can sabotage your job hunt. Record a businesslike greeting on your phone voicemail. Be aware that prospective employers are likely to type your name into a search engine or may try to view your social network pages. Before you begin your job hunt, you should remove any questionable material of a personal nature. The best course of action is not to post such material online in the first place.

If you are including a photo on your slate, a professional "head shot" in business attire is best. Avoid glamour shots or casual photos. You may also have the option of grabbing a frame from one of your standups or studio appearances.

Video montage

"Montage" is an editing term which refers to a sequence of short clips. Its purpose on a résumé reel is to quickly show the full range of your journalistic skills. Most hiring managers observe *the ten-second rule*: if they don't like the first ten seconds of your work, they will click out of your reel before viewing the rest of it. You've already learned the rule of *best video first* in visual storytelling. It's even more important to carefully consider the first images on your reel, the initial impression which can make or break your chances of being hired.

Don't waste the employer's time. He or she has to view dozens, maybe even hundreds, of reels for a typical job opening. If you are applying for an on-camera position, we should see you at your best in the very first frame of video. The typical montage will go on to include a minimum of three or a maximum of eight short clips, but should not run longer than one minute. You'll want to show a variety of newsgathering situations such as a serious breaking story, a light feature, a demonstration standup, a live report, and so on. It is not necessary to include the entire standup in a montage and it is okay to include a standup that we'll see again later as part of a complete story. The editing should move the sequence along at a brisk pace, but keep the fancy digital transition effects to a minimum and focus on the content.

Think of the montage as the tease that gets the hiring managers past the first ten seconds. If they don't click out of your video during or after the montage, they have made the commitment to seriously consider more of your work. Use only the clips that show you at your very best. You should have a consistent look that is appropriate to each story. Don't make radical changes in your appearance and leave them guessing which hairstyle represents the person they are hiring today.

Complete story packages

Now that the manager has a positive first impression, he or she wants to know if you can tell a compelling story. You should select a maximum of three strong packages showing a variety of skills, from hard news to light features or enterprise reporting. Don't pad your reel with work that is second-rate. "Grab their interest from the first shot and don't let go," advises Rich Everitt of Talentapes.com. "We select the very best material and that's all we show."

Producer reels

Field producer reels are similar to reporter demos, except that the montage will show a range of story content instead of on-camera appearances. Think of it as the opening of a show that's all about your skills as a journalist. Use compelling sound bites, natural sound and video to draw the hiring manager into the rest of your tape. Newscast producer reels may need to be longer than ten minutes. Edit your program to eliminate commercial breaks and any material, such as a reporter package, the sports segment or the weather forecast, that you did not produce. Your goal is to give your prospective employers a taste of your writing style, your news judgment and the flow of your program. Include headlines and teases, especially if you wrote them. Your cover letter can further explain your editorial decision-making and news philosophy.

Anchoring or digital hosting

Should you include it on your demo reel? Some employers might think you are sending a message that you'd rather not go out in the field to do the nuts and bolts of reporting. Others may want to know if you have the potential to develop into an anchor. Either way, you may choose to include a clip of anchoring in your opening montage, or a longer sample of your studio work after the reporting on your reel. You should only include anchor work if it is of professional quality.

The Importance of Networking

Even in the high-tech world of multimedia, a successful job hunt cannot be conducted on the Internet alone. You need to make personal contact to move to the front of a long line of candidates. Join professional organizations and attend their meetings to meet others in your chosen profession. Your school's alumni network is a good source of successful people who may be willing to advise you. If you know someone who is currently working at the news organization where you are applying, ask if they would be willing to hand-deliver your materials with a personal recommendation. A professor with past experience in the industry may be willing to phone or e-mail a contact on your behalf. Keep in touch with those you meet during internships and contact them again as possible references and advisors for your job hunt. This is not a time to be shy about asking for help.

Entrepreneurial Journalism: Being Your Own Boss

The changing media landscape rewards people with good ideas and the will to make them a reality. You may be able to make a living as a freelancer, or you could strike out on your own by starting a web site.

"There's not a great future in working for mainstream media," says Christopher Harper, who teaches in Temple University's Multimedia Urban Reporting Lab. "The future is for smart, hardworking students to band together, create their own media and make a business out of it."

"Entrepreneurial journalism" is the idea that multimedia storytellers can go into business for themselves. The Internet certainly makes the barrier to access non-existent. Expense is minimal. With a laptop and an idea, the thinking goes, you can make your own job right out of school. Create a web site and start making money. Unfortunately, it's not that simple. The reality is that while many have tried, many more have failed. Making money from a web site, however great the content may be, is a long, slow process.

Applying an entrepreneurial model to the creation, maintenance, and marketing of a web site requires some very specific skills, many of them having more to do with business than journalism. One way to acquire such skills is to enroll in business courses while you're still in college. Taking an example from the Chapter 6 profile of James Lee, you might even consider business as an additional field of study, along with your journalism/communication major. If you've already graduated, think about enrolling in targeted business courses at a local community college or university. Focus on those that teach business startup skills, including ways to finance your venture.

There are many resources available online to get you thinking about the entrepreneurial path. In 2009, the Poynter Institute for Media Studies in St. Petersburg, Florida, began offering seminars for those who want to learn from the experiences of those who successfully launched their own news web sites. Its web site (www.poynter.org), offers online resources linked to "The Future of Entrepreneurial Journalism," including "The Top Mistakes that Startups Make (and How to Avoid Them)" and "Top 10 Sources of Funding for Startups." In addition, New York's Paley Center for Media offers a useful video resource entitled "Real Tales for the Real World: Education of the Entrepreneurial Journalist" online at www.paleycenter.org.

Here are some factors to consider when deciding if being a journalism entrepreneur is right for you:

- Do you have enough money to sustain yourself in the short term?
- How original is your idea? Have others tried it before?
- If it has been tried, why didn't it succeed?
- Does it have an audience "niche" – that is, do you have idea that serves a need not currently being served in the media marketplace?

Telling Your Own Story

Finding your place in a changing industry can be time-consuming and filled with setbacks. Focus on the qualities that make your power performance stand out: Are you unflappable during breaking news? Are you an insightful interviewer? Do you have a passion for uncovering new information? Do you capture images that others will want to download and share? Does your background enable you to develop the stories that are often overlooked? The power profiles in this book provide role models for storytelling in the multimedia world, but it is up to you to tell the story that is uniquely your own.

Multimedia Exercises

1. Compile a list of job openings by going on company web sites and job listing sites.
2. Go to a demo tape site like www.talentapes.com and view the work samples with a critical eye. Which applicant would YOU hire?
3. Assess your body of work. Do you have enough material to put together a multimedia portfolio? If not, what is missing and how will you get it done?
4. Write your résumé. Proofread it carefully and then show it to someone else to proofread again.

5. Write a cover letter, and ask a friend, a teacher or someone at your internship to read it. Have you given the manager a good reason to hire you?
6. Talk to working journalists, such as recent graduates of your school, about how they landed their first jobs.
7. Role-play a job interview, anticipating the questions you might be asked and preparing your responses.
8. Research a specific job opening. Determine what the employer is looking for, including the key words you should include in your résumé and cover letter.
9. Assemble your multimedia portfolio.

Works Cited and Further Reading

Becker, L. B., Vlad, T., and Olin, D. "2008 enrollment report: slow rate of growth may signal weakening of demand," *Journalism & Mass Communication Educator*, 64(3) (2008): 232–257.

Bureau of Labor Statistics. U.S Department of Labor. "Writers and Editors," in *Occupational Outlook Handbook, 2009–2009 edition. US Bureau of Labor Statistics*. N.p. 29 Apr. 2008. Accessed 27 Aug. 2009. Retrieved from: http://www.bls.gov.

Mangan, Katherine. "Stop the presses! revamped journalism courses attract hordes of students," *Hot Topics in Journalism and Mass Communication*. AEJMC, 22 Sept. 2009. Accessed 15 Apr. 2010. Retrieved from: http://aejmc.org/topics/tag/enrollment/. Why students are drawn to journalism education programs emphasizing multimedia and entrepreneurial journalism.

Nielsen, Jakob, and Loranger, Hoa. *Prioritizing Web Usability*. Berkeley, CA: Pearson-Peachpit-New Riders, 2006.

Papper, RTNDA/Hofstra University Annual Survey, 2009.

COURTESY WJLA-TV

KRIS VAN CLEAVE

WJLA-TV

Job: TV News Reporter, ABC 7 and News Channel 8
Market: Washington, DC
Hometown: Los Angeles, CA
Education: University of Southern California, BA Broadcast Journalism, 2002
Career Path:

Internships: ABC News, Los Angeles Bureau, KTLA-TV
Producer, *Cyberguy Report*, KTLA-TV, Los Angeles, CA
Freelance reporter, KTLA and KSWB-TV, San Diego, CA
Reporter, KOAA-TV, Colorado Springs, CO
Reporter, XETV, San Diego, CA
Reporter, WJLA-TV, Washington, DC

On making the most of his internships.

I started interning the second semester of my freshman year in the ABC News Los Angeles bureau tape library. I was a research intern and the youngest intern they ever had. It was a network newsroom and it was union, so there was only so much I could do myself, like logging tapes. The takeaway was seeing how some of the best people in the business do their jobs. And it was my first introduction to things like office politics and the egos that go along with television, the things you don't learn in a classroom.

During my sophomore year, a professor pushed hard for me to intern at KTLA with Kurt the Cyberguy. It turned into a huge platform that was a launching pad for me.

Kurt Knutsson was a big believer in "How much can you do?" He gave me the ball and let me run. I was setting up interviews and stories, I was doing some of the interviews and I graduated to writing the pieces and editing. I spent a year as his intern and by the end of that time I thought of myself as an off-air reporter. The beat was anything we could brand as technology and how it can make your life better. We covered anything from somebody planning a wedding online, to a new gadget, to hanging out with a celebrity who had launched a new web venture.

I was hired as Kurt's producer at the end of my sophomore year. After the September 11th terrorist attacks we did stories on military technology, the things that were being used in the war that had just started. In my opinion that was the technology news of the day. We were one of the first to start reporting on the file-sharing site Napster, when music sharing was becoming the Wild West of getting anything online and the courts were trying to shut it down. We were there for the Internet boom and bust. There was more work than we could do.

Here's what I did well: I found mentors at the TV station, people who were willing to help. There are people like that at every television station. What helped me stand out was that I worked hard. One of the nightside reporters at KTLA, Ted Garcia, allowed me to ride along to get a feel for what it was like. I went out on a story with Ted and his photographer. I had kind of zoned out and Ted said, "What are you doing? You're writing this story. Start working. And when we're done we'll see which script is better and that's the one we'll track." Ted could write a script in 15 minutes max, so I wasn't anywhere near done when he was done. And his story was much better. At the end of the night, he said I could come back next week. Every Friday night, for a whole summer, I rode along. By the end of the summer of my sophomore year in college, I was being trained in how to be a writer by a really talented reporter and immediately implementing those skills by producing in the Cyberguy unit.

How did you balance the job and internships with what you were learning in your college journalism courses?

Getting my degree in journalism filled in the blanks that I had skipped over at warp speed. There were things I needed to learn. I didn't know how to be an investigative reporter. My storytelling needed work. College gave me a chance to process what I was learning at KTLA. Technology stories, if you just do them about some inanimate object, are really boring. So I had to learn that the stories had to be about people. Knowing how to use characters and people in a story takes some time and I needed to learn that in school and doing campus journalism.

So when KTLA assigned you to go on the air with a story about student reaction to the 9/11 attacks, you were ready?

I had the crew for an hour. We talked to some young people, put together a panel and did it live on the morning news, one week after the attacks. The executive producer liked that story and said, "What are you going to do next?" I had read about a surge of military enlistments, and that was my generation. We did that story. KTLA also sent me to their sister station in San Diego to fill in for one of the reporters. When it was time to put my tape together, I was a producer who had been building a reel and riding along with news crews. I wanted to go on the air and be the exception to the rule that you can't start in a big market like Los Angeles. My executive producer said that would do me a huge disservice and she was right. I had experience, but I was a very green reporter. I'm really glad I got to make my mistakes in front of 30,000 people instead of 300,000.

What did you learn during your first full-time reporting job at KOAA-TV in Colorado Springs?

It was culture shock. I had always lived in big cities, and in my mind I had moved to a quaint little town in the middle of nowhere. It was not an easy change for me to make. Being the new kid was nothing new because I had moved a lot growing up.

I worked a lot. The first six months you're there, you are just happy to be on the air and making your slot. After that first six months, people start to get a little cocky. Really what you're doing is you've now reached the level of maybe being adequate at the job. I got a feel for the live shots. And the market, because of its proximity to Denver, was really about storytelling and finding the characters and writing to video and doing these really visual stories.

Not long after I got there, the war with Iraq began and the Air Force academy had a sexual assault scandal. The reporter covering the military couldn't do both, so I inherited the sexual assault scandal. A few months later, he left and I became the military reporter. In that town it's the beat you want to have, because there are five military installations. You had 25,000 local troops, out of a town of 400,000, deploying to Iraq. I had the best beat in the world because there was always a story. It wasn't always good. I think I did 37 memorial services or funerals for service members. There were two months where I did that almost every day. It doesn't hurt if you are timid the first few times because it comes across as sympathetic. I found that, often, military families wanted to tell their story or the story of their loved one, the fallen hero. It was hard, but sometimes you end up being bonded in strange ways to people. We went with one widow and her six-month-old daughter to pick up her husband's body with a full military police escort. It was the only flag-draped casket from that entire war that I ever saw.

After two years in Colorado Springs, what did you learn at your next job in San Diego, as a reporter for the morning show at XETV?

I got a lot of experience doing live shots where the camera was on me for a long time. You rely as much on your personality as you do the facts. After the morning show was done, I could do whatever story I wanted. We did a lot of stories at Balboa Naval Medical Center on how they were helping wounded service members put their lives back together.

I had the freedom to be a "Big J" journalist there. We did a story about sex offenders near schools. I got to know a California Department of Justice agent who runs the sex offender compliance task force in San Diego. It became one story after another. We ultimately won an Emmy after we did a story on a 12-step program the state runs for sex offenders. To me, it sounded like a bad idea for a reality show: Let's release a violent sex predator into the community and see what happens. We went to the hospital, spent time and interviewed patients. One story involved talking to pedophiles about how they picked their victims.

We also won a sports Emmy and a Murrow award. I wanted to do a story on 30-somethings who are crazy skateboarders. The photographer was motivated and I brought a handicam. Skateboarding is such a big part of the culture in San Diego. Here are guys who should have given this up years ago going down hills at 40 mph.

Describe a typical day for a reporter at WJLA-TV in Washington and how multimedia technology has affected your job.

I wear two hats. Some days I'm a special projects reporter. Other days I'm a general assignment reporter and I come in at 11 a.m., knowing that I'll probably be in the A block at 5 p.m. You walk in and you're behind the eight ball. It's a fever pitch. You have to make your calls and get on the road. I subscribe to countless list-servs for neighborhoods and police. You'd be shocked at the stories that come out of that. Sometimes the victim's contact e-mail is right there. Same with Twitter. It's a great tool for young journalists. If one of your followers sends something like "My dog got attacked by a coyote, that sucks," it can develop into a story. My BlackBerry is attached to me at all times. I can follow the news of the day on CNN, the *Wall Street Journal*, CNBC or the *Washington Post* and have access to things like Facebook and Twitter. I couldn't imagine a day without it.

Most memorable story.

I covered the aftermath of the Virginia Tech shooting on April 16, 2007, when a student gunned down 32 people before killing himself. There was a moment that stands out. It was the day after, I'd already interviewed a couple of families that lost loved ones and one of the families was trying to give us a picture of their daughter. We somehow ended up inside the restricted area where all of the families were. Just the sense of awful loss permeated the room. You could hear sobbing. It wasn't something we could ever put on TV, but the ten minutes that we spent in that room waiting for a picture was so haunting. At that moment the story was real.

Best advice for multimedia journalists.

Don't become just a mike holder. Don't just stand there and regurgitate. Make one extra call. Knock on one extra door. You never know what you're going to get.

Also, be patient. It's going to take time to get a job. Once you get a job, you're thinking about how to move on the next job and it's not time yet. There's a reason why the contract in your first job is two years; you need it. Then you move on to your second job and at some point you start thinking about the end game: Who do I want to be when I grow up? The whole industry is in flux and our jobs are going to be different. If you can roll with the punches of being a daily television news reporter, you can adapt to changes.

LILA KING

Senior Producer, CNN.com

Job: Manage iReport.com, a user-generated community web site for citizen journalists
Market: International
Hometown: Atlanta, GA
Education: University of Georgia, comparative literature and philosophy, 1998
Career Path:
  Freelance radio journalist in Atlanta
  Documented the restoration of the vintage Fox Theater
  Joined CNN as a webmaster in 2001

In its first 18 months, iReport.com generated 100,000 video, photo and text submissions. How would you describe your job?
I've always been focused on interactive storytelling and iReport since its beginning in 2006. I call myself the ring-leader. I'm responsible for the site and its development and its priorities and the editorial team.

Why should multimedia journalists get involved?
iReport.com is the simplest way to magnify your voice on a story the rest of the world needs to hear. It's a direct line to CNN from across the world into the news agenda meeting every day. When the producers and reporters get together and decide what we're going to cover and how we are going to focus our resources, iReport is at the table with what's top of mind in the community, what's getting the most activity and what people are most interested in.

Most viewers s became aware of the site during live coverage of the Virginia Tech shootings in 2007, when a student gunman killed 32 people and himself. A student submitted his cell phone video to CNN through iReport.
It was the internal "aha!" moment, when producers across CNN … for the first time really felt the impact of the platform. It's the signature video of the event and as the story was breaking it helped CNN to confirm the details that actually the shooting was much more serious than we initially had thought. Hearing the gunshots and the number of them in that really chilling video is one of the ways that CNN was able to confirm what was actually happening.

How did iReport make use of viewer submissions during the 2009 election protests in Iran?
This story was only being reported through citizen journalists, people on the ground who have cameras and sometimes are at great risk taking pictures and shooting video and sharing their stories. We've been working on developing a model for making user-generated content a meaningful part of the way CNN approaches the news every day.

How do you sort through all the pictures and video?
We try so hard to look at everything that comes in. It's just not possible. iReport.com is built in a way to enable community activity in terms of clicks, sharing, uploads and comments to help elevate the most urgent and interesting pieces of the site.

When it started in 2006, it was a series of upload forms. Ninety percent of what came in never saw the light of day. We recognized at the end of 2007 when we were seeing about 10,000 iReports every month and only about 900 of them actually went out to the world. There was an enormous missed opportunity for great, interesting content that people needed to hear. It didn't feel right for CNN to be sitting on top of all of it.

We built iReport.com as an open invitation to post any kind of story from any place in the world. We built the system with a lot of algorithms to help community activity on the story surface the ones that need to be paid attention to.

Some contributors are designated as "superstar" reporters. How does that work?

It's a crazy mathematical formula that takes into account the number of stories and how many have been on CNN and how many times they get shared and commented on. It's all in the math. There's a system of tags and assignments that we post every day as a way for people to get involved and suggest ideas. We post assignments based on what we think will be the most interesting and relevant to CNN producers. Then we look for what jumps out within a particular assignment. For example ... memories of (pop music star) Michael Jackson. It's a whole new way to write an obituary: people's snapshots of the times that they met Michael Jackson back in 1983, or how much they loved him and wore a white glove.

If your dream is to be a CNN reporter, is iReport a good way to have your work noticed?

Absolutely! If I were a journalism student today and I wanted my work to be seen by CNN, I would look at the assignment desk on iReport.com. There's a list of what CNN producers are after. I would look for ways to answer the questions there in my own local community. One of the things I love so much about iReport is that it surfaces stories from places you almost never hear about. Places that don't have bureaus or staff reporters.

We joke on the iReport team that we have a bureau in this small town in Iceland because there is one man who basically reports every interesting and noteworthy thing that happens. And it's absolutely fascinating. It gives you a glimpse of a corner of the world you otherwise would never really see. Those stories end up in the CNN bin all the time.

Several of the iReporters who are frequent contributors ... distribute their own content using other social media tools. There are buttons on every story that make it easier to post to Facebook, Twitter or e-mail to your friends. If you get the word out and people click on your iReport and add comments to it, it will increase your chances that it will catch the eye of someone at CNN.

Describe the "vetting process" you use to verify the accuracy of the videos that are chosen to be shown on CNN.

Before anything goes on CNN we call the submitter back and confirm the details, do fact checking and the "capital J" professional journalism. There's feedback that goes in to that too. If you contribute something that's local and interesting, there's a pretty good chance that someone from CNN is going to call you back and talk with you about your story and help you to craft it to make it even more powerful.

So iReporters get exposure and experience, but no money?

We don't pay our reporters for contributions. However, CNN has a licensing business called Image Source that licenses footage to other news outlets and documentary filmmakers. iReport is part of that catalog and when iReports are licensed, CNN shares the licensing fee back with the iReporter.

Because it's a community-driven site, it's important to live and breathe by the rules of online communities. When people upload to ireport.com they grant CNN a non-exclusive license to their content, so they are perfectly free to upload to YouTube or their blog or sell it to a local news affiliate if they have a buyer.

The exposure and experience can be really great. We started an iReport internship program and brought an iReporter in and paid him to work with us for the summer as a part of the team because his work was so exemplary.

What's your best advice to contributors?
The advice is to spread your stories as far as you can. iReport is a great way to be seen by producers on a national and international news desk. CNN producers take classes on how to use iReport. There are hundreds of people at CNN actively involved.

Does that mean that someone at CNN will edit your report?
What's great about iReport that it's truly collaborative. It's more than the footage, it's the person and their back story and the context they can bring to the event. Our reporters are not just contributing photos and video. We call them and interview every iReporter who ends up on CNN and direct quotes from their stories end up on CNN. It's important that we look at the iReporter and their experiences as well as their footage. It's very global. I'm proud to say we have CNN iReports from all seven continents, even scientists working on a ship in Antarctica.

How do you handle situations where contributors are putting themselves at risk to get a story?
That's something we've been wrestling with. We talk every day about how to be very careful and mindful of the danger people may be putting themselves in. Our usual practice is to credit our contributors, but very often during the Iran story we've chosen not to reveal the identities of our reporters.

Are there some ethical lines that iReporters should not cross?
The rules are the same as for CNN journalists. We've published some community guidelines and helpful tips on how to approach sticky situations.

What's the biggest mistake that would-be contributors make?
Sending photos of really low resolution. They don't look great on TV or on the web. But there's always an exception to every rule. If it's an incredible news event the world has never seen, it doesn't matter how big it is or how small it is. The fact that it exists is fantastic. Also, pay attention to the audio quality. It can be a limiting factor.

What is your advice to multimedia journalists?
I would say to above all be curious and trust your instincts about what you think is interesting and newsworthy and needs telling. Very often, professional journalists and aspiring journalists can fall into the template of what we're "supposed" to do. But ultimately great stories come from great personal passion to tell them.

How do you see the future of multimedia journalism?
I really think it's going to be more of a true collaboration. I don't see a day when citizen journalism will replace traditional journalism. I think traditional journalism will come to embrace the power and the possibility of citizen journalism in a more meaningful way and the two will learn to work … together. The best examples so far are the ones where CNN's global expertise in newsgathering and its resources come up against the absolute passion and will and amazing tech savvy of the contributors who feel strongly that stories need to be told. When those two things come together, you really get the whole picture.

Index

Power Performance: Multimedia Storytelling for Journalism and Public Relations, First Edition. Tony Silvia and Terry Anzur.
© 2011 Tony Silvia and Terry Anzur. Published 2011 by Blackwell Publishing Ltd.